GET
SMART

PHILOSOPHY

GET
SMART

THE BIG IDEAS
YOU SHOULD KNOW

PHILOSOPHY

MARCUS WEEKS

Quercus

Contents

INTRODUCTION   7

Existence and being   8
What is everything made of?   12
The nature of reality   16
Materialism vs idealism   20
Kant's transcendental idealism   24
German idealism – Kant to Nietzsche   28
Subjective reality   32
Mind and body   36
Cogito, ergo sum   40
Other minds   44
Self and identity   48
Consciousness   52
Artificial intelligence   56
The existence of God   60
Christianity, Islam and philosophy   64
Free will   68
Agnosticism and atheism   72
The problem of knowledge   76
Plato vs Aristotle   80
Scepticism   84
Rationalism vs empiricism   88
Different kinds of truth   92
Good and evil   96
The good life   100
Relativism   104
Is and ought   108

Kant's categorical imperative 112
Utilitarianism 116
Existentialism 120
Chinese philosophy 124
Buddhism 128
Politics, society and the individual 132
Justice 136
Liberty 140
The Rights of Man 144
The social contract 148
Political realism 152
Political power 156
Political ideologies 160
What is beauty? 164
What is art? 168
Reason and logic 172
Fallacies and paradoxes 176
Scientific enquiry 180
The problem of induction 184
Logic and mathematics 188
Analytic philosophy 192
Tractatus Logico-Philosophicus 196
Linguistic philosophy 200
Continental philosophy 204

GLOSSARY 209
INDEX 215
ACKNOWLEDGEMENTS 223

Are you a genius?

Check off the topics as you master them in increasing levels of difficulty.

Mind-blowing
- German idealism – Kant to Nietzsche
- Analytic philosophy
- *Tractatus Logico-Philosophicus*
- Linguistic philosophy
- Continental philosophy

Formidable
- Kant's transcendental idealism
- Existentialism
- The problem of induction
- Logic and mathematics

Tough
- Materialism vs idealism
- Subjective reality
- Free will
- The problem of knowledge
- Rationalism vs empiricism
- Different kinds of truth
- Good and evil
- Relativism
- Kant's categorical imperative
- Utilitarianism
- The social contract

Tricky
- Existence and being
- The nature of reality
- Mind and body
- Other minds
- Self and identity
- Consciousness
- Artificial intelligence
- The existence of God
- Agnosticism and atheism
- Plato vs Aristotle
- Scepticism
- Is and ought
- Justice
- Liberty
- *The Rights of Man*
- Political realism
- Political power
- What is beauty?
- What is art?
- Fallacies and paradoxes
- Scientific enquiry

Fundamental
- What is everything made of?
- *Cogito, ergo sum*
- Christianity, Islam and philosophy
- The good life
- Chinese philosophy
- Buddhism
- Politics, society and the individual
- Political ideologies
- Reason and logic

Introduction

Anybody can be a philosopher. In fact, in one way or another, *everybody* is a philosopher. Because philosophy is all about thinking, rather than knowing stuff — Socrates was considered to be the wisest man in Athens, and was certainly one of the greatest of all philosophers, but he professed to know nothing. More than that, he was a great philosopher *because* he started from the standpoint of knowing nothing.

But through the ages, philosophers have applied their rational thinking to some of the biggest and most fundamental questions about the world and our place in it, and come up with ideas to explain things. And some knowledge of the ideas and thought processes of the great philosophers can help us to think about those things too. That's how you can get smart in philosophy; by finding out what they had to say, and how they came to their conclusions. You'll find that they've thought about the same things as you — the big questions about life, the universe and everything — and will give you food for thought.

It's those ideas that this book is all about. Each section deals with a different branch of philosophy, covering questions about what exists and the nature of existence (metaphysics), about religion and religious belief, about what makes us who we are, about how we know what we know (epistemology), about morality, politics and even what we consider to be beautiful. And each chapter follows the same format, with an introduction to the main idea, and five 'Are You a Genius?' questions that give you a chance to test your knowledge of the main schools of thought on the subject. The answers are on the last page of each chapter, but see if you can work out the answers for yourself after reading the 'Ten Things a Genius Knows' topics that form the main body of each chapter. These lead you through key aspects of the topic, discussing its history, main ideas and unsolved questions. 'Talk like a Genius', meanwhile, provides some talking points that might make for interesting conversation, and if you're still having difficulty getting to grips with the subject, then the 'Bluffer's Summary' should allow you to at least *pretend* you know what you're talking about.

Don't be misled, though. Although there are 'true or false' questions accompanying each idea, philosophy is seldom so black and white: philosophers often disagree — sometimes having diametrically opposing theories — and there is no 'right' or 'wrong' answer, only more or less convincing arguments and counterarguments. Most likely, if you're anything like me, you'll be attracted to some philosophers and their way of thinking, and remain unconvinced by others, but will be reluctant to come down definitively on one side or another. That's the nature, and the beauty, of the subject.

So, the thoughts, ideas and arguments presented in this book, which are only the tip of an immense iceberg of philosophical enquiry more than 2,500 years old, may not provide you with definitive answers. They will, however, give you a framework for thinking about the world around you and your place within it, and, I hope, a deeper understanding of the perennial questions tackled by philosophers.

Marcus Weeks

Existence and being

'The basic drive behind real philosophy is curiosity about the world, not interest in the writings of philosophers.'

BRYAN MAGEE

Some time in the sixth century BCE, an intellectual movement like none before began in ancient Greece. It was inspired by a group of thinkers who challenged conventional wisdom and were fuelled by their curiosity about the world around them. They were not satisfied with religious and superstitious descriptions of natural phenomena, and instead sought rational explanations. Western philosophy grew from the ideas of these thinkers, and its first concern was to try to understand the nature of the Universe and all that exists within it. This became the branch of philosophy known as metaphysics.

It all began with a search for explanations of the Universe and everything in it. A big ask... how much do you know about it?

1 The word 'metaphysics' means beyond or after physics, and comes from the title given to those of Aristotle's writings that came after the ones labelled as 'physics' in his collected works.

TRUE / FALSE

2 Some philosophers, including Pythagoras and Aristotle, use the word 'cosmos' to mean the world or Universe, because of its implication of an ordered system.

TRUE / FALSE

3 Questions of religion, such as whether God exists, are not considered to be within the scope of metaphysics.

TRUE / FALSE

4 Ontology is concerned with the nature of things that have a concrete existence, that are made of physical matter, as opposed to those things that have only a metaphysical existence.

TRUE / FALSE

5 The metaphysical question of what does and does not exist in reality is the central question of existentialism.

TRUE / FALSE

TEN THINGS A GENIUS KNOWS

1 What metaphysics is
One of the first aims of philosophy was to provide a rational explanation of what the world is made of, the fundamental concern of metaphysics. From the enquiries of the early philosophers with their various theories of the physical Universe, the subject expanded to examine not simply what is there, what exists, but also the nature of what exists, and even the nature of existence itself. Science, which itself evolved from the philosophical investigation of the natural world, has increasingly found answers to questions about the physical world, but the fundamental questions of existence remain the province of metaphysics.

2 The world and the Universe
For philosophers the words 'world' and 'universe' have slightly specialized meanings. For example, when we talk of the early philosophers seeking explanations of the world, we mean everything that they experienced, including the Sun, Moon and stars. The world in this sense is the totality of empirical reality, everything it is possible to experience, and for many philosophers this means everything that exists. But because some philosophers – idealists – believe that there is more to reality than is possible for us to experience, the word 'universe' has taken the meaning of total reality, including any transcendental world that may exist – a concept even more all-encompassing than the scientific notion of our physical Universe.

3 Branches of metaphysics
Over time, the scope of metaphysics broadened as philosophers began to examine the nature of the material from which the Universe is made. This raised questions of the properties of that material, and even whether there are both material and non-material substances. From these questions, several branches of metaphysics emerged: questions of existence, what sorts of things can be said to exist, and what exists in reality form the branch of ontology; other major branches examine the philosophical basis for religion, and the concept of mind.

4 Ontology
Generally considered the most central branch of metaphysics is ontology, the study of being, existence and reality. In brief, ontology tackles the questions of whether something exists, what sort of things can be said to exist, and the way that we perceive what exists. To find answers, entities are examined and categorized according to their characteristics, such as their physical properties, their substance or essence. Another primary concern of ontology is to establish what we mean by existence, being, or reality. For example, can an abstract concept, such as justice, be said to exist in the same way as a concrete object, such as a rock? Can there be such a thing as a non-material substance?

5 What is reality?
In a broad definition, reality is the state of things that are real as opposed to imaginary, things that actually exist. Philosophers use the word in a rather narrower sense, however, particularly in the context of metaphysics. Reality for them is the 'realm' in which all real things exist. For example, everything that exists in the Universe is often referred to as 'total reality'. Where philosophers may disagree, though, is in the nature of reality and what can be said to be real: some consider reality to consist only of physical entities with a concrete existence, while others argue that abstract concepts, and even immaterial entities, are equally real.

6 **What existence is**
There is a subtle distinction to be made between what we can say is real, and what exists. One of the most fundamental topics of ontology is what exactly we mean when we say something exists. According to materialists, the only things that exist are concrete objects, composed of a material substance, and subject to physical laws; everything else is a result of the workings of these material things. But it is also argued that abstract things, such as love or courage, have an existence too, and even imaginary beings such as unicorns, which exist as a concept in our minds, but patently do not exist in reality.

7 **The categories of being**
Clearly, there is a difference in the kind of existence of a concrete object, such as a rock, and an abstract concept, such as justice. They have different 'ways of being' and in order to explore the concept of existence, ontology examines the characteristics of things that are said to exist in order to classify them into categories of being. The most obvious distinction is made between things with a concrete existence, and those with an abstract existence. Within the former is the category of physical objects; in the latter are such categories as the properties of physical objects, relations between them, events, concepts, ideas and propositions. A particularly controversial category, the mind, has spawned a separate branch of metaphysics – 'philosophy of the mind'.

8 **Why there is something rather than nothing**
As well as examining what existence is, metaphysics faces the more difficult question of why anything exists at all. As long ago as the fifth century BCE, Parmenides argued that it cannot be said of nothing that it exists, so there must be something. Some two thousand years later Gottfried Leibniz explained it in terms of what he called sufficient reason: 'The sufficient reason … is found in a substance which … is a necessary being bearing the reason for its existence within itself.' Perhaps the most straightforward answer, and one that reflects a peculiarly British disdain of metaphysics, was Bertrand Russell's dismissive 'I should say that the Universe is just there, and that's all.'

9 **Objective and subjective reality**
The aim of science is to give an objective description and explanation of the world, and it is arguably the aim of metaphysics to provide an objective description of reality and existence. But this assumes that what we call reality exists independent of us, something that some philosophers would dispute. We too have an existence, and many things said to have an abstract existence are dependent on our existence. And although it is we who are seeking that objective description of reality, we have a uniquely subjective perspective, a sense of what it is like to be, which is also a legitimate subject of ontological enquiry.

10 **Perception of reality**
Until the beginning of modern philosophy, which has roots in the Renaissance, it was assumed that it would be theoretically possible to know all there is to know about the Universe. But philosophers such as John Locke and Immanuel Kant pointed out that our ideas of reality are shaped and limited by the way that we perceive it. We can only know as much of reality as our senses and the structure of our minds allow us to, and there may be more to total reality than we are capable of apprehending.

TALK LIKE A GENIUS

❧ Metaphysics is the branch of philosophy most often stereotyped as the search for the answer to "the ultimate question of life, the Universe and everything", but in practice the question is not as simple as that. ❧

❧ Martin Heidegger believed that the question "Why is there something rather than nothing?" is the fundamental question of metaphysics. And perhaps he had a point; it involves not only the nature of what exists, but the concepts of cause and effect, and time and space, and how they relate to existence. ❧

❧ It seems that William Shakespeare anticipated Locke and Kant and their idea of a limit to our knowledge of reality, when he has Hamlet declare: "There are more things in heaven and earth, Horatio, than are dreamt of in your philosophy". ❧

1 TRUE – Aristotle himself called the subject 'first philosophy', but the idea of 'beyond physics' is apt.

2 TRUE – The word 'cosmos' is contrasted with its opposite, 'chaos'.

3 FALSE – The philosophy of religion is a distinct branch of metaphysics.

4 FALSE – Ontology is the branch of metaphysics concerned with the nature of existence.

5 FALSE – Existentialism is concerned with the implications for the individual of his or her own existence.

THE BLUFFER'S SUMMARY

The Universe, or total reality, comprises everything that exists; the question is, what can be said to exist in reality?

What is every-thing made of?

'We can speak and think only of what exists.'

PARMENIDES

It is generally accepted that Western philosophy has its origins in the ideas of a group of thinkers in the ancient Greek town of Miletus. The problem that preoccupied them was a metaphysical one: what sort of thing is everything in the world made of? Various explanations were proposed, starting with the suggestion that all matter is one substance in different forms, and then that it is formed by combinations of elements or atoms. Some of the ideas seem to us today naive at best, and at worst wildly wrong, but many were remarkably prescient of modern science.

Everything that exists consists of some sort of substance or matter, but what exactly is 'matter'?

1 Anaximander described the world as a sphere suspended in space, held in place by being equidistant from all the other heavenly bodies.

TRUE / FALSE

2 Heraclitus likened reality to a flame: it has the appearance of a physical object but is actually a visible process.

TRUE / FALSE

3 Empedocles's idea of matter being composed of four immutable elements was dismissed by other philosophers at the time, and only much later revived by medieval alchemists.

TRUE / FALSE

4 One of the reasons the atomist theory did not catch on is that it stated that atoms move about in empty space, and the idea of a void was unacceptable to Greek philosophers.

TRUE / FALSE

5 Xenophanes was the first philosopher to challenge the idea of monism with his suggestion that everything is made of water and air.

TRUE / FALSE

TEN THINGS A GENIUS KNOWS

1 **The pre-Socratic philosophers**
The early Greek philosophers are often referred to as the 'pre-Socratics', to distinguish them from the more human-centric philosophy initiated by Socrates in Athens. The first of these that we know about was Thales, who founded a school of philosophy in Miletus. He believed that everything, all matter, consists of a single substance, water, but what was unique about his pedagogic method was that he encouraged his students to debate his ideas, and come up with alternatives. Which they did: Anaximander rejected the idea of the Earth like an iceberg emerging from the water on which it is floating, instead suggested it is hanging in space, and Anaximenes suggested it is a flat disc floating on air.

2 **Monism**
The reason why Thales's insight was revolutionary is that he arrived at it by rational thought, dismissing conventional wisdom. He reasoned that water is found everywhere (Miletus was a port on the coast of modern Turkey, close to the Greek islands of the Aegean). It occurs in different forms – solid, liquid and gas – and it is essential to all forms of life, so it is the one substance or element from which everything is made. Although the argument seems simplistic today, the idea of monism, that everything consists of one type of substance, is essentially the same as that of materialism in modern philosophy, and the theory in physics that all matter is energy.

3 **Heraclitus**
News of the Milesian philosophers and their revolutionary ideas spread around the Greek communities of the eastern Mediterranean. In Ephesus, just along the coast from Miletus, Heraclitus picked up on the ideas and developed a completely different way of thinking about them.

What substance the world is made of was less important to him than the nature of that substance, and he suggested that it is not a simple unchanging thing, but a process, everything is flux. Reality, he argued, is a dynamic system, not a steady state, and is inherently unstable. Things come into existence, go through processes of transformation, and cease to exist, because each entity is in a state of tension between opposing, contradictory tendencies, just as a path on a mountain is both the way up and the way down.

4 **Xenophanes**
Among the next generation of philosophers from the same coastal region was Xenophanes of Colophon. He accepted the Milesian argument that everything in the world is composed of a material substance, but was not satisfied with the idea that it was composed simply of water. He was also familiar with Heraclitus's theory of opposites, and by combining the two ideas he made the game-changing suggestion that all matter, rather than one element in various forms, could be composed of two elements in different combinations. And, he reasoned, the notion of tension between opposites suggests that the two elements are water and air.

5 **Parmenides**
Heraclitus's theory of a constantly changing reality was controversial. Parmenides of Elea, for example, argued that the idea of something 'coming into existence' made no logical sense: something cannot come from nothing, because we can't talk of nothing as if it exists. Everything that exists, then, has always existed; and because it cannot become nothing, it always will exist. This eternal reality, he argued, is also unchanging, a single immutable entity. Reality is uncreated, and its existence is therefore necessary, and it is characterized by uniformity and changelessness.

6 Empedocles and the elements

Although impressed with Parmenides's logic and the attractive idea of an eternal Universe, Empedocles found it impossible to square with the obviously changing nature of the world in which we live. He did, however, manage to find a way of reconciling these conflicting ideas by returning to Xenophanes's notion of elements. Empedocles suggested that there are, in fact, four eternal, unchanging elements – earth, water, air and fire – which, when combined in different proportions, form all the different kinds of matter. Change comes about from the opposing external forces of attraction and separation, which he called 'Love' and 'Strife' bringing about these different combinations of elements.

7 The atomists

At much the same time as Empedocles proposed his theory of elements, a collaboration between Leucippus and his protégé Democritus came up with a slightly different explanation of permanence and change. Instead of elements, they suggested that everything is composed of minute, indivisible particles, which they called atoms (from the Greek *atomon*, 'uncuttable'). These are indestructible, and move about freely in empty space, coming together in different configurations to form the various substances. When a substance decays, its atoms separate and then reform with others in new configurations to make different substances.

8 Alchemy

While the idea of atoms was widely dismissed until the 19th century, Empedocles's notion of four elements quickly gained acceptance, and remained the predominant way of thinking about the make-up of the physical world in medieval times. In the Islamic 'Golden Age', scientists and philosophers developed alchemy, a forerunner of modern chemistry and physics, based on a combination of the idea of the four elements and astrology, and given scientific credibility by a process of observation and experimentation.

9 The scientific revolution

Meanwhile, in Europe, it was theology rather than philosophy that provided explanations of the nature of the physical Universe until the so-called scientific revolution began in the Renaissance. Based at first mainly on the observations of astronomers such as Copernicus and Galileo, it presented a mechanistic view of the Universe that laid the foundations for the modern subjects of physics and chemistry, and a methodical scientific approach to replace the speculation of the ancient Greek philosophers.

10 Modern science and the nature of the Universe

Despite very different methods of enquiry, modern science remains indebted to the early philosophers. Ideas that were at first dismissed as uninformed, such as the elements, atomism and so on, reappeared in modern scientific explanations of chemistry and physics. Even the simple idea of monism, that matter consists of a single substance, was revived by Einsteinian ideas of matter and energy. In retrospect, it can be seen that the theories of the early philosophers are in fact very sophisticated, and often show an understanding at a deep level of physical principles, but that they had neither the methodology to explore it nor the vocabulary to express it.

TALK LIKE A GENIUS

⸆ The first philosophers were Greeks, living in what is today the holiday resort coast of Turkey. The ideas of just a handful of thinkers spread across the Mediterranean as far as Italy in just a few generations, and quite literally changed the way we look at the world. ⸵

⸆ It's easy to ridicule the theories of the earliest philosophers, but sobering to realize that they came up with concepts of matter, elements, atoms and more that have shaped scientific thinking right up to the present day. ⸵

⸆ It's indicative of our attitude to the ancient Greek philosophers that we often refer to them as the pre-Socratics, as if they were primitive forerunners of the "real" philosophy that started with Socrates in Athens. ⸵

1 FALSE – He did believe it was suspended in space, but thought it was drum-shaped.

2 TRUE – Heraclitus described reality as a process rather than a substance.

3 FALSE – The idea appealed to Aristotle, and it was incorporated into his metaphysics – which in turn influenced medieval thinkers.

4 TRUE – Many agreed with Parmenides that we can't say of nothing that it exists.

5 FALSE – His idea was fundamentally monist: everything consists of matter, but that matter is composed of two elements.

THE BLUFFER'S SUMMARY

The early Greek philosophers reasoned that everything that exists must consist of a single substance – matter – but it can take many forms.

The nature of reality

'The more unintelligent a man is, the less mysterious existence seems to him.'

ARTHUR SCHOPENHAUER

The arrival of Socrates on the scene was a turning point in the history of philosophy. Philosophers before then, despite their divergent theories, are often lumped together as 'the pre-Socratics', whose only real concern was the question of what the world is made of. To an extent this is true, but an oversimplification, as the seeds of the ontological debate of the nature of existence were sown before the time of the great Athenian philosophers. However, it was Plato and Aristotle who really moved the discussion from what everything is made of, to questions of existence itself. Their ideas of the nature of reality were incorporated into medieval Christian philosophy, and later helped to shape modern concepts of the limits of what we can know of total reality.

Let's see how much you really know about reality...

ARE YOU A GENIUS

1 Pythagoras left his native island of Samos and set up a cultlike community in Crotone, southern Italy, dedicated to the study of the mathematical basis of all reality.

TRUE / FALSE

2 Socrates concerned himself with questions of morality and politics, and contributed little, if anything, to the ontological debate.

TRUE / FALSE

3 It was the ancient Greek belief in a world inhabited by the gods that suggested the concept of an ideal, non-material world to Plato.

TRUE / FALSE

4 Thomas Aquinas explained that the essence of a thing, its qualities, is distinct from its substance, and that God, having created a thing of substance, then endows it with its essence.

TRUE / FALSE

5 The primary and secondary qualities, according to Locke, are the two ways we perceive reality; first with our senses, and then as ideas in our minds.

TRUE / FALSE

TEN THINGS A GENIUS KNOWS

1 **The nature of existence**

The early Greek philosophers posed the basic metaphysical question of what substance everything is made of, but from this emerged a deeper question of what kind of thing that substance is. The branch of metaphysics dealing with the nature of existence, 'ontology', first flourished in Athens, as philosophers led by Plato and Aristotle examined the properties or characteristics of things that exist, or can be said to exist, to understand the nature of the Universe, and also to establish what things are eternal and unchanging in a world of apparent change and decay.

2 **Pythagoras**

Perhaps the first to shift the focus to the underlying nature of the Universe, rather than the substance from which it is made, was Pythagoras, more than a century before the Athenians. Pythagoras, like many philosophers since, was a brilliant mathematician, and this coloured his approach to philosophy. He discovered that patterns of things in the natural world could be described in mathematical terms, and conformed to the rules of mathematics. From this, he inferred that the whole of the Universe (or 'cosmos' as he preferred to call it), is orderly and systematic, and characterized not by its substance, but by its form; and the structure of the cosmos is determined by the universal and unchanging laws of mathematics.

3 **Plato's Forms**

Pythagoras's ideas of the nature of the cosmos had a profound effect on Plato in particular. He found the notion of a universal form on which everything that exists is based appealing, as he intuitively felt that the fundamental nature of the Universe is changeless and permanent. Like Parmenides, he believed that the change we see in the world is an illusion. From these two notions, he developed the theory of a realm of Forms (sometimes called 'Ideas'), which are eternal and unchanging, an ideal, immaterial reality that is the template for the illusory physical world we inhabit and experience with our senses. The Forms exist as abstract ideals or 'universals' – archetypes of the many different kinds of things in the world – and the properties that characterize them.

4 **Aristotle's four causes**

The alternative view of reality proposed by Aristotle was more straightforward. Everything that exists is what we can experience here in this world, there is no other reality. And the structure that we see in that reality is not determined by ideal Forms, but by what Aristotle calls 'causes', by which he means what makes things the way they are. Everything is made of some kind of matter, yet it is not the substance, but the way that matter is organized – its form – that makes a thing what it is. Aristotle identified four causes that determine the particular form of things: the material cause (the substance from which a thing is made); the formal cause (the structure or intended structure of the thing); the efficient cause (the external agency that has brought it into existence); and the final cause (the reason for its existence, its purpose or aim).

5 **An eternal Universe**

In Plato's theory, the earthly world we live in is impermanent and subject to change, but the world of Forms is the eternal and immutable reality. Aristotle rejected the idea of a separate, immaterial reality, arguing that everything that exists is subject to change, but that the Universe is eternal. His argument referred to the notion of cause: if the Universe is not eternal, it must have had a beginning – and what then was its cause? What brought it into existence? And if there was a cause, what caused the cause? To accept the idea that the Universe is not eternal involves the idea of an uncaused cause, which Aristotle dismissed as having no logical sense.

6 The problem of universals

With the advent of Christianity, religious belief replaced philosophy in metaphysical descriptions of the world. But medieval philosophers gradually incorporated Greek philosophical ideas into Christian doctrine. Plato's theory of a world of ideal reality dovetailed quite neatly into the Christian idea of the divine realm of heaven, but the notion of the Forms, or universals, was more difficult to square with Christianity. Thomas Aquinas tackled this problem of universals by explaining that the properties of things, what he called their essence, are distinct from their existence. For example, we can describe the characteristics of a unicorn, even though no unicorn exists. The essence of everything is in that divine realm, and as God has created everything according to his design, essence precedes existence.

7 Realism vs nominalism

But in tackling the problem of universals, Aquinas opened up a debate that divided Christian philosophers. On the one hand, there were the 'realists', who wholeheartedly accepted the Platonic notion that the universals, the properties of things, have a real independent existence in an ideal immaterial world. On the other were the 'nominalists', such as Peter Abelard, John Duns Scotus and William of Ockham, who argued that the properties do not actually exist, but are only words that we use to describe things.

8 Locke's primary and secondary qualities

The question of the properties of things that exist was later taken up by John Locke in his exploration of the way that we perceive reality. In his *Essay Concerning Human Understanding*, Locke distinguished between what he called primary and secondary qualities. The primary qualities are those properties that are independent of our experience of them, things that can be objectively measured and quantified, such as physical dimensions, motion and number. Secondary qualities are those that we perceive with our senses, which Locke explains produce sensations in our consciousness, and are therefore subjective. Secondary qualities cannot provide us with objective facts about reality in the way that primary qualities do.

9 The limits of experience

Locke goes on to explain that our understanding of the nature of reality is restricted by our experience of it; we get our information about reality from our experience of the qualities of things, which we perceive as 'ideas' – sensations, feelings and thoughts. We can only apprehend those ideas in our minds, not the things themselves, so we have no direct experience of reality.

10 Bishop Berkeley

Bishop George Berkeley made a striking inference from Locke's description of the way that we perceive things. All we can directly apprehend are the ideas in our consciousness; we have only indirect experience of the world, we experience only the qualities of things. So if all we perceive are ideas, we have no reason to believe that anything exists except ideas. Things, then, only exist in the mind of the perceiver: they only exist if they are perceived or are the perceiver. If that is the case, reality is immaterial and material substance does not truly exist.

TALK LIKE A GENIUS

❛ In Raphael's famous fresco, *The School of Athens*, the two great philosophers Plato and Aristotle are depicted centre stage, and their respective gestures reflect their divergent philosophies: Plato is pointing heavenwards, while Aristotle's palm is facing down to Earth. ❜

❛ It was Plato who really stirred things up in ontology by introducing the notion of a non-material dimension to reality. Although Aristotle steadfastly tried to quash the idea, once it was part of the debate, it wasn't going to go away ❜

❛ The problem of universals was a hot topic among medieval Christian philosophers. It was not disputed that there is a realm containing the ideal Forms of things, but the question was whether their properties also existed in that realm as distinct entities. ❜

❛ Berkeley's immaterialism seems to fly in the face of science, until you consider the idea in quantum physics that reality is not composed of simple concrete entities, but is essentially probabilistic, and affected by the intervention of an observer. As Albert Einstein wryly put it, "Reality is merely an illusion, albeit a very persistent one." ❜

1 TRUE – Pythagoras demanded devotion to a life of strict asceticism and scholarship from his followers.

2 TRUE – From what we are told by his contemporaries, Socrates kept his metaphysical opinions, if he had any, to himself.

3 FALSE – The Greeks did not regard the gods, or their home on Olympus, as non-material.

4 FALSE – Aquinas argued that the essence is the 'template' God uses to design the substantial entity.

5 FALSE – The primary qualities are measurable and objective, the secondary qualities sensory perceptions and subjective.

THE BLUFFER'S SUMMARY

After centuries of philosophy describing a physical Universe, Plato tells us it is an illusion, and that reality is non-material.

Materialism vs idealism

'To exist as an idealist is an extremely strenuous task, because existence itself constitutes a hindrance and an objection.'

SØREN KIERKEGAARD

The task the early Greek philosophers set themselves was finding a rational alternative to religious explanations of the world. As a result, their attention was focused very much on the physical aspects of the world, its structure and the material from which it is made. But with Plato came a different way of looking at reality, with his idea of the existence of a non-material realm. Thus began a major division in ontology, between materialism and idealism, which has persisted up to the present day.

A material or a non-material world, or maybe a combination of the two? The jury's still out, but can you judge which philosophers had a grasp of reality?

1 Until Descartes proposed his theory of dualism, philosophers believed that the world is either entirely material or entirely non-material.

TRUE / FALSE

2 Empiricism, the view that our knowledge of the world comes from our experience of it, implicitly assumes a materialist view of reality.

TRUE / FALSE

3 Spinoza was expelled from the Jewish congregation in Amsterdam for what were regarded as heretical views amounting to pantheism.

TRUE / FALSE

4 For the materialist, abstract concepts, such as justice, and mental states, such as consciousness, obviously exist, but their existence is derived from things in the material world.

TRUE / FALSE

5 While Christian theologians accept Plato's idealist explanation of reality, Aristotle's philosophy is regarded as heretical.

TRUE / FALSE

TEN THINGS A GENIUS KNOWS

1 **Material and non-material**

The pre-Socratic philosophers were, in the main, preoccupied with establishing the nature of the matter of the Universe and, without rejecting any notion of anything non-material, regarded it as irrelevant. This position, that reality is fundamentally material, and that things that do not have a concrete existence derive in some way from material entities, is the basis for materialism. In contrast, Plato proposed that reality is ultimately non-material, an ideal realm. This view, idealism, is more compatible with most religious beliefs. Between the extremes of materialism and idealism are various forms of dualism, suggesting total reality consists of both material and non-material entities.

2 **Plato's ideal world**

Plato disliked the materialist ontology of the pre-Socratics and was particularly incensed by the atomists' assertion that nothing exists except atoms (matter) and empty space. He accepted that matter is real, that the world we perceive with our senses is material but is impermanent and imperfect; it is only given its reality by the eternal and unchanging world of ideal Forms. Similarly, our physical bodies are material, and therefore impermanent and imperfect, but our souls are non-material, eternal and unchanging, and give us the power of reason by which we can directly perceive ideal reality.

3 **Aristotle's material world**

Despite the teachings of his mentor, Plato, Aristotle followed very much in the footsteps of the early philosophers. The world we live in is material, and that is the one we should be examining, not searching for something 'beyond' or 'under the surface' of what we experience: this is the only world that exists in reality. He went further, however, than simply asserting that everything is made of matter. What makes things distinct from one another, what makes them what they are, is not the material that they are made of, but their structure, or form. And this is determined not by some otherworldly ideal Form, but by the four causes (see page 17).

4 **Materialism and physicalism**

The first known Greek philosopher, Thales, proposed the idea that everything is composed of a single substance – water. Although the suggestion seems simplistic, the idea of monism – that reality consists of one sort of substance – developed into the materialist standpoint that the fundamental substance of reality is matter. All non-material concepts, abstract ideas, mental states and so on, are the consequence of the existence of material things. As science has progressed, however, materialism has had to take on board concepts, such as energy, space, time and even antimatter, which are undeniably physical in nature, without being composed of matter, and many philosophers today use the word 'physicalism', in preference to materialism.

5 **Idealism**

While there is a long tradition of strictly materialist philosophers who reject outright the existence of any non-material entities, there are many fewer absolute idealists. Even Plato acknowledged the existence of the material world, and the only major philosopher to suggest that reality is solely immaterial was Bishop Berkeley. But, just as materialism explains non-material things as a result of material interactions, idealists hold that the material world is a secondary reality, and as we experience it with our far-from-perfect senses, is an illusory one. The primary reality, from which everything is ultimately derived, is immaterial and is perceived with our minds or consciousness rather than our senses.

6 Idealism and religion

Naturally, for most religions, the straightforward materialist view is antithetical to their doctrines. The existence of a god or gods, and of a heavenly kingdom, do not fit in to the materialist description of a reality composed entirely of matter. Unsurprisingly, religious philosophers, especially those in Christian medieval Europe, have been more attracted to Platonic ontology, asserting the primacy of the ideal, but at the same time admitting the existence of the material.

7 Dualism

What Plato proposed with his theory of Forms was not absolute idealism, but a kind of metaphysical dualism. Things have a material existence, but derive this from an ideal world, and people have a physical body and an immaterial psyche – a view compatible with religious belief in gods, spirits and souls. Even the down-to-earth Aristotle was not so dogmatic as to reject the existence of the psyche. But the idea of dualism really took off with René Descartes, when he described the distinction between body and mind (see page 37), and our having at the same time a material and immaterial existence.

8 Spinoza and property dualism

Benedict Spinoza was brought up in the Jewish faith, but increasingly opposed the idea of separate earthly and heavenly realms and felt that there was somehow a spiritual element to the natural material world. He similarly rejected Cartesian dualism, but believed that simple monism gave an inadequate description of reality. Instead, he developed a theory that combined ideas of monism and dualism, known as 'property dualism'. Reality, according to Spinoza, consists of a single substance, but has various attributes or properties of both a physical and mental or abstract nature. He described this single substance as 'God-or-nature', explaining that God does not exist as a distinct entity, but is present in everything that exists.

9 Hume and metaphysics

If Spinoza had difficulty accepting the traditional distinctions between the material and the ideal, David Hume had a problem with the whole subject of metaphysics. In a no-nonsense attitude that anticipated British philosophers in the 20th century, he dismissed it by saying: 'If we take in our hand any volume; of divinity or school metaphysics, for instance; let us ask, Does it contain any abstract reasoning concerning quantity or number? No. Does it contain any experimental reasoning concerning matter of fact and existence? No. Commit it then to the flames: for it can contain nothing but sophistry and illusion.'

10 Science and idealism

As science advanced and provided an increasingly comprehensive description of the physical world, philosophers tended more and more to adopt a materialist standpoint. But in the 20th century, scientific discoveries, and the establishment of 'soft' sciences such as psychology and the social sciences, have led to a reappraisal of idealism, or at least some form of dualism. Neuroscience, for example has shown that mental states are physical processes in the brain, but psychology suggests the existence of something non-material as well. Similarly, the social sciences show that ideas, beliefs and values, while having only an abstract existence, have a real influence in the physical world.

TALK LIKE A GENIUS

❛ In everyday usage the words "materialism" and "idealism" have misleading connotations. The philosophical materialists are not devoted to money and material goods, nor are the idealists hopeless dreamers. Materialism is simply a belief that reality consists of matter, and idealism that it doesn't. ❜

❛ Until Plato came along, the prevailing view was essentially monist and materialist. When he suggested the possibility of a non-material world, philosophers were given the opportunity to see reality as dualist in nature, or even to adopt a position of idealist monism. ❜

❛ Science has tended to explore the material world, those things that can be learnt about empirically. But it has become clear that we can observe some non-material things empirically, such as energy, space and time, and so must consider that they have a real existence in the physical world. And if we do that, should we not also admit the physical existence of observable phenomena, such as psychological states? ❜

1 FALSE – Plato, who introduced the idea of a non-material reality, did not deny the existence of the material world.

2 FALSE – Although many empiricists rejected the notion of an ideal world, Berkeley showed it was possible to be an empiricist and an absolute idealist.

3 TRUE – And at around this time, aged 23, he adopted his Latin given name Benedictus rather than the Jewish Baruch.

4 TRUE – Materialism does not deny the existence of non-material things, but that they do not have an independent existence.

5 FALSE – Thanks largely to Thomas Aquinas, Aristotelean philosophy was gradually incorporated into Christian doctrine.

THE BLUFFER'S SUMMARY

While materialists believe reality consists ultimately of matter, and idealists that it is ultimately non-material, there's room in the middle for a dualist view.

Kant's transcendental idealism

'It is precisely in knowing its limits that philosophy exists.'

IMMANUEL KANT

By the middle of the 18th century, the division in philosophy between materialists and idealists had been deepened by the ongoing epistemological debate between empiricism and rationalism. Empiricists argued that we acquire knowledge from our experience of the material world, rationalists that it comes from reasoning and innate understanding of eternal truths. In his critical look at these approaches, Immanuel Kant argued that our experience of the world is structured by the mind's inbuilt capacity to shape sensory perceptions. So our knowledge of the world is limited to the world as we perceive it, not the world as it is. From this, Kant developed a form of 'transcendental idealism' that dominated philosophy in the following century, inspiring many, but also provoking a reaction in others.

Kant knew there is a limit to our knowledge. What's the limit of yours about him?

1 Kant was born and died in Königsberg, and never travelled further than 16 km (10 miles) from his home town.

TRUE / FALSE

2 The idea of critical philosophy, examining and judging all previous theories to determine their validity, is attributed to Kant.

TRUE / FALSE

3 The term 'thing-in-itself' was coined by Kant to describe an object as it actually is, independent of our perception of it, as opposed to its outward appearance as we perceive it.

TRUE / FALSE

4 In Kant's transcendental idealism, reality consists of the 'phenomenal', the material world we experience with our senses, and the 'noumenal', an immaterial world that we cannot perceive.

TRUE / FALSE

5 According to Kant we do not use reason to determine what is morally good or bad, but have *a priori* knowledge of ethics.

TRUE / FALSE

TEN THINGS A GENIUS KNOWS

1 **Immanuel Kant**
Kant was born in Königsberg (then in Prussia, now in the Russian Kaliningrad Oblast), where he studied philosophy at the university. The predominant philosophical ideas there were rationalism and idealism, and in particular the philosophy of Gottfried Leibniz. Although a gifted philosopher, Kant broadly accepted these views for some years, and contributed little that was innovative. Until, that is, he was 'awoken from his dogmatic slumber' by reading David Hume, whose down-to-earth scepticism had an electrifying effect. Kant then set about subjecting all theories of philosophy to scrutiny, in what he described as critical philosophy.

2 **The *Critique of Pure Reason***
Having been educated in the continental tradition, Kant naturally tended to the rationalist idea that reason is the source of our knowledge of everything. And so the first target of his critical philosophy was reason itself, 'the faculty of reason in general, in respect of all knowledge after which it may strive independently of all experience'. In his magnum opus, the *Critique of Pure Reason*, Kant examines the arguments of both rationalists and empiricists to establish the extent to which our senses and intellect can give us knowledge of metaphysics. His conclusions about the nature of our experience of the world formed the basis for a new metaphysical interpretation of total reality, distinct from idealism and realism, which he called 'transcendental idealism'.

3 **A unified system of philosophy**
Central to Kant's thinking were the connections he made between metaphysics and epistemology; our understanding of the nature of reality is dependent on the way that we experience and gain knowledge of it. As well as attempting to reconcile the apparently opposing ideas of rationalism and empiricism, and idealism and materialism, he aimed to construct a unified system of philosophy combining metaphysics, epistemology and ethics. Others before him had made similar connections, but Kant was the first philosopher to do so on such a grand scale, in a comprehensive single system.

4 **The structure of our experience**
In the *Critique of Pure Reason,* Kant recognizes that we experience the world empirically with our senses, but we have some rational understanding of it too. But more than that, he argues that our experiences are shaped by the way that our minds work. We have an innate understanding of the concepts of time and space, and cause and effect, and this attribute of the mind structures the experience we have of the information from our senses. Space, time and causality are, therefore, an inherent part of our experience of the world. But, Kant points out, our experience of things is always of the world as conveyed by our senses – what he calls the 'phenomenal world' – and we have no access to things as they actually are.

5 **Limits of human apprehension**
We can have knowledge of some things empirically, but because of the way that the mind structures experience in terms of space, time and causality, we are limited in what we can perceive and understand. Our experience is limited to those things that conform to the same temporal, spatial and causal rules that are an integral part of the way we understand things. So we cannot know of everything that exists, total reality; we cannot experience or have any understanding of anything that exists outside of space and time.

6 The thing-in-itself

Kant explains this idea of our limited ability to apprehend things by likening what we perceive with our senses as a mere representation of a thing itself, in the same way as a painter presents us with a picture of an object. No matter how accurate a portrayal the painting is, it is not the object itself; and no matter how detailed our perception of something is, it is not the thing as it is, but a mental representation. What we can't experience is the thing as it actually is, the true nature of its existence, what Kant refers to as the 'thing-in-itself'.

7 Phenomena and noumena

The distinction between what is and is not possible for us to apprehend is the core of Kant's metaphysics, and hence the whole of his philosophy. In place of the stark dualism that posits the existence of separate material and non-material worlds, he says that there is the world as we experience it, and the world as it is in itself. The world that is accessible through our senses and intellect is the world of 'phenomena', things as they appear to us; but reality also consists of 'noumena', things as they are, independent of our concepts of them.

8 The transcendental

Kant described this metaphysical concept of the phenomenal and noumenal world as 'transcendental idealism'. He ascribed a particular meaning to the word 'transcendental': rather than referring to things that transcend the possibility of human understanding, he used the word to mean knowledge not of things, but of the way that it is possible for us to perceive things as things, to know of them before we experience them. Our knowledge does not conform to objects, he asserted, but rather the other way around, objects conform to our knowledge. The 'idealism' part of his philosophy refers to the concept of the noumenal, that which is outside the world of sense experience and in that sense ideal, but not strictly in contrast with the material.

9 Kantian ethics

The relationship between metaphysics and epistemology is made clear in Kant's transcendental idealism, but less obvious is the connection with other branches of philosophy. Yet in his comprehensive system of philosophy, Kant manages to include ethics, politics and even aesthetics. Ethics in particular is very much an integral part of this system. Reason, he argues, governs our moral actions, but the source of our morality is the innate understanding we have of the 'laws' of morality, in the same way that we have an innate understanding of the physical laws of space, time and causality. We can use reason to recognize moral decisions in the world, and to follow them as a matter of moral imperative.

10 The foundation of German idealism

Kant felt, with some justification, that he had, with transcendental idealism, reconciled the differences between rationalism and empiricism, and made a case for an idealist interpretation of reality. His ideas marked a significant turning point in European philosophy, inspiring a century of German idealism. Some, such as Georg Hegel and Arthur Schopenhauer, built on his concept of idealism; for others, such as the materialists Ludwig Feuerbach and Karl Marx, he provoked a reaction that culminated in Friedrich Nietzsche, a long way from Kant's idealism.

TALK LIKE A GENIUS

❛ Not convinced by either rationalist or empiricist descriptions of how we understand the world, Kant embarked on a critique of both. What he concluded is that both our senses and our reason limit what we can apprehend about reality – so there is far more to it than we know or can ever know about. ❜

❛ We only experience what our senses and psychological make-up allow us to experience, and they shape the way we perceive the world. So what we take for reality is just how it appears to us, not how it actually is. ❜

❛ When we perceive phenomena, we interpret them in terms of their existence in time and space, and their cause and effect, because those are the parameters set by the structure of our minds. But there are aspects of reality outside those parameters, noumena, which we have no way of apprehending. ❜

THE BLUFFER'S SUMMARY

Kant argued that both our empirical and rational understanding of reality is limited, and that there is a whole world we can never know about.

German idealism – Kant to Nietzsche

> 'The real is the rational, and the rational is the real.'
>
> GEORG WILHELM FRIEDRICH HEGEL

Immanuel Kant is widely regarded as the foremost of the philosophers of the Enlightenment, and his influence over the next century was immense. At a time when, elsewhere, the revolutionary mood was turning philosophers' attention more to matters of morality and politics, his focus on metaphysics and epistemology inspired philosophers in the German-speaking world. At the same time Germany, as the home of the Romantic movement, was becoming the cultural centre of Europe. Philosophy flourished in this atmosphere and spawned a succession of German idealist philosophers, and those that reacted against the movement, that spanned the 19th century.

From Kant to Nietzsche, German philosophy dominated the scene. How much of it have you taken in?

1 Although it is convenient to talk of a century of German idealism, Germany was not a single country, but a confederation of independent sovereign states.

TRUE / FALSE

2 Fichte made his name as a philosopher with an anonymously published book. His *Critique of All Revelation* was well received, but largely because it was assumed from the title that it was by Kant.

TRUE / FALSE

3 Schelling's obsession with Nature was a reaction to rapid industrialization and urbanization in Germany and the loss of human connection with the natural world.

TRUE / FALSE

4 A student of Hegel's, Feuerbach, ended up reacting strongly against his idealism. His inversion of Hegel's ideas to a materialist and atheist perspective was a significant influence on Karl Marx.

TRUE / FALSE

5 The concept of the universal will was inspired by Schopenhauer's studies of Buddhist philosophy.

TRUE / FALSE

TEN THINGS A GENIUS KNOWS

1 19th-century philosophy
In the last decades of the 18th century, much of Europe was in turmoil. In France, the revolution and its aftermath dominated people's minds, and philosophical theorizing was the least of their concerns. At the same time, Britain was coming to terms with the implications of the Industrial Revolution, the first country to do so, and the tradition of materialist, empiricist thinking evolved into utilitarianism, a framework for moral and political philosophy. Meanwhile, in Germany, as the Enlightenment period drew to a close, there was the beginning of a distinctly German cultural movement, Romanticism, with ideas that echoed Kant's idealism.

2 Romanticism
The Romantic movement emerged as a reaction to the emphasis on scientific rationalization of the previous century, and the potentially dehumanizing effect of industrialization. Spinoza's idea of God-or-nature provided a much needed spiritual dimension to philosophy, which was reinforced by the rigour of Kant's exposition of transcendental idealism. And this chimed with artists who were contemporaries of Kant, including the writer Wolfgang Goethe, composer Ludwig Beethoven and painter Caspar David Friedrich. The defining features of Romantic art was its emphasis on emotional expression, and a personal viewpoint of the world, but above all, a fascination with Nature, often depicted as a noumenal entity beyond our experience of the phenomena of the natural world.

3 The legacy of Kant
Kant's *Critique of Pure Reason* had little impact when it was first published in 1781, but through the 1780s news spread of its importance. Several hundred pages of dense prose did not make it an easy read, but its central message of the limits of our understanding of metaphysics imposed by our reason struck a chord with philosophers dissatisfied with the scientific rationalization that characterized the Enlightenment. This opened up the possibility of a number of different interpretations of idealism; some, like that of Schopenhauer, built on the ideas of phenomena and noumena, while others took a more radically idealist approach – or even, in the case of Feuerbach, used it as a starting point for a purely materialist philosophy.

4 Johann Gottlieb Fichte
One of the first of Kant's followers was Johann Gottlieb Fichte, who came across his writings in the 1790s, and after studying them in great detail developed his own idiosyncratic version of idealism. Despite the centrality of the concept, Fichte rejected the idea of the noumenal thing-in-itself, and instead proposed a form of absolute idealism. As Kant had shown, we cannot derive scientific laws from empirical evidence, but have innate knowledge of them. It is from this, Fichte argued, that we deduce external reality; the 'I', the knowing mind, creates this external reality, the 'not-I', which as a creation of the mind, must be ideal. As it is, therefore, a creation of a knowing subject, and one that is free to make moral choices, the nature of reality must be not only ideal, but essentially moral.

5 Friedrich Schelling
Fichte's absolute idealism provoked a strong reaction, not least from Kant, who rejected it completely. But in Friedrich Schelling, it prompted an essentially Romantic interpretation of idealism. Schelling was a part of the circle of intellectuals at the centre of the German Romantic movement, and deeply influenced by their view of Nature. He argued that Fichte's idea made no sense, a knowing subject cannot exist independently, but depends on being a part of reality for its existence. And in his view, Nature is total reality, of which we are

a part. Life and Nature are inseparable, so reality is a living thing, an ongoing creative process. The culmination of this is human creativity, in which we manifest our oneness with Nature, and Nature demonstrates its self-awareness.

6 Schopenhauer: will and representation

Of all Kant's admirers, Schopenhauer followed most closely the central themes of transcendental idealism. He understood and took on board Kant's distinction between phenomena and noumena, but put his own spin on the idea in *The World as Will and Representation*. The phenomenal and noumenal are not two separate worlds, nor simply that which we can and can't apprehend, but the same world experienced in two different ways. We experience the world from outside, through our senses as representation (as Kant had described our experience of phenomena), rather than the thing itself. But we experience the world from within as will, which is what controls our actions.

7 The universal will

The will that we experience from within, according to Schopenhauer, is something that is inherent in everything. And because it is noumenal, outside the realm of space and time, it must be universal. We can experience our own will, but it is only a part of the universal will that pervades reality. And because we experience it from within, we can only experience our own will; we can experience the representation of other things, but not their inner will. Nor can we have access to anything but our own small part of the universal will, which is beyond our apprehension, meaningless to us, yet having influence over the individual wills that control our actions.

8 Hegel: reality as a historical process

Schopenhauer revered Kant, and was fiercely critical of those who strayed too far from the ideas of transcendental idealism. He was particularly vehement in his criticism of Hegel, who, like Fichte, dismissed the idea of the thing-in-itself. Hegel suggested that reality is a single entity, in which the thinking subject and the object of its thoughts, the external world, are one and the same. This thinking subject he described as consciousness, whose essential characteristic is *Geist*, or spirit. And both external reality and consciousness are subject to change and evolution; reality is not a material entity but a historical process that manifests itself in the spirit of the consciousness at any one time, the *Zeitgeist*.

9 Marxian materialism

Somewhat surprisingly, Hegel's so-called 'absolute idealism' made a deep impression on the materialist Karl Marx. What appealed to Marx was the logic with which Hegel explained the process of history in dialectical terms – that opposing ideas presented themselves as a thesis and antithesis that resolved into a synthesis, the next stage of historical development. Marx was keen to give the study of history some philosophical credibility, and so substituted materialism for idealism in Hegel's framework to analyse the historical process in terms of economics, politics and the class struggle. The thinking subject of this historical reality is consciousness, but a consciousness of those material elements, rather than a mysterious *Geist*.

10 Nietzsche: metaphysics is dead

By the end of the 19th century, German idealism had come a long way from Kant's original, and in an increasingly scientific and secular world, had run its course. Among those sounding its death knell was the natural descendant of the German idealists, Friedrich Nietzsche. As a young man he had been impressed by Schopenhauer, especially the idea of a mindless, amoral universal will, yet he later rejected not only idealism, but metaphysics in general, shifting the focus from external reality to human beings, and their ability to fulfil their potential in life.

TALK LIKE A GENIUS

❝ It all started with Kant. Schopenhauer followed in his idol's footsteps, and developed the ideas of transcendental idealism still further, while Hegel and others used it as a springboard from which to take off into new realms of idealism. And, of course, there were those who reacted against it, striking out in new directions, like Marx and Nietzsche. ❞

❝ Interestingly, although inspired by Kant, many German idealists rejected the idea of the thing-in-itself, and opted for a broader interpretation of idealism. Hegel even suggested that reality is neither phenomenal nor noumenal, but a process. ❞

❝ Hegel's description of reality as a historical process provided a pivotal point for Marx to turn German idealism upside down. Where Hegel spoke of an idealist *Geist*, Marx simply replaced this with the materialist concepts of economic, social and political conditions. ❞

WERE YOU A GENIUS?

1 TRUE – Until German unity in 1866, there was no German nation state.

2 TRUE – He later published several more books under his own name.

3 FALSE – Industrialization was slow in Germany, and did not become significant until the late 19th century.

4 TRUE – Marx acknowledged his debt to Feuerbach for showing how Hegel's philosophy could be subverted.

5 FALSE – Schopenhauer apparently reached the strikingly similar idea independently, and only later studied Indian philosophy.

THE BLUFFER'S SUMMARY

Kant's legacy: a century of German philosophy developing from the starting point of his transcendental idealism.

Subjective reality

'We are ourselves the entities to be analysed.'

MARTIN HEIDEGGER

At the end of the 19th century, the influence of German idealism was on the wane, and British philosophers were in the ascendancy. The influence of Bertrand Russell's analytic philosophy led to an almost complete dismissal of the importance of metaphysics, as such questions about the world were increasingly considered more the realm of science than philosophy. Meanwhile, however, there was a change of direction among European philosophers in the wake of German idealism, towards a more subjective approach to metaphysics. For them, the nature of total reality was less important than our experience of it and, in particular, the way we experience our own existence.

Are we alone responsible for finding meaning in our own existence?

ARE YOU A GENIUS

1 The idea of reality as a process was first posited by Heraclitus, and revived by Hegel, but Bergson gave it a distinctively 'continental' spin by describing our subjective experience of it.

TRUE / FALSE

2 The pragmatist view is that we can never get a complete understanding of total reality, but by participating in it our understanding increases step by step.

TRUE / FALSE

3 The *Lebenswelt* that Husserl refers to is the world as it is perceived by an individual over the course of a lifetime.

TRUE / FALSE

4 In *Being and Time*, Heidegger reaches the conclusion that being, existence, is not only defined by time, but that its primary characteristic is temporal – being actually is time.

TRUE / FALSE

5 Instead of attempting to define existence, Sartre contrasts it with non-existence, nothingness, in order to show that it is up to us to find significance in life.

TRUE / FALSE

TEN THINGS A GENIUS KNOWS

1 **From objective to subjective reality**
Advances in the physical sciences in the 20th century reinforced the idea that our understanding of the world is better informed by science than philosophy. Materialism and physicalism became the dominant modes of thought, and it was felt that science was the only means we have of getting an objective view of the nature of external reality. But this left room for a different approach: it is impossible to take an objective 'God's-eye-view' of total reality, but we can ignore the things that can either be objectively explained by science or are beyond our apprehension. What is possible, then, is to have a first-person perspective, and examine our subjective experience of the world, and our experience of existence.

2 **Henri Bergson**
Henri Bergson was one of the first philosophers to adopt this approach, describing how, individually, we have a direct experience of reality. Much influenced by Charles Darwin's theory of evolution, Bergson regarded reality not as a stable state, but as a process, a continuous flow. We are a part of this continuum, and, as such, the flow of reality and our experience of it are the same thing. This direct experience of reality is distinct from the perceptions of the external world we have from our senses, which, Bergson explains, have evolved merely to tell us what we need to know for our survival.

3 **Charles Sanders Peirce**
At much the same time, a distinctly American approach to metaphysics emerged. The American pragmatists, led by Charles Sanders Peirce, argued that we experience the world not as observers, but as participants, and our knowledge of external reality comes from this practical first-hand experience. Because that knowledge is restricted to our experience, it is incomplete. But gaining knowledge is a cumulative process: if we find, in practice, that our knowledge matches reality, we can use it as a base for further knowledge; but it may be that our further practical experience provides a more accurate (or more useful) picture of reality, on which we can base our participation in the world.

4 **Edmund Husserl and phenomenology**
As a German born in the middle of the 19th century, Edmund Husserl came from the German idealist tradition and, like others, used Kant as a springboard for his own ideas. He accepted Kant's description of phenomena and noumena, but felt that this had led philosophers into a blind alley, chasing the idea of the noumenal, when that is beyond our apprehension. What he suggested was concentrating instead on the phenomenal, the things we can experience, and 'bracket out' the unanswerable questions of the noumenal. In this way, his phenomenology looks not at total reality, but the *Lebenswelt*, the world we live in, so that we can subject our first-person experience of it to scientific examination.

5 **Heidegger's *Being and Time***
Husserl's idea of 'bracketing out' anything that we cannot apprehend and focusing on those things that we can, was taken up in the next generation of German philosophy by Martin Heidegger. But Heidegger went one step further, suggesting that instead of just excluding the noumenal, philosophers should not examine the phenomenal either, but the being that experiences it; it is our subjective experience that constitutes reality. In his words, 'We are ourselves the entities to be analysed.' We can only know the nature of being from experience of our own existence, and that, Heidegger argued, is defined by our awareness of time. We become aware of being born into a world that existed before us, and of our death as the end of our existence. Our experience of the time in between clarifies for us what it means to exist.

6 **Maurice Merleau-Ponty**
Heidegger's suggestion that our philosophical enquiry should centre on the existence of the subject – ourselves – introduced the idea of a truly subjective metaphysical perspective. Continuing this train of thought, the French philosopher Maurice Merleau-Ponty took the idea a step further, proposing that we do not examine our own existence as subjects, but rather our subjective experience of that existence – what it is like for us to exist as individuals – which he believed can help us challenge our everyday assumptions and see the world more clearly.

7 **Existentialism**
Heidegger and Merleau-Ponty are sometimes described as 'existentialists', but the term is more properly applied to those French philosophers, such as Jean-Paul Sartre and his partner Simone de Beauvoir, who took the 'bracketing out' of unanswerable questions to its extreme. It is not important, they argued, to understand the nature of things that exist in the world, or even our own existence. There is no point in speculating about the nature of existence, but instead we should examine the meaning of existence, what our existence means for us. With that comes the realization that we alone are responsible for finding meaning in our own existence (see page 120).

8 **Continental philosophy**
The extremely subjective approach of existentialism excluded almost all aspects of traditional metaphysics, and concentrated more on the moral and political implications of existing as a human being. This reflected a general trend following the Second World War, from theoretical to practical applications of philosophy, especially in the social sciences. In France especially, the generation that succeeded the existentialists developed a distinctively 'continental' philosophy concentrating on ethical, political and aesthetic aspects of society, leaving metaphysical questions either unanswered or the province of the natural sciences (see pages 204–7).

9 **Anglo-Saxon rejection of metaphysics**
The idea that metaphysics is not a meaningful subject for philosophical enquiry had been held for some time by many British philosophers. It is the task of science, they said, to provide explanations of the physical world, and philosophy's role is to provide a rational framework for their investigations and a way of critically judging their findings. In place of metaphysics, focusing on the things that science can and cannot tell us, philosophy has turned its attention to the practice of science itself.

10 **Modern science and metaphysics**
Today, the majority of philosophers have abandoned idealism in favour of a broadly physicalist understanding of reality. But modern science has, in some cases, provided questions as well as answers: the Big Bang theory, for example, describes the beginning of space and time and a finite Universe, reviving an ancient metaphysical conundrum; and discoveries in quantum mechanics challenge even the most informed physicist's conception of the nature of matter.

TALK LIKE A GENIUS

⁶ Over the course of the 20th century, philosophers have tended to progressively abandon metaphysics. In part, this is because many have taken a physicalist standpoint, and put the onus on the sciences to provide empirical answers. But others have clung to the remnants of Kant's idealist tradition, and accepted that there are things we cannot know or understand, and have simply chosen to exclude them from their philosophies. ⁹

⁶ If we take Husserl's suggestion that philosophy should "bracket out" the noumenal, what is left is reality as we perceive it. And it's only a short step from examining that subjective reality to turning the mirror on ourselves and considering our own existence. ⁹

⁶ Once we ourselves, rather than external reality, are the subject of philosophical examination, metaphysics takes a back seat to questions of morality, politics, language and philosophy of mind. ⁹

1 TRUE – Unlike Heraclitus and Hegel, Bergson had the benefit of knowledge of Darwin and the idea of constant evolution in nature.

2 TRUE – Science and philosophy present only a partial picture of reality at any one time, but it is expanding incrementally.

3 FALSE – The *Lebenswelt* is the world all of us live in, the world that we can perceive, equivalent to what Kant called the 'phenomenal world'.

4 TRUE – In much the same way as Bergson describes reality as a process, Heidegger equates our being with time.

5 TRUE – We cannot know how we came to exist or why, but we can choose our own purpose before we cease to exist.

THE BLUFFER'S SUMMARY

An end to speculation about the things we can't know, and a focus on the things we can know – especially ourselves.

Mind and body

'It is not necessary to ask whether soul and body are one, just as it is not necessary to ask whether the wax and its shape are one.'

ARISTOTLE

The idea that we have a soul, or spirit, as well as a physical body is common to most religions, and the nature of this has been the subject of debate among philosophers from the ancient Greeks to the present. They sought an explanation for what we intuitively feel, that we have a consciousness – a sense of identity, emotions and reason – that is distinct from our bodies and apparently immaterial. Theories about this aspect of our being have gradually evolved from mystical and religious ideas of spirits and souls to modern ideas of mind, which have their origins in Descartes.

Until comparatively recently, most philosophers believed in the existence of the soul. Do you know what changed their minds?

1 The Greek concept of psyche was something quite separate from the religious belief in an immortal soul.

TRUE / FALSE

2 Descartes laid the foundations for the modern philosophy of mind by characterizing the immaterial aspect of human existence as a 'thinking thing' rather than a spiritual entity.

TRUE / FALSE

3 If the mind is, as Descartes asserts, immaterial, it is not susceptible to empirical examination, and descriptions of it cannot be objectively verified.

TRUE / FALSE

4 Most philosophers today deny the existence of an immaterial mental substance, and believe that mind is a product of physical processes in the brain.

TRUE / FALSE

5 Philosophy of mind, like metaphysics and epistemology, has become largely redundant in the light of recent scientific advances.

TRUE / FALSE

TEN THINGS A GENIUS KNOWS

1 Philosophy of mind

The branch of philosophy known as philosophy of mind is a relatively young one, only gradually becoming a distinct field of metaphysics after Descartes revisited the ancient question of whether mind and body are separate entities. From this mind–body problem, as it became known, the scope of philosophy of mind has broadened to include such subjects as perception, consciousness, self and identity, and artificial intelligence. Many of the questions it has addressed were later taken up, and to some extent answered, by the new sciences of psychology and neuroscience in the 20th century, but fundamental questions of the nature of mind remain the subject of philosophical debate.

2 The immortal soul

The origins of our conceptions of mind can be traced back to ancient religious beliefs, some still held today, that beings have an immaterial spirit, a life force, as well as a physical body. This is analogous to the idea in most modern religions, of an immortal soul, the indestructible essence of a person (it is something not generally ascribed to non-humans), which is distinct from the impermanent physical body. It is often also characterized as the seat of morality and of emotions, but not necessarily of mental faculties, such as intellect, as is the modern concept of mind.

3 The soul and the afterlife

The soul, as it is conceived in religion, is immaterial and so has an independent existence from the physical body. When we die, the soul continues to exist in some form of afterlife, either reincarnated into another physical body, or in an immaterial realm, such as heaven or hell. Belief in the existence of immaterial substances such as souls, and immaterial realms distinct from earthly existence, has persisted in secular philosophy as idealism and has been disputed by materialists.

4 The psyche

The ancient Greek philosophers, whose aim it was to find rational rather than religious explanations of things, had a somewhat more sophisticated notion of the soul. To them the 'psyche' included the life force and the soul of a person's being, but also the mental faculties – what we today would call the mind. These included memory, consciousness, character and morality, but above all reason, the capacity for rational thought. For Plato, the psyche exists independently, an immaterial and immutable entity that can give us access to the ideal world of Forms. In contrast, Aristotle characterized the psyche as the actualization of a being that gives it life and identity, and as such cannot have a separate existence from the physical body.

5 The nature of mind

In modern philosophy of the mind, the concepts of soul and spirit have been almost completely subsumed into the general concept of mind, as philosophy has distanced itself from religious belief. Rather than considering it as a spiritual entity, the essence of a being, philosophers have characterized it as the seat of consciousness, where our sensory perceptions are experienced. It gives us our feeling of self and identity and, more than that, it is the part of our being that is capable of thought and reasoning. This also makes it the seat of moral responsibility.

6 The mind–body problem

The mind–body problem raised by Descartes lies at the heart of philosophy of mind. If the mind is a separate and distinct entity from the body, what kind of thing is it? As with many philosophical concepts, we have an intuitive idea of what it is, but it is not easy to define. We know that the brain is the physical thing that receives information from our senses, but the brain is different from the mind; is there, then, an immaterial thing, the mind, that does our thinking and feeling, or does it consist of the thoughts and feelings themselves? This raises the metaphysical question of whether the mind actually exists as an immaterial substance – something denied by physicalists – or is merely an abstract concept.

7 Mind–body interaction

Descartes's dualist idea that mind and body are separate and distinct divided opinion among philosophers. For some, idealists, the concept of an immaterial mind chimed with their view that reality is primarily non-material, while of course materialists rejected the idea outright. But even for those who accepted mind–body dualism, there was a problem: our material bodies provide our minds with sensory information, and our minds control the movement of our bodies. They may be distinct entities, but cannot be entirely separate, as they interact with one another – the question is, how?

8 Human and non-human minds

Another idea, inherited primarily from the Abrahamic religions, is the concept that only humans have a soul. Animals were considered lesser beings, and although sentient to a greater or lesser degree, are not capable of moral responsibility, an essential element in the spiritual make-up of the soul. As late as the 18th century, it was widely believed that non-human animals were akin to automata, without consciousness or the capability of rational thought. Ideas have changed, of course, and today it is generally accepted that many animals are not only conscious, but have intelligence, and may even be capable of making moral decisions.

9 Other people's minds

A more fundamental problem for the study of the mind is that a person can only have direct experience of his or her own mind. Each of us knows what it is like to perceive things, to think, to have ideas and experience consciousness, but it is introspective and subjective. When we talk about the mind, we are basing our ideas on a sample of one, the only mind we have access to, and making an assumption that other people's minds are at least similar. There is some evidence to believe that is the case, of course, but we can never be certain.

10 The mind as software

The advent of computer technology, and the possibility of developing artificial intelligence to match our own, provided a handy metaphor for the mind and brain. The modern materialist or physicalist concept of the mind is that it is a function of the brain, rather than a separate thing; what exists is the brain, what it does is the mind, analogous to hardware and software in computer science. The operation of the brain is mechanical, but it still thinks rationally and can make moral decisions. But even those who accept the analogy feel intuitively that something else constitutes 'self' (see pages 48–51), an entity or agency overseeing our experiences and controlling our thoughts and actions, whether it be a soul, a mind or just consciousness. As Jerry Fodor put it, 'If there is a community of computers living in my head, there had also better be somebody who is in charge; and, by God, it had better be me.'

TALK LIKE A GENIUS

❛ A problem in philosophy of mind is that we have intuitive ideas of what our mind is and how it operates – and those ideas may not match reality; the notions of an independent spirit or soul are attractive, but a matter of belief rather than rational thought ❜

❛ In an interview with an Italian newspaper, Daniel Dennett explained his physicalist concept of the mind and soul as a mechanical operation, and now treasures the headline given to the article: "YES, we have a soul but it's made of lots of tiny robots." ❜

❛ In recent times, the status of philosophy of mind has been called into question by physicalist philosophers, who deny the existence of a mind as a concept distinct from physical processes. The prospect of real artificial intelligence reinforces that view, but some problems of mind seem impervious to purely physicalist explanation. ❜

THE BLUFFER'S SUMMARY

The mind is the part of our being that provides us with thoughts, ideas, emotions and consciousness, but its existence is debatable.

Cogito, ergo sum

'I am therefore, precisely speaking, only a thinking thing, that is, a mind, understanding, or reason.'

RENÉ DESCARTES

The modern branch of philosophy concerned with the study of mind originated largely from the ideas of René Descartes. In his *Discourse on the Method*, published in 1637, he set out to tackle the problem of scepticism and find an incontrovertible truth on which to build a scientific method of enquiry. But perhaps the most influential part of this work was his famous statement, '*cogito ergo sum*', which formed the basis of his theory of mind–body dualism, that the mind and body are separate and composed of two distinct substances, immaterial and material.

Turn your mind to the subject of dualism and see if you are the genius you think you are.

1 Descartes never actually used the phrase '*cogito ergo sum*' in Latin, but used the French '*je pense, donc je suis*'.

TRUE / FALSE

2 Avicenna's image of a man floating in space is an early description of the sensation of being separated from one's body that comes with sensory deprivation.

TRUE / FALSE

3 Descartes was not the first to come to the conclusion, that 'if I am thinking I must exist'. It is a concept mentioned by Aristotle and others, and even earlier in the Hindu Upanishads.

TRUE / FALSE

4 By describing mind–body dualism as the existence of a ghost in the machine, Ryle clarified the distinction between the immaterial nature of mind and the mechanistic nature of the body.

TRUE / FALSE

5 Putnam devised his brain in a vat story to prove Cartesian dualism incoherent, but a shallow understanding of it has meant that it is often thought of as confirming it.

TRUE / FALSE

1 René Descartes

Descartes is widely regarded as the first great modern philosopher, laying the foundations for what came to be known as continental rationalism, and philosophy of mind. Descartes was also a brilliant and innovative mathematician, and believed that the methodical, step-by-step procedures of mathematical proofs could be used as a model for investigations in the natural sciences. His *Discourse on the Method* explained this rational approach to science, but necessarily touched on issues of metaphysics, including a detailed discussion of the nature of the mind.

2 The deceiving demon

Descartes argued that, just as mathematical proofs start from an axiom that is taken to be true, scientific and philosophical enquiry should proceed from a certain truth. However, we can be deceived – he asks us to imagine an evil demon capable of tricking us into believing things that are not true. The only way to counter this demon's deceits is absolute scepticism: we should doubt everything, all the information from our senses, and even our thoughts and ideas. Whatever cannot be doubted must be a certain truth from which to proceed.

3 I am thinking, therefore I exist

It would seem that if the demon is capable of deceiving all our faculties, there could be nothing we cannot doubt. But here was Descartes's game-changing insight: he realized that there must be something to do all the doubting, a being that is thinking. His original words *'je pense, donc je suis'* (better known as *cogito ergo sum*), are usually translated into English as 'I think, therefore I am', but are perhaps better understood as: I am thinking, therefore I exist. This was the one indubitable truth that Descartes had been looking for as a foundation for knowledge. At the same time, however, it implied a metaphysical statement of the nature of the 'I' that he had shown exists.

4 Cartesian dualism

In a later examination of *cogito ergo sum* (often simply referred to as 'the cogito'), Descartes elaborated on those metaphysical implications. He realized that the 'I' that was doing the doubting was a 'thinking thing', and that therefore thinking is the defining characteristic of the 'I' that exists: the 'I' that I am is a thinking thing. The mind, then, is what I know exists, and what makes me who I am. I have an idea of myself as a being that thinks, which is distinct from my body; and whereas my body is made of material substance, my mind is made of non-material substance.

5 Avicenna: the flying man

Descartes was not the first to reach this conclusion. In the early 11th century, the Islamic philosopher Avicenna described his 'flying man' thought experiment. He imagined a man floating in space, blindfolded and deprived of all sensory perceptions. With no information coming to him from the external world, he is, nevertheless, aware of his own existence, which is distinct from his physical experience. Avicenna infers that he has a 'soul' or 'self' with no physical substance, that coexists with his physical body.

6 The brain in a vat

A 20th-century version of Descartes deceiving demon idea came from Hilary Putnam, who provided a striking metaphor with which he hoped to expose the weakness of the original argument. Rather than a demon, he asks us to imagine an evil scientist, who keeps a brain in a vat of fluid, wired up to a computer that provides it with a completely credible virtual reality. The question Putnam poses is, if the brain does not know it is a brain in a vat, how can we know that we are not being similarly deceived? Is the existence of our minds really an indubitable truth?

7 Descartes's seat of the soul

In Descartes's dualism, the body and mind are not only distinct, composed respectively of material and immaterial substance, but also separate in that they have independent existence. As Descartes explained, the physical body is not capable of thought, and mental substance does not exist in space. Yet there has to be some relationship between the two, as the body sends sensory information to the mind, and the mind is capable of directing the movement of the body; there has to be some point of contact for the two to interact. The obvious answer, to Descartes, was that this interface is somewhere in the brain (he suggested the pineal gland, which he called the 'seat of the soul'). Other adherents to this form of dualism suggested that the link between mind and body is through God.

8 Dualism vs monism

The relationship between material body and immaterial mind was a real problem for some philosophers, and Descartes suggestion of a point of contact between two fundamentally different substances in the (physical) pineal gland was far from satisfactory. Those who could not accept this mind–body dualism divided into several schools of thought, based on some form of monism: some opted for physicalism, the view that everything is essentially physical; others for idealism, that everything is essentially non-material; and some a 'neutral monism', such as Spinoza's idea that everything is of one substance but has both mental and physical properties.

9 The ghost in the machine

The physicalists were the most forthright in their criticism of Cartesian dualism. Among them was Gilbert Ryle, who dismissed the explanation of the existence of a non-material mind as the equivalent of finding a ghost in the machine. Descartes, he said, had confused things that belong in different logical categories, and then presented them as comparable opposites. By presenting mind and body as substantially different entities, Descartes was making a category error similar to thinking of 'the electorate' as an immaterial substance distinct and separate from the people who vote.

10 Psychology and the science of the mind

Cartesian substance dualism became less and less popular in the 20th century, with advances in science and a general trend in philosophy towards a materialist view of the world. Yet, although the quasi-mystical idea of two substances, material and immaterial, was no longer prevalent, vestiges of the dualism between mental and physical persist, even in modern science, in the distinction between brain and mind. And although the two disciplines frequently overlap, we have on the one hand psychology, the science of non-material mind and behaviour, and neuroscience, the science of the physical brain and nervous system.

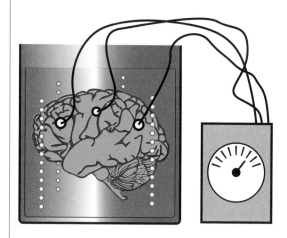

TALK LIKE A GENIUS

❛ Interestingly, even people who would pooh-pooh the idea of our minds being made up of some non-material substance refer to the determination of a heroic sportsman as "mind over matter". ❜

❛ To explain what he meant by a category mistake, Ryle gave the example of the tourist in Oxford who had visited all the college buildings and libraries, but could not locate the university. ❜

❛ There have been numerous takes on the deceiving demon idea in popular culture, indicating a reluctance to dismiss Cartesian mind–body dualism completely. The Matrix trilogy of movies, for instance, is basically an elaboration of Putnam's brain in a vat scenario. ❜

THE BLUFFER'S SUMMARY

I am thinking, therefore I exist as a thinking thing, a non-material entity distinct from my physical body.

Other minds

'We have no conception of Mind itself, as distinguished from its conscious manifestations.'

JOHN STUART MILL

A particular problem with philosophy of mind – that of objectivity – was put into the spotlight when philosophers sought to give their knowledge a more scientific foundation. To do this would require observation of many different minds, but the only mind that we can have any direct experience of is our own. We are, therefore, faced with basing our theories of mind on the subjective evidence of introspection, and whatever indirect evidence there is that it is representative. There are several philosophical objections to assuming what goes on in other people's minds, or even if they have minds at all.

Find out if you really know what goes on in other people's minds.

1 Other minds can never be scientifically studied because general conclusions cannot be drawn from a single instance, and the only evidence we have is subjective.

TRUE / FALSE

2 It is impossible for my sensory experiences to be different from other people's if we all have the same sensory organs and nervous systems.

TRUE / FALSE

3 If a person does not respond to any physical stimulus, we can assume that they have no consciousness; so we can assume that a person who responds to a stimulus has consciousness.

TRUE / FALSE

4 Wittgenstein touches on the problem of other minds in his discussion of public and private language, and the metaphor of the beetle in a box.

TRUE / FALSE

5 If the workings of minds can be explained in purely physical terms, the problems of zombies and other minds can be scientifically solved.

TRUE / FALSE

TEN THINGS A GENIUS KNOWS

1 **Access to other minds**
A fundamental difficulty of philosophy of mind is that the object of its study is not something that lends itself easily to examination. Quite apart from the question of whether or not mind exists as an entity, or is simply an abstract concept, we cannot generalize with any confidence about the way minds operate, without knowing what goes on in other people's minds as well as our own. And, by the very nature of mind, we can have no first-hand objective experience of any other mind than our own. As a result, the problem of how much we can know about other minds has itself become a subject of interest for philosophers of mind.

2 **The problem of introspection**
As the only mind I can have direct access to is my own, it is my primary source of information in any study of mind. But such introspection raises questions of the validity of that information for a philosophical or scientific study of anything but my own mind. There is an epistemological problem of how I can acquire any certain knowledge of other minds, but also a question of whether I am justified in projecting my conceptions of mind onto other minds. Using just one particular instance – my own mind – to infer by induction a general rule, is as inconclusive as assuming that because my dog has three legs, all dogs have three legs. But being overly sceptical about the similarity of my mind and others runs the risk of solipsism, the conclusion that the way my mind works is the only way minds work, or even that mine is the only mind that exists.

3 **Analogy with one's own mind**
It was John Locke who first touched on this problem of other minds, and suggested that if we can have any knowledge of them at all, it has to be indirect and by analogy with our own. This argument from analogy was set out more fully by J.S. Mill, who agreed that while it gives no solid basis for knowledge of other minds, it is not an irrational belief. The argument found defenders in the 20th century too, using Ludwig Wittgenstein's arguments against private language (see page 202) to justify the analogy; as other people describe the inner workings of their minds in the same way that I do, and we can understand one another, we are referring to similar things.

4 **Sensory information**
Although we have no means of directly observing mental processes – seeing inside the minds of other people – we can examine the outward, physical bodies with which they experience the outside world. Physical sensations are picked up by our sensory organs and transmitted to the brain, where we experience them with our minds. And as we all have the same, or at least similar physical sensory apparatus, we can assume that our brains are receiving similar information, in the form of neural signals. But is this sufficient to assume we experience things in the same way?

5 **Subjective experience**
Even if my brain is receiving the same information from my senses as other people's, I cannot be sure that we process that information in the same way. The fact that some people find the taste of Brussels sprouts delicious, and others find it disgusting suggests that we do not experience sensations in the same way. What I see as red, for example, others see as what I would call green, yet because we all refer to it with the word 'red' we assume we are seeing the same thing. The argument from analogy would seem to be weakened by the subjectivity of our sensory experience.

6 Responses to stimuli

Locke's notion that other people's minds are analogous to our own was based on their outward behaviour, and how it is similar to our own. The best explanation for the similarity of our behaviour is that we all have similar minds that cause us to behave the way we do. This is most obviously observable in people's reactions to stimuli: if I prick you with a pin, you will cry out, just as I would. If I treat you kindly, you will smile, and so on. But even this is not conclusive evidence: I cannot know from your reaction that you actually experience pain or pleasure the same way that I do, if at all.

7 Consciousness

There are a couple of assumptions in the process of making an analogy of other minds with our own: that other people's minds work in the same way as my own, but more fundamentally that other people, in fact, have minds – and that is just as much in dispute. To experience things requires more than just sensory input, there must also be consciousness, and it is perhaps this that we need evidence of, in order to establish if other minds exist. After all, some responses are involuntary, reflex actions, and do not involve any conscious thought; so it is not inconceivable that all the responses we observe in others are purely physical, without the need for consciousness. Once again, without direct access to other minds, we cannot be completely sure.

8 Neuroscientific evidence

We may not be able to see into other people's minds, but with modern methods of scanning and monitoring neural activity, we can see into their brains. We now know that all human brains work in very similar ways, and in similar circumstances show similar patterns of electrochemical activity. It is possible, for example, to distinguish between conscious and unconscious brains, in the strict medical sense of the words. This reinforces our intuitive, commonsense notion that we all have similar minds, but still does not conclusively show that our subjective experiences are the same.

9 Philosophical zombies

To illustrate the problem of other minds, modern philosophers such as Daniel Dennett and David Chalmers have made reference to zombies. Not the undead creatures of horror films, or even the mythological voodoo beings, but philosophical zombies: people who in all respects are indistinguishable from us, but have no consciousness. They react to things as we do, but actually experience nothing. If you prick them, they cry out, but they feel nothing. But if they are indistinguishable from other people, how can I know who is or isn't a zombie – or even if I am the only person that has consciousness, that has a mind.

10 Suspending scepticism

Just because I cannot be completely certain that other minds exist does not prove that they don't. It would be perhaps more irrational to make that assumption than to assume that they do exist. Common sense, intuition and modern science present a compelling case for believing that zombies do not exist, that other people have minds, and that they are similar to my own. But this is not sufficient for certain knowledge.

TALK LIKE A GENIUS

❝ It's reassuring that philosophers of mind describe the mind in the same way as I subjectively experience it, in terms of ideas, memories, consciousness and so on, confirming my intuition, but I have no rational grounds for believing other people's minds are like that. ❞

❝ We rely on the evidence of responses to stimuli or verbal reports to know whether or not a person has the same mental experiences as we do, and that they're not a zombie. But we all know from experience how easy it is to fake a reaction when the situation (an unwanted gift, for example) demands. ❞

❝ Wittgenstein made the point that if minds are, in fact, distinct from bodies, it should be just as easy to imagine a table feeling pain as it is to imagine another person feeling pain. But the point is, it isn't. ❞

WERE YOU A GENIUS?

1 FALSE – If we dismiss Cartesian mind–body dualism, it is theoretically possible to have an objective understanding of other minds.

2 FALSE – Even if our physical bodies are identical, how we perceive that sensory information may still be totally different.

3 FALSE – While it is difficult to simulate a non-reaction, especially to a painful stimulus, the converse is easy – and some responses are in any case involuntary.

4 TRUE – The 'later Wittgenstein' examines the problem of understanding a person's inner experience from the language they use.

5 TRUE – Physicalists assert that consciousness in another person can be detected by physical means.

THE BLUFFER'S SUMMARY

Other people's minds are like a closed book to us; we can only assume what's going on inside them from outward appearances.

Self and identity

'We experience ourselves, our thoughts and feelings, as something separate from the rest. A kind of optical delusion of consciousness.'

ALBERT EINSTEIN

While ancient Greek philosophers had explained that it is the soul, or psyche, that is the essence of a person, what makes them who they are, modern philosophers have sought to understand our subjective sense of self. From Descartes's famous *cogito* onwards, philosophy of mind has taken a first-person perspective, as it necessarily involves more subjective introspection than any other field of philosophy. And in examining the concept of self, the philosophy considers not only what makes us who we are, but also our awareness of our existence as individuals.

The oracle at Delphi famously gave the advice 'know thyself'. But do you know how we know what our self is?

1 As our minds are a blank slate at birth, Locke argues, our sense of self comes from our experiences of the world.

TRUE / FALSE

2 Hume asserts that it is impossible for us to have the kind of 'God's-eye' overview that is implied by the notion of an inner experiencing entity.

TRUE / FALSE

3 Kierkegaard described the self as 'a relation that relates itself to itself or is the relation's relating itself to itself in the relation'.

TRUE / FALSE

4 In *Being and Time*, Heidegger says that one can be aware of existence, and of the passage of time, but not of oneself.

TRUE / FALSE

5 Hobbes originated the story of the Ship of Theseus to illustrate his theory of continuity of identity.

TRUE / FALSE

TEN THINGS A GENIUS KNOWS

1 **The self**
Each one of us is a unique individual. And each of us also has an awareness of existing as a separate and distinct being. This is, of course, partly because of our unique physical bodies, but our minds, too, have distinguishing features that make us essentially who we are. The features we exhibit to the outside world – our physical characteristics, behaviour, personalty and opinions for example – constitute what we can call our identity. The self, on the other hand is how we experience that uniqueness from within, from a first-person perspective. We may have a sense of this essential self as the 'agent' that controls our actions and thoughts, or the being that gives us consciousness, and experiences the world with that consciousness.

2 **Locke: an association of ideas**
Numerous theories have attempted to explain this sense of self. Among the first was John Locke in *An Essay Concerning Human Understanding*, which describes the self in terms of a continuity of consciousness. Locke explains that we do not directly experience things in the external world, but the 'ideas' of those things, the information received from our senses. The ideas in our minds also include our reactions to these sensations, our reflections on them, opinions, thoughts and memories, and it is the associations we make between those ideas that are, together, what we consider as our selves.

3 **Hume: the bundle theory of self**
Over time, we feel that not only our physical bodies, but also our ideas change, yet we feel an underlying sense of being the same person. David Hume explained that this is not because there is some mystical unchanging core self, but that we are at any one time a 'bundle of perceptions' that are continually evolving, changing from moment to moment. When we turn our mind inwards, we are only conscious of the particular 'bundle' at that time, not of a separate self that is having those perceptions, and Hume concludes that there is, therefore, no self to be found.

6 **Self-awareness: Heidegger and Merleau-Ponty**

European philosophy in the 20th century adopted an increasingly first-person perspective, tackling issues of metaphysics in terms of our individual experience. This culminated in existentialism, which developed from the notion of self suggested by Martin Heidegger. We get our feeling of a sense of self, he argued, from our being aware of our own existence, of the time between birth and death and what we experience within that time frame. Maurice Merleau-Ponty took this concept of self-awareness a step further, suggesting that our sense of self is not simply an awareness of existence, but an awareness of our own consciousness – we are both subject and object of our awareness.

5 **William James: me and I**
William James was both a philosopher and a pioneer of the new science of psychology, and his theory of self bridged the gap between the two disciplines. James argued that a person's sense of self consists of two distinct conceptions, which he called the 'empirical me' and the 'pure ego'. They correspond to the concepts of 'me' and 'I' in statements such as 'I know it was me who did that': the 'me' consists of a material self (a body and physical attributes), a social self (the self we present in different social situations), and a spiritual self (a personality, and the moral values and opinions we hold); the 'I' is the purely thinking self, which experiences and controls, and perceives the stream of consciousness (see page 53), giving us our sense of self.

6 The self and consciousness

It is helpful to consider a few thought experiments to avoid an overly introspective approach to examining this sense of self. For example, many philosophers have pointed to the importance of consciousness, being aware of our ideas and perceptions, to our feeling of self. If we consider a philosophical zombie (see page 46), we intuitively feel that, although it has a physical identity, its lack of consciousness prevents any sense of self. On the other hand, a brain in a vat (see page 41), if it is wired up cleverly enough, will be conscious, and therefore have a sense of self – but is not aware of how illusory this is.

7 The self and memory

An important feature of our sense of self is that it is founded on more than just our experiences (our perceptions, feelings, thoughts) at any one time; it also includes our memories of past experiences. It is those past experiences that, collectively, have made us who we are now, and their memories persist in our present. But if memories tell us how we became who we are today, they also remind us that we are no longer the same, we have changed, perhaps radically, but still feel we are essentially the same person, the same self, and that there is an element of continuity to our sense of self.

8 The ship of Theseus

The idea of continuity of identity in something that is constantly changing can be illustrated by a story recounted by Thomas Hobbes. On a long voyage, Theseus instructs the crew of his ship to replace any timbers that are showing signs of wear each time they stop off for supplies. By the time the ship eventually reaches its destination, every single piece of it has been replaced. But Theseus and his crew still identify the ship as the one they set sail in. So it is with our bodies, which replace cells as they die off so that we are literally not the person we were 20 years ago; and our minds are changing in a similar way, yet there is a continuity to our sense of self.

9 The brain transplant

There is, however, a limit to how far we can take the Theseus's ship analogy. In the case of the ship, we are talking of its identity, the way that it is recognized from outside, which is not comparable to the subjective, first-person sense of who I am. These days it is possible to transplant almost any organ from one human into another, and, theoretically at least, replace a whole physical body. And yes, the recipient would still retain the same sense of self – so long as the brain was the only organ not transplanted. Something in that complex physical mass of neural networks is what gives us a sense of self.

10 The teleporter thought experiment

Let's return to the story of Theseus's ship: an enterprising merchant follows Theseus on his voyage and collects all the discarded timber from his ship, then rebuilds it exactly as it was. Which now is the ship that Theseus set sail in? Now, imagine a 'teleporting machine' that works by making a duplicate of me in a remote location, at the same time destroying the original. The replica is exact in every detail, including my memories, thoughts and ideas. But it isn't me, even though it thinks it is. And if there was a malfunction, and the original was not destroyed, there would be two identical mes. Naturally, I know I am me, but the replica not only appears to be me, but has the same sense of self as I do.

TALK LIKE A GENIUS

❝ The idea of continuity is a vital ingredient in a sense of self. Take any well-established string quartet, for example: the personnel may have changed completely over the last 50 years, and the repertoire too, but they still think of themselves as the same group. ❞

❝ The importance of experience and memory to notions of self is perhaps most noticeable by its absence, as in the case of people with dementia. From an outsider's perspective, they lose an essential part of their identity, and on the inside they feel a loss of self. ❞

❝ If it were possible to somehow separate all the "software" – the thoughts, experiences and memories, and so on – from our physical brains and transplant it into a younger brain, we could keep our selves alive indefinitely. ❞

WERE YOU A GENIUS?

1 TRUE – Self is the association of ideas in our minds, which ultimately derive from our experience.

2 TRUE – When we introspect, we only see our experiences, not a self having those experiences.

3 TRUE – This description is at the beginning of *The Sickness unto Death*, written under the pseudonym Anti-Climacus.

4 TRUE – It is our awareness of being and time that gives us a sense of self, according to Heidegger.

5 FALSE – The story is a paradox discussed by several ancient Greek philosophers.

THE BLUFFER'S SUMMARY

There is a continuity to the constantly changing bundle of experiences that gives me an enduring sense of self.

Consciousness

'Human consciousness is just about the last surviving mystery.'

DANIEL C. DENNETT

In almost every aspect of philosophy of mind, reference is made to consciousness – indeed, consciousness is an inherent part of what we call 'mind'. However, despite our intuitive understanding of consciousness, it has eluded precise definition until comparatively recently. As with other concepts in philosophy of mind, opinion has changed over the centuries since Descartes. With the advent of the modern sciences of psychology and neuroscience, philosophers have tended increasingly towards physicalist definitions of consciousness, yet none has yet satisfactorily explained the subjective experience we are all familiar with, of being aware of our perceptions, thoughts and intentions.

Despite advances in the scientific and philosophical understanding of the mind, consciousness remains an elusive concept. Is it a mystery to you?

1 An explanation of consciousness is a concern not only for philosophy, but also in psychology, neuroscience and medicine.

TRUE / FALSE

2 William James developed his concept of a 'stream of consciousness' from the device used by novelists, presenting a series of related subjective thoughts and experiences.

TRUE / FALSE

3 Some cognitive scientists, including Dennett, believe that consciousness will eventually be explained in terms of the computational faculty of neural networks.

TRUE / FALSE

4 In 1974, Nagel was the first to challenge the strictly physicalist dismissal of consciousness in his article, 'What is it like to be a bat?'

TRUE / FALSE

5 With his phenomenology, Husserl hoped to explain consciousness in terms of our ability to experience phenomena.

TRUE / FALSE

TEN THINGS A GENIUS KNOWS

1 What consciousness is

Consciousness is one of those phenomena we all understand intuitively, but struggle to define. A broad, commonsense definition involving awareness of having thoughts in our minds is broad enough to be used in everyday situations, but tells us little about the nature of consciousness. We can describe various aspects of what we experience as consciousness, our awareness of what is going on in our minds, but not how it is that we are aware of that. And as philosophers, psychologists and neuroscientists seem to have different ideas of the nature of consciousness – for example, whether it is subjective or objective – perhaps there are several different elements contributing to our experience of consciousness.

2 Locke's definition

As with the concept of 'self', it was John Locke who first suggested a definition of consciousness, a definition that established a concept of consciousness that has shaped modern ideas in the subject. In brief, he defined it as the 'perception of what passes in a man's own mind'. A simple but pithy phrase that went beyond the shallow idea of consciousness as awareness of the external world, or even simple self-awareness, and instead described it as an awareness of what is happening in the mind: not just having ideas, thoughts and perceptions, but having the experience of having those ideas, thoughts and perceptions.

3 Forms of consciousness

The definition of consciousness is different in different contexts. In medicine, for example, it is a state of awareness of sensory experience, contrasted with unconsciousness. There is also a more practical definition, of knowing things, and knowing how to do things. There are also what Locke called 'reflective ideas', our ability to use our reason to make sense of our sensory perceptions. But for the philosopher, consciousness is the sum of all these things and more: it is the perception we have of being conscious, of knowing and of thinking.

4 James: stream of consciousness

David Hume, in his 'bundle' theory of self (see page 49), described how the conscious mind is continually changing, moving from one thought, one perception, to another with amazing rapidity. This idea of the changing nature of our consciousness was picked up by the American philosopher and psychologist William James. While he agreed with Hume that we are only conscious of what is happening in our mind at any given time, he did not see it as being a kaleidoscopic series of momentary perceptions, but rather a flow of experience of thoughts and perceptions, for which he coined the term 'stream of consciousness'.

5 Gilbert Ryle: a misleading concept

Descartes's mind–body dualism cast a long shadow, and the idea of not just mind, but mental states such as consciousness, being somehow separate from the physical body, persisted well into the 20th century. But Gilbert Ryle set the physicalist ball rolling by dismissing Cartesian dualism as finding a 'ghost in the machine', and explained how it has misled us into thinking of that intuitive feeling of consciousness as something separate from the rest of our existence. It would be more helpful to our understanding of consciousness, he suggested, if we considered the person as a whole, as an individual interacting with the world, with both physical and mental perceptions.

6 Physicalist explanations

In the second half of the 20th century, Cartesian dualism was widely rejected in favour of a monist, physicalist approach to philosophy of mind. Physicalists, in the main, denied the existence of consciousness completely, dismissing it as an illusion. Various physicalist explanations of consciousness emerged. Behaviourism, which had become a major school of thought in psychology, held that we do not have an introspective perception of mental states, but that they are a disposition to certain sorts of behaviour. A slightly different approach, 'functionalism', was taken by philosophers including Hilary Putnam and Jerry Fodor. It held that mental states are entirely defined by their role as a function, in terms of their causes and effects.

7 What it is like to be a bat
The problem for some philosophers, including a number who rejected Cartesian dualism, was that strict monist physicalism and its purely mechanistic explanation of mind ignored or dismissed the subjective, intuitive sense we all have of being conscious. Thomas Nagel was uncomfortable with what he saw as a reductionist approach to the question of consciousness. In his essay 'What Is it Like to Be a Bat?', he argued for the validity of a subjective experience of mind, what we understand as consciousness. It is impossible for us, he says to think of what it is like to be a bat for the bat, as every conscious being has its own perspective. There is a 'subjective character of experience', as he puts it, a consciousness of what it is like to be a particular being, and that is missing in purely physicalist explanations.

8 The subjective experience of consciousness
Another philosopher who could not accept the purely physicalist explanation of mind is John Searle. He felt that the argument had become polarized: on the one side, the physicalist idea of a totally physical world, and on the other, the subjective but undeniable experience of consciousness. He suggested the two views are not incompatible, that our subjective experience of consciousness is the perception of the physical processes happening in our brains.

9 Phenomenal and access consciousness
In recent years, the majority of philosophers have accepted physicalism, but without dismissing the subjective experience we recognize as consciousness. Instead, some have tried to further define the ways in which we experience it. Ned Block, for example, has suggested that there are two distinct types of consciousness: phenomenal (P-consciousness) and access (A-consciousness). He describes P-consciousness as simple experience of sensory information, emotions and so on, which he calls 'qualia', our subjective experience of the world. A-consciousness, however, is the process by which that information is available for us to reason, talk and act. The information is there for us to access when we introspect.

10 A scientific explanation of consciousness
Today, most philosophers agree that what we experience as consciousness is a product of physical processes in the brain. There is, however, no consensus as to whether the 'problem of consciousness' can be answered by science. Some, like philosopher and cognitive scientist Daniel Dennett, believe that an increased knowledge of the higher-order workings of the brain will lead to a full understanding of the nature of consciousness. Others are more sceptical. John Searle, for example, argues that although consciousness is a combination of physical biological processes, it is much more than the sum of its parts – and how that comes about is, as yet, beyond scientific explanation.

TALK LIKE A GENIUS

❝ In his definition of consciousness as "perception of what passes in a man's own mind", Locke marked it as different from other mental states, as it is the subjective awareness of those mental states and ideas. ❞

❝ Philosopher David Chalmers refers to the "hard problem of consciousness", to distinguish it from the mechanisms of perception comparatively easily explained in physical terms. Although many philosophers accept this distinction, some – and many cognitive scientists – dispute that it is any different from other questions of mind. ❞

❝ While it is easy to describe and define the subjective experience of consciousness, as John Searle points out, the mystery is: "how does a lump of fatty tissue and electricity give rise to this experience of perceiving, meaning or thinking?". ❞

THE BLUFFER'S SUMMARY

The problem of consciousness is not defining the subjective experience of consciousness, but explaining how we come to have it.

Artificial intelligence

'May not machines carry out something which ought to be described as thinking but which is very different from what a man does?'

ALAN TURING

Although computer science as we understand it today only took off in the mid-20th century, ideas of artificial intelligence date back to the Renaissance, when philosophers such as Hobbes began to compare the workings of the human mind to automata and calculating machines. As the technology became ever more sophisticated from Babbage's programmable Analytical Engine onwards, the potential for some kind of artificial intelligence became a reality. Alan Turing, a pioneer of computing and artificial intelligence, recognized the possibility, and even suggested that, in the foreseeable future, machines would show evidence of intelligence. But the philosophical question then is: can a machine think in the same way as a human?

Modern computers behave in an apparently intelligent way, but can a computer match your intelligence?

1 One of Descartes's arguments against any form of artificial intelligence was that machines are incapable of speech.

TRUE / FALSE

2 The idea that machines can't have minds because they lack consciousness is countered with the fact that modern computers can examine their own systems, for example, to trace bugs.

TRUE / FALSE

3 The Turing test is based on a party game known as the 'imitation game', in which one player asks questions of two other players, and from their written responses tries to tell which is which.

TRUE / FALSE

4 In 1972, a computer program called ELIZA passed the Turing test, by responding to questions in the manner of a paranoid schizophrenic, convincing a panel of psychiatrists that it was human.

TRUE / FALSE

5 According to a strictly physicalist view, the question is not so much whether machines can think in the same way as humans, as whether humans think in the same way as machines.

TRUE / FALSE

1 Can machines think?

The emergence of artificial intelligence (AI) as a field of study in computing science stimulated a debate among psychologists, cognitive scientists and philosophers. At its most basic, the question was: can a machine think? But this is not as simple a question as it seems. On one level, it is a question of whether a machine can have the ability to solve problems intelligently; but a more searching question arises as to whether machine intelligence of this sort is comparable to human intelligence, whether it can be said to be really thinking – and the converse, whether human thinking is simply a mechanical process. Finally, there is the more philosophical question of whether a machine can have a mind in the same way that humans have, with mental states, consciousness and a sense of self. And if they can't, how do we?

2 Animals as automata

Long before the invention of computers, philosophers touched on some of the basic issues of artificial intelligence. In the 17th century, mechanical toys were all the rage, including some very sophisticated automata, such as Jacques de Vaucanson's duck, which walked, flapped its wings, ate, drank and defecated. These were obviously machines, not living things, but many people, Descartes and Hobbes among them, saw no difference between man-made and natural animals – only humans have a mind (or soul), and all other creatures are merely physical. Descartes considered it a mistake to interpret their mechanical activity as evidence of a mind or consciousness.

3 A mechanistic view of the Universe

The late Renaissance was a time of extraordinary scientific discovery, especially of the physical laws governing everything. This replaced religious and mystical explanations with a mechanistic model of the Universe. For Descartes, these physical laws applied to material things and physical beings, but not the immaterial human mind. But for Hobbes, the mechanistic character of everything included the human mind. 'Reason', he argued, is 'nothing but reckoning'; our brains and what they do are merely mechanical. And if they are mechanical, then machines are theoretically capable of the same kind of thought. The battle lines were drawn by Descartes and Hobbes for the debate: 'Can machines think?'

4 The appearance of intelligence

While the physicalist approach to the question appears to be the more scientific, Descartes had identified a chink in its armour. As with de Vaucanson's duck, we may be deceived by appearances into thinking that machines have intelligence, and assuming that they therefore have a mind. Machines, such as the computers that can now compete with chess grand masters, do not actually make decisions, but are programmed to analyse all possibilities and their outcomes and act on one that fits certain criteria. Hobbes would respond by saying that surely that is exactly what we do when we make a decision.

5 The Turing test

Alan Turing, considered the 'founding father' of the modern science of artificial intelligence, was uncomfortable with the question 'can machines think?' It depends, he said, on our definition of 'think'. Instead, he preferred to talk of whether or not machines can have intelligence, and suggested that if a machine behaves as intelligently as a human being, then it is as intelligent as a human being. He devised the famous 'Turing test' to determine whether a machine was capable of such intelligence. It pits a computer and a human against one another, answering questions put to them by an interrogator communicating via text on an electronic link. If after questioning them the interrogator cannot tell which is human and which the machine, the machine has passed the test; it behaves as intelligently as a human, so can be said to have intelligence.

6 Human versus machine intelligence
According to Turing, it is more accurate to say that a machine has intelligence than that it thinks. A machine can be said to be thinking, but it probably thinks in a different way from us. Computers have now come to outstrip humans in their capability to store data, perform calculations and so on, but does this demonstrate a superior intelligence, or just a different kind of intelligence? And if we turn the comparison around, can we really understand the human mind by analogy with computers? Thomas Nagel thinks emphatically not, describing this line of reasoning as a 'gigantic waste of time'.

7 Soft machines
Nevertheless, the analogy between brain and computer is attractive, and has been adopted by a number of physicalist philosophers. Following on from Gilbert Ryle's 'ghost in the machine' rejection of Cartesian dualism, philosophers including Hilary Putnam and Jerry Fodor suggested a purely physical model of the mind known as functionalism. This viewed humans as 'soft machines', and explained the workings of the human mind in terms of inputs and outputs, similar to the way in which a computer processes information. The brain is essentially the hardware, and the mind the software.

8 The Chinese room
A number of philosophers found the purely physical comparison of computer and mind unsatisfactory. We intuitively feel that the human mind has something that a machine can never have, despite its ability to show intelligence. To show the flaw in the Turing test, John Searle proposed the 'Chinese room' thought experiment. He imagines an English-speaker, with no knowledge of Chinese, in a room containing a library of instruction books.

Written information comes into the room in Chinese characters, to which the English-speaker must respond. To do this he refers to the library, which tells him which Chinese characters constitute an appropriate response. He writes these down and passes this out of the room. To someone outside the room the responses are exactly what would be expected of a Chinese speaker, but without any understanding of the Chinese texts. As well as showing that the information can pass through the 'mind' of a machine without any understanding, Searle undermined the functionalist idea that the human mind is reducible to input and output of data.

9 Consciousness and feelings
Searle's argument was that a human mind is different from a computer in one important respect: it has understanding of the information in its thought processes, and that implies consciousness and other mental states. Not that these are some mysterious immaterial substance, as Descartes suggested, but identifiable all the same. According to Searle, machines may show intelligence, but do not, and cannot, have consciousness. Even ardent physicalists, such as Daniel Dennett, would agree that even a perfectly programmed computer model of a human would give merely the appearance of consciousness. But if machines are made with the same sort of neural networks as humans, it is difficult to put up a good argument as to why they shouldn't have similar mental states.

10 Strong and weak AI
The science Turing helped establish, AI, has advanced to the stage where machines have, in some respects, become indistinguishable from humans, but cannot really be said to be thinking. There is a distinction to be made between what Searle called strong and weak AI. According to strong AI, a computer programmed cleverly enough would have a mind in the same way as humans do; according to weak AI such a computer would merely be a model of a mind, simulating the way that it works.

TALK LIKE A GENIUS

❝ The argument is cut and dried for Descartes and his followers: machines cannot be made with the immaterial substance that constitutes mind. For those who reject Cartesian dualism, however, the jury's still out. ❞

❝ Although we intuitively feel that a man-made machine cannot have a mind like ours, and there are good rational arguments to back this up, it is a seductive idea that repeatedly features in science fiction, and the Holy Grail of AI. ❞

❝ Searle's Chinese room thought experiment demonstrated how computer programs are mindless processors of data, but we are still left with the possibility of building organic "machines" that replicate human brains, and the nagging doubt that they might be capable of having a mind. ❞

THE BLUFFER'S SUMMARY

Even if we could make a machine physically identical to a human, it still might only *appear* to think as humans do.

The existence of God

'It is incomprehensible that God should exist, and it is incomprehensible that He should not exist.'

BLAISE PASCAL

Western philosophy developed out of our human curiosity, seeking explanations for phenomena in the world around us, but based on reason rather than belief in supernatural causes. Yet, with very few exceptions, religions are founded on a belief in some sort of supreme supernatural being – God – generally credited with the creation of the Universe. To overcome this apparent incompatibility of religion and philosophy, some thinkers, especially the medieval Christian philosophers, sought rational arguments to prove the existence of God. Others, however, produced counterarguments, and suggested that it is a matter of faith, not reason, and that the existence of God cannot be proven.

A number of philosophers remained unconvinced by arguments for the existence of God; do you know why?

1 As a counterargument to the 'problem of evil', Leibniz asserted that God could conceive of infinite universes, but only one can exist; God is good, so the Universe He chose is the best of all possible worlds.
TRUE / FALSE

2 Scientists have shown that the Universe has not always existed: before the Big Bang, there was nothing. If so, the cosmological arguments for the existence of God will be proved correct.
TRUE / FALSE

3 According to Berkeley, things only exist if they are perceived by a subject; as we can perceive God through the Universe He created, He must exist.
TRUE / FALSE

4 Using Russell's argument, that all rational arguments for the existence of God are inconclusive, it is as irrational to believe in God as it is to believe in the tooth fairy.
TRUE / FALSE

5 In weighing up the probabilities of his wager, Pascal concludes that there is a rational argument for believing in God.
TRUE / FALSE

TEN THINGS A GENIUS KNOWS

1 Belief, faith and reason

Philosophers have debated endlessly the question of how much we can claim to know something to be true. When a philosopher says they believe something is the case, it is the conclusion of a reasoned argument or line of thought, after examination of all the available evidence. Religious claims, however, are often not based on reason, but on faith, and that may be a blind faith with no basis in evidence or rational argument. While many religious believers are content simply to have faith, others have sought rational grounds to support their beliefs, most importantly belief in the existence of God.

2 Thomas Aquinas: the Five Ways

The problem of reconciling faith and reason was a fundamental concern for medieval philosophers, because the Christian Church held the monopoly of scholarship and learning in Europe. A number of arguments were advanced for the existence of God, and in the 13th century the leading philosopher of the time, Thomas Aquinas, made a methodical study of the most important ones in what he called the Five Ways. Three of these – the arguments of the unmoved mover, the first cause, and the necessary being – are considered to be variants of the cosmological argument, that the existence of the Universe as it is, demonstrates that there was a creator God. Similarly, the teleological argument is based on the evidence of a deliberate design or purpose in the Universe, which proves it had an intelligent creator. The argument from degree, or ontological argument, takes a different approach, based on the necessary existence of a supremely perfect being.

3 The cosmological argument

Christian dogma asserts that the Universe has not always existed, and that it was created by God.

Although the idea of an eternal Universe without beginning or end had been hotly debated by Greek philosophers, Aquinas took the Aristotelean notion of cause as the basis for his arguments. He argued that nothing can cause itself, but must be caused by something, and if we trace back the chain of events, we come to the cause of the existence of the Universe itself. It cannot always have existed, and moreover there must have been something to cause it to exist, a 'first cause' or 'unmoved mover'. And that first cause, he says, is God.

4 The Big Bang theory

Critics have pointed out a couple of flaws in the cosmological argument. The idea of a first cause raises the logical question: what caused the first cause? Perhaps there is an infinite regress, rather than a finite beginning to everything. Another unjustified assumption is that the first cause must be God. Modern cosmology, in the form of the Big Bang theory, gives an alternative, evidence-based explanation for the origin of the Universe, and at the same time solves the problem of both a first cause and infinite regress. All time and space came into existence with the Big Bang, so notions of 'before' it are meaningless: there was no time or space in which something could exist. In Bertrand Russell's words, 'The Universe is just there, and that's all.' But even that has a counterargument, that God the creator exists outside of time and space.

5 The teleological argument

The natural world is filled with examples of complex things that function beautifully and suit their environment. The teleological, or intelligent design, argument suggests that these couldn't have come into being by accident, but have been deliberately created with some design or purpose. There must, then, exist an intelligent creator, God, who is sometimes likened to a divine watchmaker. Once again, scientific evidence, in this case Darwin's theory of evolution by natural selection, provides a counterargument.

6 Idealism and religion

An alternative counter to the teleological argument is provided by an inversion of its premise. Credited to Epicurus, the 'problem of evil' turns the argument that there must be a God because everything in the world is wonderful on its head. It begins by stating the fact that there is evil in the world. Why doesn't God prevent it? If he wants to, but can't, he isn't omnipotent. If he can, but won't, he isn't benevolent. and if he is neither omnipotent nor benevolent, why call him God?

7 The ontological argument

The 'argument from degree' referred to by Aquinas is an ontological argument first proposed by Anselm of Canterbury in the 11th century. God, he claimed, is 'that than which nothing greater can be thought'. Imagine the greatest possible being. If that being is perfect in every way, but only exists in your imagination, not reality, it isn't the greatest possible being – one that exists both in your imagination and in reality would be better. So the greatest possible being must exist in reality; and that greatest possible being is God. An elegant argument, but not without its critics, including Hume and Kant, on logical grounds. But perhaps the simplest was Gaunilo of Marmoutiers' 'lost island' counterargument, which used the same logic to demonstrate the existence of a lost island more perfect than any island in existence.

8 Berkeley and the mind of God

George Berkeley's 'immaterialism' (see page 18) provides yet another argument for God's existence. According to Berkeley, material things only exist as ideas in the mind of the perceiver, they cannot exist without being perceived. Common sense, however, tells us that things continue to exist, even when there is nobody there to perceive them – they don't suddenly cease to exist, or leap into existence. This, Berkeley says, is because they are being perceived by God; things exist in the mind of God, who is the 'Spirit' that is the cause of our perception.

9 Bertrand Russell's teapot

Bertrand Russell pointed out a fundamental problem with all rational arguments for the existence of God. None of them can be conclusive, as there is no factual evidence, and you can choose to believe in all sorts of things if you don't have to provide evidence as a basis for a rational argument. It is also difficult to refute an argument by trying to prove the non-existence of something. As an example, he facetiously claimed to believe in the existence of an invisible teapot orbiting the Sun: although he could not provide rational arguments to support his claim, he challenged anyone to prove him wrong.

10 Pascal's wager

Blaise Pascal was primarily a mathematician and a pioneer of probability theory. He was also a theologian, and slightly mischievously illustrated one of his theories of probability with a wager about whether it is more rational to believe or not believe in the existence of God: you can choose either, but what do you stand to gain or lose? If you choose not to believe, if you are right you lose nothing and gain nothing, but if you are wrong you face the huge loss of eternity in hell. If you choose to believe, however, if you are right you get an infinite gain, eternity in heaven, with minimal loss that you follow his laws.

❛ There are three main arguments for the existence of God: that the Universe had to have been created by something; that the Universe shows evidence of intelligent design; and that there is a being that is more perfect than the most perfect being imaginable. All three have been shown to be flawed, but that doesn't prove that God doesn't exist. ❜

❛ Pastafarians, who claim to believe in the invisible flying spaghetti monster, highlight the problem of the burden of proof. If asked to prove it exists, they respond by asking for proof that it doesn't. ❜

❛ Pascal never intended his wager to be an argument for the existence of God, but a demonstration of a mathematical idea. The stakes (eternity in either heaven or hell) assume that, if there is a God, He is the God envisioned by Christianity. ❜

❛ David Hume offered sound logical criticisms of all the arguments for the existence of God, but also poked fun at them, saying that not only is it presumptuous to assign characteristics, such as omnipotence, to God, but on the evidence of the Universe as it is, He would have made a better job of it if He were omnipotent. ❜

1 TRUE – Leibniz, a Christian, did not accept the argument that evil contradicts God's omnipotence or benevolence.

2 FALSE – The Big Bang theory states that absolutely nothing – no unmoved mover, necessary being or first cause – existed before the Universe came into being.

3 FALSE – Material objects only exist in the mind of a perceiver, but God is the subject, not the object, of perception.

4 TRUE – Russell's argument is a logical one, that something has to be shown to be true, not assumed for lack of contrary evidence.

5 FALSE – His conclusion is that if it were simply a matter of choice, then a rational person would choose to believe in God.

THE BLUFFER'S SUMMARY

All arguments for – and against – the existence of God are inconclusive, and it is generally accepted that it is not provable either way.

Christianity, Islam and philosophy

'Therefore do not seek to understand in order to believe, but believe that thou mayest understand.'

AUGUSTINE OF HIPPO

Philosophy in the classical world had been dominated by the Greek thinkers, even in the Roman empire that succeeded the Greeks. But as the classical era was drawing to a close, Christianity was beginning to establish itself as the predominant force in western Europe. With a virtual monopoly of learning and scholarship, the Church ruled cultural life, and was suspicious of anything that contradicted Christian dogma. But medieval scholars sought ways to integrate into Christian doctrine the philosophical ideas of Plato and Aristotle. During this period, another religion was founded – Islam – which had a very different attitude towards philosophical and scientific enquiry.

Medieval philosophers struggled to reconcile conflicting claims of religion and philosophy. Do you know how they did it?

1 *The Consolation of Philosophy* enjoyed enormous popularity in the Middle Ages, as it explained that Aristotelian philosophy complements, rather than contradicts, Christian doctrine.

TRUE / FALSE

2 Plotinus was the first of the Christian philosophers to integrate Platonism into Christian doctrine.

TRUE / FALSE

3 Augustine was raised as a Christian, but abandoned the faith in his teens and joined the Manichaeans, then studied philosophy before returning to Christianity when he was in his 30s.

TRUE / FALSE

4 In a thought experiment, Avicenna described a man floating in space, deprived of all sensory information, to demonstrate that mind (or soul) and body are separate and distinct.

TRUE / FALSE

5 The great centres of learning established in the Islamic 'Golden Age' were strictly secular, as theology was considered the province of the mosques.

TRUE / FALSE

TEN THINGS A GENIUS KNOWS

1 **Christian doctrine versus philosophy**
The core beliefs of Christianity are based on a historical narrative, the life and teachings of Jesus, and are accepted as articles of faith rather than conclusions of reasoning. Because of that, anything that appears to contradict or cast doubt on Christian dogma is regarded as heretical. And so, in the early Christian Church, philosophical ideas were subjected to careful examination to ascertain whether they were compatible with Christian belief, and were only gradually accepted.

2 **The early Church**
Although Christianity originated in Roman-occupied Judaea, the Christian Church was founded in Rome, where it was regarded as a rather exotic cult. It was monotheistic, unlike the Graeco-Roman religion, and demanded faith in the revelations of Jesus, the Son of God, which was at odds with the emphasis on learning and debate in Graeco-Roman culture. Nevertheless, Christianity gradually became integrated into the host culture, and some early Christian thinkers took an interest in its philosophy, which at the time was either Roman stoicism or Platonism. In time, these ideas were deemed acceptable, and even used to support some Christian beliefs.

3 **Neo-Platonism**
Probably the most influential Roman philosopher of that time was Plotinus, whose ideas developed the mystic side of Plato's philosophy. Many Christian thinkers were attracted to this neo-Platonism, as it was later called, as its interpretation of Plato's eternal world of Forms chimed with their belief in a Kingdom of Heaven. In Plotinus's philosophy, reality is in the realm of the Forms, and is apprehended by the intellect, it is mental, so that to exist is to be thought; this matched the Christian idea that the world was created in the mind of God. For Plotinus there are three levels of being: the Soul, where we exist; the Intellect, where we have access to the reality of the Forms; and the One, the transcendental, which Christians took to mean being at one with God.

4 **St Augustine**
Augustine of Hippo was one of the first Christian philosophers, and one of the most influential. Before adopting the Christian faith, he studied philosophy, and was inspired by neo-Platonism. He was particularly struck by the idea of an eternal, non-material world of ideal Forms, and that our immortal soul is in that realm. Despite the fact that this was not part of Christ's teaching, through Augustine's writings it later became accepted as part of Christian doctrine. In his book *The City of God*, he developed the idea further, explaining that the laws governing our behaviour also belong in three realms: God's laws are ideals in the immaterial realm, while here on Earth we have natural laws created by God, and man-made laws governing our human societies. But faith, he maintained, precedes reason, and philosophy, for him, was merely to support his beliefs, not create them.

5 **Boethius: *The Consolation of Philosophy***
Augustine was certainly the first great Christian philosopher, but he was one of the last of the classical world. During his lifetime, the Roman empire collapsed, and Europe entered the so-called Dark Ages, a period of cultural decline and political turmoil that was to last several centuries. The Christian Church struggled to survive, and philosophy all but disappeared as Europe was overrun by Germanic invaders. One philosopher, Boethius, managed to continue with his work, translating the few surviving texts of Aristotle, but he became embroiled in the conflict between warring tribes, and was sentenced to death. He was a Christian, but the book he wrote in prison before his execution, *The Consolation of Philosophy*, showed he turned not to his faith but the ideas of stoicism and neo-Platonism.

6 Scholasticism

It was not until the 11th century that the Church – and philosophy – re-emerged as a cultural force. But by then Christian doctrine had absorbed much of Plato's philosophy, and the problem now was to reconcile that with what was known of Aristotle, which was, at that time, restricted to his writings on logic. These, however, were to have a profound influence, as they provided the methodology of logical reasoning on which the medieval universities were based, known as scholasticism. Being Christian institutions, the academics in them increasingly used Aristotelian reasoning to support Christian dogma.

7 Thomas Aquinas

Anselm of Canterbury, who proposed the ontological argument for the existence of God (see page 62), is credited with introducing Aristotelian reasoning to the Christian centres of learning. Subsequently, scholasticism produced a succession of Christian philosophers, including Pierre Abélard and Roger Bacon, but by far the most influential was Thomas Aquinas. Aquinas sought not simply to reconcile the differences between Aristotle's philosophy and Christianity, but to show that they are actually compatible. With systematic reasoning, he showed that Aristotle's assertion that the Universe has always existed does not contradict the Bible's account of God creating it: God created the Universe with a beginning, but could have created a Universe that is eternal. He concluded that, as both reason and Christian doctrine are God-given, it is impossible for them to be contradictory.

8 Greek philosophy and Islam

The Christian philosophers' interest in Aristotle didn't come out of the blue. From about the 11th century, texts by the Greek philosophers were becoming available in Europe for the first time, having been preserved, translated and annotated by Islamic scholars. Islam, founded in the seventh century, flourished while Christianity struggled, but, more importantly it had a reverence rather than a suspicion of scholarship and discovery. Philosophy, and especially the scientific philosophy of Aristotle, was considered complementary to theology, and reason regarded as God-given.

9 The Islamic 'Golden Age'

In a remarkably short time, Islam became a major religion with adherents across the Middle East, into Asia and Africa. With its respect for scholarship, it encouraged the establishment of 'houses of wisdom' in the major cities, which attracted thinkers from across the region. The accepted source of knowledge were the works of the Greek philosophers, and philosophers including Avicenna and Averroes developed a distinctive Islamic philosophy from their commentaries on these texts. Aristotle was especially admired, and his emphasis on empirical observation and methodical analysis inspired a wealth of scientific enquiry and discovery. When this knowledge found its way into Europe, it inspired Christian scholasticism, but also the beginnings of a scientific tradition that would be in conflict with Christian dogma.

10 Desiderius Erasmus

At the end of the 15th century, the medieval period was coming to an end as Renaissance ideas took hold. Science, reason and humanism challenged the authority of the Church, and it was becoming increasingly difficult to reconcile the latest ideas and discoveries with Christian doctrine. Many Christian thinkers were frustrated by the continual philosophical debates about theology, especially when the corruption in the Church was being exposed and a Protestant Reformation was imminent. The solution, according to Desiderius Erasmus, is simple: religion is based on faith, not reason, and combining the two is impossible. Faith is about an individual's relationship with God, and cannot be subject to reason, and once philosophy becomes involved it simply leads to fruitless theological intellectualizing.

TALK LIKE A GENIUS

❛ The early Christian Church was established in the Roman empire, where stoicism and Platonism were almost the only schools of philosophy. Because of that, the philosophical aspects of Catholic doctrine are based largely on neo-Platonism. ❜

❛ While Christianity was initially hostile to Aristotle's philosophy based on empirical evidence and logical reasoning, Islam embraced it, and consequently made scientific advances long before Europe. ❜

❛ By adopting Aristotelian methodology, scholasticism produced many of the finest medieval Christian philosophers, but also led to rifts in the Church over the philosophical justification for minor points of dogma – just the sort of theological intellectualizing that prompted Erasmus to urge a separation of reason from faith. ❜

THE BLUFFER'S SUMMARY

Medieval philosophy was dominated by the attempt by Christian philosophers to reconcile their dogma with philosophical reasoning.

Free will

'Man can do what he wills but he cannot will what he wills.'

ARTHUR SCHOPENHAUER

Belief in an omnipotent creator God is common to many religions, as is the concept of sin, of disobeying His moral laws. And this poses a philosophical problem: if God is omnipotent, and also omniscient, then He either determines our actions or knows of them in advance. Yet if they are predetermined, how can we have free will to go against His authority, or have any moral responsibility for our actions? The problem of reconciling the idea of free will is not confined to religion, however. Determinist philosophers believe that everything, including our own actions, is causally determined by prior events, a view that is difficult to reconcile with our subjective impression of having free will.

You're free to check your knowledge of determinism, but are you destined to failure?

1 Free will and determinism can only be regarded as compatible if we accept the idea of an omnipotent God determining our freely chosen actions.

TRUE / FALSE

2 Philosophers have identified logical determinism, where events in the future can be determined as true or false in the present.

TRUE / FALSE

3 Although Hume intuitively felt that we have free will, his reason told him that everything in the physical world is causally determined; since our decisions are not separate from the physical world, they are also causally determined.

TRUE / FALSE

4 Schopenhauer argued that we cannot be held morally responsible for our actions because, although we have physical freedom to do what we will, we have no moral freedom to will what we will.

TRUE / FALSE

5 The will to power, cornerstone of Nietzsche's atheistic philosophy, is only possible because we have free will.

TRUE / FALSE

TEN THINGS A GENIUS KNOWS

1 The problem of free will

We have a strong intuitive feeling that we have the ability to make conscious decisions, that we have the free will to do as we want. But is there any real justification for that belief? Our religious faith in an omnipotent God may contradict that idea; this theological determinism, as it is called, is the view that God controls or foresees our actions. Causal determinism poses a similar dilemma, but instead of God, the laws of nature or science determine events; everything is caused by whatever happened previously, and it is not possible for things to happen in any other way. The problem of free will is a question of whether we have any control over our actions, and to what extent they are determined by external factors.

2 Boethius on free will

The problem of free will is especially relevant in Christianity, with its concept of original sin and the free choice of Adam and Eve to eat the fruit of the tree of knowledge of good and evil. The theological debate still goes on, but the philosophical dilemma was tackled in the early sixth century by Boethius. He argued that free will and theological determinism are not incompatible. God is omniscient and knows in advance what our thoughts and actions will be, but He has granted us free will to do what we choose. So, He knows what that choice will be (even if we change our minds): He foresees, but does not control, our future thoughts and actions.

3 Moral responsibility

It is an important belief in many faiths that we are responsible for our behaviour and, in the Abrahamic religions in particular, that we will have to account for it in some future life. That, however, presupposes that we have at least some degree of free will to choose between good and evil, that our actions are not entirely predetermined. The idea that only freely willed actions merit blame or credit is also true in secular circumstances, and has implications for our attitudes to crime and punishment, and reward for good behaviour. If everything is causally determined by external factors, our actions are inevitable and we have no moral responsibility for them.

4 Hard and soft determinism

Philosophers disagree about the extent to which our behaviour is determined, and how much freedom we have to choose. At one end of the scale, there is 'hard' determinism, the view that free will does not exist, and that either God or the scientific laws of cause and effect determine everything we do and think. At the other end is libertarianism (not to be confused with political libertarianism, see page 142), the view that we have free will and moral responsibility, which is only constrained by physical factors. And somewhere between the two is 'soft' determinism, the view that our nature is shaped by external factors, such as inheritance and upbringing, but otherwise we are free to make choices.

5 Compatibilism and incompatibilism

A similar categorization of theories of free will and determinism classifies them as either compatibilist or incompatibilist. Compatibilists hold that we do indeed have free will, and this is our freedom to choose what to do, but that this may be constrained by external factors that are causally determined, emphasizing the difference between freedom of will or choice, and freedom of action. Incompatibilism, on the other hand, is the view that free will and determinism are logically contradictory. Among them are the hard determinists who deny the existence of free will and claim that every event is determined, and extreme libertarians who believe we have free will and deny determinism.

6 John Locke: the locked room

In answer to the question of free will, John Locke replied, 'I think the question is not proper, whether the will be free, but whether a man be free.' To explain this, he gave the analogy of a sleeping man who, unbeknown to him, is locked in his room. When he wakes, he decides not to go out. He believes that this decision is freely made, but really he has no other choice. Locke argues that there is a choice in mind, which he can make freely, but in order put this into practice there must be an absence of constraint. The will is determined by a desire to do something, but the man is only free if he has the freedom to choose and the power to do otherwise.

7 Kant: free will and the noumenon

Immanuel Kant proposed a different solution to the problem of free will. Like many philosophers, he recognized the intuition that we have the ability to make conscious choices, and reasoned that we have both free will and moral responsibility. He also accepted the determinist arguments, but suggested that our physical bodies, like the whole material world, are in the realm of the phenomenal and so are subject to scientific laws; but acts of free will take place in the noumenal world, and so are not subject to those laws, and so are not causally determined.

8 Schopenhauer: physical and moral freedom

Arthur Schopenhauer also addressed the problem of free will and moral responsibility in terms of the phenomenal and noumenal. He, too, recognized that we all believe we have free will, but argued that we should understand the distinction between physical freedom (the absence of physical constraints on our actions), intellectual freedom (the mental ability to make a rational decision) and moral freedom (the absence of necessity to do something). Phenomena, things in the material world, have no free will, but will – our urges and desires – is a noumenon and is itself free. While we may be physically free to do what we will, we are driven to action by this will, which is not in our control: we cannot will what we will.

9 Nietzsche: unfree will

In characteristically iconoclastic fashion, Friedrich Nietzsche rejected the concept of free will absolutely, dismissing our intuitive sense of it as human-centric arrogance. He was especially critical of the idea because of its association with the Judaeo-Christian religious morality that he despised, but also because he, inspired by Schopenhauer, believed in a universal will that governs our behaviour. This he describes as an 'unfree will' that determines our actions, although the question of whether it is free or unfree is less important than the strength of the will to power.

10 Free will and existentialism

Perhaps the most libertarian stance by any major philosophical movement is that of the existentialists. For them, free will is taken for granted, and it is the sudden realization of the reality of free will, the freedom to do as we choose and the responsibility that entails, that defines the 'existential crisis' that frees us from the idea that our lives are determined by external factors.

TALK LIKE A GENIUS

6 Although free will and determinism seem to be polar opposites, and impossible to reconcile rationally, philosophers have been reluctant to reduce the problem to an "either-or" question, and have sought some kind of compatibility between the two. 9

6 If God had exercised His omnipotence to deny us free will, we would bear no moral responsibility for our actions and could face the Day of Judgement without fear. 9

6 Hard determinism fits well with a scientific interpretation of the Universe. A person who understood all the laws governing the physical Universe, and knew everything that has ever happened could predict what, inevitably, is going to happen in the future. 9

6 Faced with the choice between Schopenhauer's gloomy picture of us at the mercy of some external determinist will, and the optimism of the existentialists' absolute freedom, it's not difficult to understand why we prefer to believe we have free will. 9

WERE YOU A GENIUS?

1 FALSE – So-called compatibilist philosophers argue that it is possible to have free will even when physical events are divinely or causally determined.

2 TRUE – Logical determinism argues that present circumstances determine whether a proposition about the future or its negation is true.

3 TRUE – Hume believed we only have the freedom to make decisions within the constraints of causally determined physical factors.

4 FALSE – A person has moral responsibility, because the essence of that person, the 'thing-in-itself', is the will, which is free.

5 FALSE – Nietzsche denied the existence of free will and adopted a fatalistic stance; the will to power is expressed in everything, and by existing we are part of destiny.

THE BLUFFER'S SUMMARY

If our actions are predetermined by God or external physical causes, our intuitive sense of free will may be an illusion.

Agnosticism and atheism

'God did not, as the Bible says, make man in His image; on the contrary man ... made God in his image.'

LUDWIG FEUERBACH

Unsurprisingly, most of the arguments for the existence of God were developed in the medieval period, when European philosophers were almost exclusively Christian scholars. But there have been those who did not accept their arguments, and either remained sceptical or disputed the existence of any deity. For much of history, they have been in the minority, partly because their ideas were considered heretical in many societies. However, after the 18th century, it was generally accepted that the arguments for the existence of God are at best inconclusive, and an increasing number of philosophers declared themselves agnostic or atheist.

Some philosophers believe, some have their doubts and others deny – do you know which is which?

1 While theists believe in the existence of a god or gods, and atheists deny the existence of any deities, agnostics simply have no strong convictions either way.

TRUE / FALSE

2 One of the charges against Socrates, for which he was sentenced to death, was impiety, not believing in the gods.

TRUE / FALSE

3 The ancient Greek philosopher Xenophanes anticipated the 19th-century idea that humans impose their own attributes on their gods, imagining them as like themselves.

TRUE / FALSE

4 Marx was raised as an orthodox Jew, but renounced his faith when he realized that religion was nothing more than 'the sigh of the oppressed creature'.

TRUE / FALSE

5 Although an increasing number of philosophers have adopted an atheist stance, none has yet presented a conclusive argument for the non-existence of God.

TRUE / FALSE

TEN THINGS A GENIUS KNOWS

1 Belief and reason
All the arguments for the existence of God have at one time or another been subjected to philosophical scrutiny, and have been shown not to satisfy the demands of a valid rational argument. Yet many people, including philosophers, continue to hold that belief, unjustified by reason. In the absence of any rational grounds for that belief, some have chosen to remain sceptical, neither accepting nor denying the existence of God. Others, however, deny that any god exists. And here there is some irony, as rational arguments for the non-existence of God are also inconclusive, making atheism a matter of belief rather than reason, too.

2 Hard and soft atheism
Belief in the existence of a deity or deities is referred to as theism – a rather less familiar term than its opposite, atheism. Atheism, however, is not so simply defined, and includes various shades of non-belief. Loosely speaking, it is the rejection of belief in God, but philosophers such as Antony Flew have suggested a distinction between positive (or 'hard') and negative (or 'weak') atheism. The hard atheist not only rejects the existence of deities, but positively asserts that they do not exist. Soft atheists, on the other hand, simply do not believe

in the existence of God; included in this category of negative atheists are agnostics, who also believe that we do not, or cannot, know if God exists.

3 Atheism in the ancient world
The main concern of the very first Western philosophers in ancient Greece was 'what is everything made of?', so it is not surprising that a number of Greek philosophers had a very materialist view of the Universe. If everything is composed of some matter, the idea of immaterial, immortal gods is difficult to explain. Many left the question unanswered, but the atomists Leucippus and Democritus explicitly denied the existence of anything other than atoms and empty space. Epicurus, who is credited with posing the 'problem of evil' (see page 62), held similar materialist views, but professed to believe in the gods – probably in fear of upsetting the authorities.

4 Scepticism
Even believers recognize the weakness of their arguments. René Descartes, a devout Catholic, defended his faith and exposed the flaws in the arguments for atheism, but also pointed out the circularity of a popular argument for belief: God exists because it says so in the scriptures; it must be true, because the scriptures are the word of God. Even more sceptical was David Hume, whose down-to-earth empiricist approach to belief in miracles tells us a lot about his attitude to anecdotal evidence, such as the word of prophets and scripture. When we witness or hear about a miracle, he says, common sense tells us it is more likely our senses are deceived, or that the testimony is false, than that the laws of nature have been broken.

5 Kant: God as noumenon
Immanuel Kant had no time for organized religion, but there is little in his philosophy to suggest whether he was a theist or not. He explained that metaphysical questions such as the existence of God,

Hard atheism
'I know that God does not exist.'

Soft atheism
'I do not believe that God exists.'

Agnosticism
'We do not or cannot know if God exists.'

the immortal soul and so on, are not capable of being answered by reason. If God exists, He is not part of our physical word, but outside time and space. In terms of Kant's transcendental idealism, God does not exist in the phenomenal world, but is a noumenon, and as the noumenal is beyond our apprehension, we cannot know of His existence.

6 Materialism and atheism

As mentioned above, materialism has its roots in pre-Socratic philosophy, but subsequently those ideas were largely ignored, especially by medieval Christian philosophers. With the so-called scientific revolution that started in the Renaissance, however, there was a revival of interest in materialist philosophy, and an acceptance of scientific, physical explanations of the Universe. Physicalists rejected, for example, the concept of an immaterial soul or mind, and many found belief in God incompatible with their materialist stance.

7 God as a human construct

Among the first of the Enlightenment philosophers to stick his head over the parapet and risk prosecution for heretical views was Voltaire. He wittily mocked the theist arguments by saying 'If God did not exist, it would be necessary to invent Him', but also suggested that 'If God created us in His own image, we have more than reciprocated'. This idea was echoed by Georg Hegel, who suggested that we project our human ideals onto God, but more forcefully by the openly atheist Ludwig Feuerbach. God, he claimed, is a human invention, an imaginary being we have created, and is nothing more than the projection of our own ideals.

8 The opium of the people

Feuerbach was one of the first openly 'hard atheist' philosophers, and his ideas had an enormous impact. Among those who were influenced by the idea of God as a human invention was Karl Marx, who saw it as fitting into his own analysis of life in a capitalist society. We have not just created a God to embody what we see as good, but also to fulfil a social function; religion is there to give comfort, reassurance and hope, and is an expression of suffering and protest against oppression.

9 Nietzsche: God is dead

Friedrich Nietzsche was also deeply affected by Feuerbach, who offered him a justification for his loss of faith. For a time, Nietzsche believed in an imaginary man-made God, but once he ceased to believe, that God ceased to exist. Humans created God to represent the values and morals of a world that no longer exists, and now we have no need for those religious explanations, 'God is dead'. And, Nietzsche, continued, just as we created Him, we murdered Him.

10 Analytic philosophy and religion

In a purely logical way, Bertrand Russell showed that the existence of God could be neither proved nor disproved. But he went on to remark that if there are no rational grounds for believing or not believing in something, why believe at all? Wouldn't you have to concede, then, that it's acceptable to believe in anything that cannot be disproved, including Russell's invisible teapot (see page 62)? Wittgenstein came at the same problem from a different logical angle, explaining that religion, like ethics, is one of the topics that is beyond the limits of our world, and so beyond the limits of language. We cannot meaningfully talk about such matters, and they do not belong in the rational discourse of philosophy.

TALK LIKE A GENIUS

❝ Even atheism is a belief. The "hard" atheist believes in the non-existence of God, just as much as the theist believes in His existence; and the agnostic believes that it is impossible to know. ❞

❝ It's difficult to know which philosophers did not actually believe in the existence of God, as it was often dangerous to express atheist or even agnostic views, as Socrates found to his cost. Hume was guarded in his critique of religion, even though he specified it was for posthumous publication. ❞

❝ In different ways, both Kant and Wittgenstein come to the conclusion that belief in God is not something that can be justified by reason, and so is not a matter for philosophical enquiry. ❞

WERE YOU A GENIUS?

1 FALSE – Agnostics are not simply unconvinced, but believe that we cannot know whether God exists or not.

2 TRUE – Socrates was accused of impiety and corrupting the minds of young people – both of which he denied.

3 TRUE – Almost 2,500 years before Hegel and Feuerbach, Xenophanes suggested that we project our ideals onto our gods.

4 FALSE – Although his ancestry was Jewish, Marx was baptized in the Lutheran church, and had a mainly secular upbringing.

5 TRUE – It is generally believed the question is unlikely ever to be satisfactorily settled by philosophical argument.

THE BLUFFER'S SUMMARY

In the absence of a convincing argument for His existence, many philosophers have questioned the rationality of believing in God.

The problem of knowledge

'All men by nature desire to know.'

ARISTOTLE

Western philosophy has its origins in our natural human curiosity about the world around us. The first concerns of philosophy were metaphysical questions about the make-up and structure of the Universe, and the search for rational rather than religious explanations. But then the question arose: 'How do we know that?', shifting the focus from the external world to the way we humans acquire our information about it. The study of knowledge – how we can know things, what sorts of things we can know and the nature of knowledge itself – is the second major branch of philosophy: epistemology.

How much do you know about how we know what we know?

1 In English, the word 'know' can refer to knowledge of how to do things, and familiarity with things, as well as propositional knowledge, but in many other languages the distinction is made by use of different words.

TRUE / FALSE

2 Epistemologists identify several different ways in which a belief can be justified as knowledge: rational argument, empirical evidence, faith and conviction.

TRUE / FALSE

3 The terms *a priori* and *a posteriori* were coined by Plato to describe innate and acquired knowledge.

TRUE / FALSE

4 Modern psychology has provided scientific evidence for theories of learning that show knowledge is acquired solely by experience.

TRUE / FALSE

5 Reason and experience are not only the sources of our knowledge, but also the means of verifying what we know.

TRUE / FALSE

TEN THINGS A GENIUS KNOWS

1 Epistemology

As with almost every branch of philosophy, a primary concern is to establish definitions. For epistemologists, the task has been to determine what we mean when we say that someone knows something, what the nature of that knowledge is and what distinguishes it from not knowing. Arising from this examination of the nature of knowledge is the question of how we actually acquire knowledge, whether it is through experience or by reasoning, or a combination of the two – a question that has divided epistemologists from Plato and Aristotle to the present day. Another aspect of epistemology concerns the extent of our knowledge, whether there are some things that we cannot know or, indeed, if we can really know anything at all.

2 Socrates

One of the first philosophers to address the problems of epistemology was Socrates, who challenged the assumptions we all have about what we know with his relentless questioning. He himself took a position of professing to know nothing, and in a series of questions challenged what people know, how they know it, what evidence they had for that knowledge and so on. Using this dialectical method, he elicited answers that demonstrated that they did not really know what they thought they knew, and showed that knowledge is a far from simple concept.

3 Propositional knowledge

We use the word 'know' in several different ways. Sometimes what we mean when we say we know something, such as we *know* that it is going to be a sunny day, is that we believe something with a degree of conviction. We also talk about knowing how to do something, and knowing a person or place, meaning that we are familiar with them. Epistemology, though, is mainly concerned with what is known as propositional knowledge, sometimes known as 'knowledge-that', as statements of this kind of knowledge typically take the form 'I know that such and such is the case'.

4 Belief and knowledge

Knowledge is a kind of belief, but believing something is not the same as knowing. Knowledge implies certainty, but even a firm belief can be mistaken, and it cannot really be considered knowledge in that case. You might believe, for example, that your friend is in the next room, because that's where she said she was going; but when you look, you discover she isn't. There is a difference between what you believed and what was the case, so that you cannot say that you really knew. In another example, you might be convinced that it will rain tomorrow, but have no good reason for that belief; even if it does actually rain tomorrow, you cannot say that you really knew that it would.

5 Justified true belief

In searching for a working definition of knowledge, Greek philosophers identified three distinguishing features: belief, truth and justification. And to be considered knowledge, belief has to be both true and justified. In the examples in the previous paragraph, you might be justified in believing your friend is in the next room, but it is not true; and if it does rain tomorrow you will be proved right, but you have no justification for believing it. On the other hand, that the Moon orbits the Earth is a justified true belief – you have been given reliable scientific evidence, and it happens actually to be the case.

6 Gettier problems

The justified true belief definition of knowledge was widely accepted until the 1960s, when Edmund Gettier showed that sometimes those criteria are not sufficient. For example, take the case of a farmer who thinks his sheep has gone missing. His friend tells him that she has seen the sheep in the field, and the farmer goes to check, and is reassured when he sees the familiar white shape. The friend also looks in the field again, and finds the sheep hidden in some bushes, while in the middle of the field there is a large white dog, which the farmer has mistaken for his sheep. The farmer believes his sheep is in the field, which is factually true, and his friend's testimony gives him justification for that belief – but it isn't right to say that he really *knows* his sheep is there.

7 Sources of knowledge
A central concern of epistemology, and one that has helped to define different schools of epistemological thought, is how we come to know something. Perhaps the most obvious way that we acquire knowledge is by experience. We perceive things through our senses, and this information constitutes our knowledge of the physical world around us. This kind of empirical knowledge is the basis of our scientific understanding of the world. In addition to this knowledge, however, we can use reasoning to draw inferences from it, providing us with further knowledge. We can even acquire knowledge of abstract concepts, such as mathematical facts, through reasoning alone; this sort of rational knowledge is not dependent on experience.

8 Rational and empirical knowledge
The two different ways we come to know something, either empirically through experience, or rationally through reasoning, can be used as justification for knowledge of a proposition. If it is known independent of any experience, a proposition is said to be knowable *a priori*, while a proposition that is justified on the basis of experience of the world is known as *a posteriori*. We can know, for example, that two plus two

equals four simply by rational inference, but to know whether it is raining outside, we need to have empirical evidence.

9 Innate and acquired knowledge
Philosophers throughout history have debated the degree to which we acquire our knowledge through either experience or reasoning, empirically or rationally. Many, like Aristotle, believed that we are born with no knowledge of any kind, and gain it though experience, which we can then analyse by reasoning to increase our understanding. Others, like Plato, believed that we have some innate ideas, which can be accessed rationally, independent of our physical senses, and these help us to understand the world that we experience.

10 An innate capacity for reasoning
Although the divide between rationalists and empiricists is very noticeable, it would be a mistake to think that they are at opposite ends of a spectrum. Empiricists do not reject the idea that knowledge can be acquired through reasoning, but only maintain that experience is the primary source of our knowledge. Similarly, rationalists (in the main) do not believe that we are born with fully formed knowledge of concepts, but rather that we have an innate capacity for reasoning; it is not ideas that exist in our minds at birth, but the potential of those ideas, and this is the primary source of our knowledge.

TALK LIKE A GENIUS

❛ The whole point of philosophy, science and any field of enquiry is to gain knowledge of the world around us and our place in it. For information to be considered knowledge and not mere belief, we must turn to epistemology to examine how reliable it is. ❜

❛ Gettier demonstrated that, in some cases, even justification and verification aren't enough for us to claim we really know something – but those cases are rare, and more often than not occur when there are extraordinary circumstances. ❜

❛ In contrast to religion, philosophy sets out to provide rational arguments to justify what we know, but it's a moot point how much of that knowledge we acquire from rational thinking, and how much from experience." ❜

THE
BLUFFER'S
SUMMARY

Epistemology is the study of knowledge: what we know, how we know that we know, and how we know what we know.

Plato vs Aristotle

'Earthly knowledge is but a shadow'
PLATO

As with all major branches of philosophy, the agenda of epistemology was set by the great Athenian philosophers, Plato and Aristotle. Their very different approaches to the questions of knowledge and how we acquire it are shaped by their attitudes to metaphysics: Plato's somewhat mystical other-worldliness and Aristotle's down-to-earth observations. The main epistemological point of contention between the two was whether our knowledge is innate and accessed by reasoning, or whether we are born with no knowledge and acquire it by experience.

Plato believed you can access knowledge by reasoning, Aristotle that you learn by experience; can you figure out how much you've learnt about them?

1 It is clear from his writings that Socrates believed all knowledge could be discovered by a process of dialectical reasoning.

TRUE / FALSE

2 Plato's allegory of the cave appears in his *Republic,* as part of the argument that only philosophers have the necessary knowledge of the world of Forms to be able to rule properly.

TRUE / FALSE

3 Aristotle was tipped to succeed Plato as head of the Academy in Athens, but because of their differences of opinion was not appointed and instead set up his own school, the Lyceum.

TRUE / FALSE

4 Our modern system of taxonomy, the classification of living things, derives from Aristotle's methodical study of the natural world.

TRUE / FALSE

5 Immanuel Kant concluded that while experience gives us knowledge of the physical world, reason gives us knowledge of the non-material world.

TRUE / FALSE

TEN THINGS A GENIUS KNOWS

1. Innate or acquired knowledge

It was Socrates, as always, who set the scene for the debate of how we come to know something. In typical fashion, he offered no answers, but posed the question. With his dialectical method of interrogation, he showed the contradictions and inconsistencies in what people thought they knew. But as well as showing what they didn't know, this method uncovered things that they didn't realize they knew; it drew knowledge out of them by reasoned argument. The implication is that knowledge is already there and can by accessed by reason, rather than learned by experience. (Remember that our knowledge of Socrates's ideas comes from Plato's writings, so this may not be Socrates's view)

2. The allegory of the cave

Plato believed that we are simply deceived into believing we know things from our experience of the world around us, and that true knowledge comes from reasoning. To illustrate his point, he asks us to imagine a cave in which prisoners are shackled with their backs to the entrance. Behind them is a fire, and between them and the fire people carry all sorts of different objects, whose shadows are cast on the back wall. All the prisoners have ever seen is these shadows, which they take for reality. If they are freed and allowed to turn round, they will at first be dazzled by the fire, then as they see more clearly, realize their mistake and understand the true nature of the objects throwing the shadows. If they then leave the cave, they will be dazzled again by the Sun, but at last will see the world outside.

3. Plato: experience is illusory

The allegory of the cave refers to Plato's theory that our experience of the world around us is illusory, a mere shadow of reality. We are deceived into thinking we know something, but it is an imperfect copy of the truth. But if the world we inhabit is imperfect and illusory, there is another realm 'out there' consisting of the true and perfect 'Forms' or 'Ideas' of which our earthly world is an imitation. Our knowledge of the world is flawed, and the only true knowledge is of this realm of Forms.

4. Accessing the Forms

Going back to the allegory of the cave, how can we break free of the shackles in order to access knowledge of reality? Plato says that this can be done by reasoning. As Socrates showed, knowledge of truths can be uncovered by his method of dialectical questioning, it is already in the mind. Plato believed that knowledge of the Forms is innate, and a form of pre-birth memory that can be recollected. The soul, or psyche, has a connection

with the realm of Forms, but is also the seat of our reasoning, which provides the key to accessing our innate knowledge of Forms.

5 Recovering innate knowledge
In the *Meno*, Plato gives an example of how this can be done. He describes Socrates in conversation with an uneducated slave boy, asking if he knows the answer to a geometric problem. The boy, of course, struggles to give the correct answer, but Socrates explains using diagrams drawn in the sand, which the boy can recognize as providing him with the solution. Plato concludes that this knowledge must be innate, and is recovered by reasoning.

6 Aristotle: knowledge through experience
Plato's protégé Aristotle rejected the whole notion of a realm of perfect Forms, and believed there is no other world more real than the one we inhabit. All of reality, all that exists, he maintained, is here in this Universe. And the only way we come to have knowledge of it is by experiencing it through our senses, not recovering some innate ideas or recollecting pre-birth memories. Yes, we have the capacity for rational thought, but that alone cannot provide us with knowledge.

7 Aristotelian methodology
Aristotle put his money where his mouth was, too. His thirst for knowledge led him to embark upon a lifelong methodical study of the natural world. From his observations, he built up an unprecedented body of knowledge of nature but, in addition, he identified many different types of living things, which he systematically classified. His knowledge of the world, he explained, came from his experience, his observations, but it was followed by reasoning to make sense of what he had observed.

8 Common characteristics versus Forms
Aristotle's classification of the natural world was based on his observation of certain common characteristics. For example, he noticed that all the things he identified as fish have scales, that all the birds have feathers and animals we call mammals do not lay eggs. He reasoned that we don't know that an animal is a dog, for instance, by comparing it to an ideal Form of dog, but by comparing it to our experience of other dogs. Over time, we experience many instances of dogs, and from their common characteristics we build up a picture of 'dogginess' – what it is that makes an animal recognizable as a dog.

9 Scientific knowledge
By using reason to analyse and make sense of experience, Aristotle was laying the foundations for a scientific method of acquiring knowledge. That observations – all that we experience with our senses – come first, and are followed by a process of reasoning, inferring from the particular instances a general rule.

10 Divisions in epistemology
The two opposing theories of how we come to have knowledge proposed by Plato and Aristotle have been echoed by epistemologists ever since. Questions of whether our knowledge is innate or whether we are born as a 'blank slate', and the degree to which knowledge is derived from reasoning or experience, were at the heart of the debate between rationalists and empiricists that dominated philosophy during the Enlightenment period and influenced different schools of thought in psychology in the 20th century.

TALK LIKE A GENIUS

❧ Alfred North Whitehead once characterized the European philosophical tradition as consisting of a series of footnotes to Plato. Maybe it would be more accurate to say footnotes to Plato and Aristotle, given the influence of their fundamentally different approaches to epistemology and metaphysics. ❧

❧ Plato's epistemology is derived from his idealist belief that reality exists in an immaterial world of Forms. Obviously, it would be impossible to have any empirical experience of it, so knowledge must already be in our minds, or accessible by using our minds. ❧

❧ Aristotle considered that the cosmos is essentially material, that reality is what we can experience with our senses, and that this is the only way we can come to have knowledge of it. ❧

❧ Despite the difference of opinion (and temperament) between Plato and Aristotle, the ideas of knowledge through reasoning and from experience are not mutually exclusive. Some things, such as mathematical proofs, can be known rationally, and others, such as scientific theories, by empirical observation. ❧

THE BLUFFER'S SUMMARY

We either come to know things by reason, accessing an ideal reality, or by experience, observing the world with our senses.

Scepticism

'In order to seek truth, it is necessary once in the course of life, to doubt, as far as possible, everything.'

RENÉ DESCARTES

As well as studying the nature of knowledge, what we know and how we come to know it, epistemology examines the extent of our knowledge: whether there are things we do not and cannot know, or even whether we can truly know anything at all. There is a long history of philosophers who have cast doubt on our ability to know things for certain, a view known as scepticism. There are, however, degrees of scepticism, ranging from the absolute sceptic's view that all knowledge is impossible, or that nothing can be known with certainty, to the view that some philosophical questions cannot be answered.

No doubt you know the limits of your knowledge with some degree of certainty, but why not test it here?

ARE YOU A GENIUS

1 Socrates is sometimes described as a sceptic, as he claimed he knew nothing except his own ignorance. Unlike the true sceptics, however, he did not deny the possibility of certain knowledge.

TRUE / FALSE

2 Pyrrho and his followers argued that all dogma – that is, unjustified propositions – should be sceptically challenged, but did not accept that their stance was itself dogmatic.

TRUE / FALSE

3 In *The Incoherence of the Philosophers* Islamic philosopher Al-Ghazali adopted extreme scepticism to demonstrate the superiority of faith over philosophy.

TRUE / FALSE

4 Kant credited Hume's scepticism with waking him from his 'dogmatic slumber', and setting him on the road to a critical system of philosophy.

TRUE / FALSE

5 From a stance of 'mitigated scepticism' Hume distinguished between the probable truth of scientific theories, and the improbability of the existence of miracles.

TRUE / FALSE

TEN THINGS A GENIUS KNOWS

1 **What scepticism is**

The word 'sceptic' was first used to describe one of the four main schools of thought after Plato and Aristotle (the others being the Epicureans, cynics and stoics), whose central principle was one of doubt. It has since become used to describe any philosophical approach that calls into question the certainty of a belief or beliefs. This may be directed at a particular belief, such as belief in the existence of God, or a more global denial that we can know anything at all. As knowledge is widely considered to be justified true belief, sceptics typically challenge either the justification for, or the truth of, a belief.

2 **The Greek sceptics**

The sophists, a group of professional advocates and rhetoricians, were among the first to cast doubt on our ability to know anything. As lawyers and political speakers, they claimed that there are two sides to any argument, and that there is no such thing as absolute truth. And without certain truth, our beliefs cannot be said to be knowledge. Following in their footsteps were the sceptics, a school of philosophy founded by Pyrrho of Elis, who argued that knowledge is not possible by challenging its logical justification. When we claim to know something, his argument went, we infer that conclusion from premises whose truth has not been established. To verify them would require further premises, which in turn would need to be justified by evidence, and so on in an infinite regress. There can be no knowledge, as there can be no ultimate justification for it.

3 **Can we trust our senses?**

The sceptics pointed out another reason for denying the possibility of knowledge: as followers of Plato, they believed that our earthly experience is imperfect, illusory and therefore unreliable, and

no basis for certain knowledge. Premises of an argument based on experience require verification before they can be accepted, and can be denied without any logical contradiction. Indeed, one of the principles of the Pyrrhic school of scepticism was that, against every statement, its contradiction may be advanced with equal justification.

4 **Cartesian scepticism**

Like Socrates, Descartes believed a good starting point for philosophical enquiry is knowing nothing. In order to do that, he suggested, we must first of all doubt everything, take up a position of absolute scepticism. In order to become such an absolute sceptic, Descartes imagined that all his senses were being deceived by an evil demon, so that he could not trust them as a basis for his beliefs, which in turn meant that he had no justification for any of his knowledge. But, if we can find just one thing that is beyond all doubt, we have a firm basis from which to establish what is or isn't true – in his case his own existence, verified by his *cogito ergo sum* (see page 40).

5 **Humean scepticism**

In contrast to Descartes, Hume believed we have to trust our senses. Nevertheless, he argued that there is still reason to be sceptical, even if our senses are trustworthy, because we only perceive a particular part of the Universe at any given moment, and then assume that is enough to give us knowledge of the world. We believe that the Universe is both unchanging and uniform – but have no rational grounds for that belief. For example, I see a pen on my desk when I leave work one night, and again when I return the next morning; naturally, I believe it is the same pen and it has been there all night. Similarly, I believe that that pen will be there in the future, unless I or someone else moves it. Although that is more than likely, I cannot be sure, and cannot say I know it to be the case.

6 Hume's 'mitigated scepticism'

The problem for Hume, who as an empiricist believed that the primary source of knowledge is experience, is that his scepticism removes any justification for our beliefs; we cannot truly know anything. To overcome the problems that lack of certain knowledge poses for disciplines such as philosophy and science, Hume adopted a stance of what he called 'mitigated scepticism', using common sense to determine what seems probable or improbable, based on our experience of the world.

7 The limits of knowledge

A number of philosophers have taken a less radical sceptical approach, suggesting that, although we can know some things, there is a limit to our knowledge. John Locke was probably the first to tackle the problem of the extent of our knowledge systematically, in *An Essay Concerning Human Understanding*. He argued that we only have direct access to 'ideas' in our minds, not reality, but that there is nothing in the mind that was not previously in the senses: all the ideas in our mind ultimately derive from our sensory experience and, therefore, 'No man's knowledge can go beyond his experience'.

8 Noumena: beyond our apprehension

Immanuel Kant set himself a similar task of defining the extent of our knowledge in his *Critique of Pure Reason*, explaining the limits of what we can know in terms of his transcendental idealism. We acquire knowledge of the world through both experience and reasoning, according to Kant, but it is only knowledge of the phenomenal world governed by the physical laws of space and time, and cause and effect, because the structure of our mind does not allow us to perceive things outside this phenomenal world. We have no direct access to things-in-themselves – the noumena – and can have no knowledge of the noumenal realm, which will always be beyond our apprehension.

9 American pragmatism and scepticism

The American pragmatist C.S. Peirce argued against adopting too sceptical an approach. While he accepted Hume's arguments that our knowledge is partial because we only experience a small part of the world at any one time, that should not mean that we must doubt everything. Instead, the pragmatist principle that all knowledge is tentative should reassure us that, by continuing our enquiries, more and more certain truth can be revealed. Nor should we adopt a kind of Cartesian scepticism, making ourselves doubt things unnecessarily. Just as we demand a justification for belief, there should be a justification for doubt, or it will hinder rather than help our enquiry.

10 Dogmatism

While it is difficult to refute sceptical arguments about the unreliability and incompleteness of sense-experience, the absolute scepticism of Pyrrho carried within it a contradiction: if we can have no certain knowledge of anything, how can we know the truth of the sceptic's argument? By saying that all knowledge is impossible, the sceptic is being paradoxically dogmatic in his scepticism. As Bertrand Russell later pointed out: 'Dogmatism and scepticism are both, in a sense, absolute philosophies; one is certain of knowing, the other of not knowing. What philosophy should dissipate is certainty, whether of knowledge or ignorance.'

TALK LIKE A GENIUS

❦ In the fourth century BCE, Zhuangzi cast doubt on our ability to distinguish reality from illusion, in his well-known story of dreaming that he was a butterfly. When he woke, he could not tell if he was a man who had been dreaming he was a butterfly, or a butterfly dreaming he was a man. Bertrand Russell's response to this dream argument was that, although he could not prove he was not dreaming, he was certain he was having experiences whether he was dreaming or awake. ❧

❦ There are very convincing rational arguments for questioning the possibility of certain knowledge, but in practice we cannot doubt the truth of absolutely everything. Instead of trying to refute the sceptics' arguments, we should apply them with a dose of common sense, as Hume and Peirce suggest. ❧

❦ While a number of philosophers have argued about the possibility of having certain knowledge, others have simply adopted a sceptical approach as a means to an end. Descartes, for example, was not fundamentally a sceptic, but adopted a hypothetical scepticism for the purpose of establishing what can be certainly known. ❧

WERE YOU A GENIUS?

1 TRUE – Socrates professed to know nothing, but did not deny the possibility of acquiring knowledge.

2 FALSE – The Pyrrhonists held that even the proposition that nothing can be known is dogmatic.

3 TRUE – Having shown that there is no philosophical basis for knowledge, Al-Ghazali advocated theology instead.

4 TRUE – Kant started work on his *Critique of Pure Reason* in reaction to Hume's scepticism.

5 TRUE – Hume asks which is more likely: that the laws of physics have been broken or that reports of a miracle are false?

THE BLUFFER'S SUMMARY

Knowledge, as opposed to belief, implies certainty, but sceptical philosophers question how much, if at all, certain knowledge is possible.

Rationalism vs empiricism

'All our knowledge begins with the senses, proceeds then to the understanding, and ends with reason.'

IMMANUEL KANT

In the late Renaissance period, the so-called scientific revolution inspired a renewed interest in philosophical enquiry, and the thirst for knowledge a renewed interest in epistemology. From what is now regarded as the beginning of modern philosophy, two distinct strands of philosophical thought evolved. In Britain, this was an empiricist tradition, the view that knowledge comes from our experience; but in mainland Europe, philosophers tended towards rationalism, the view that reasoning is the primary source of knowledge. Although Immanuel Kant bridged the gap between empiricism and rationalism, to some extent, with his transcendental idealism, the debate concerning innate ideas continued well into the 20th century.

British and continental philosophers disagreed about the source of our knowledge; do you know why?

1 The terms 'British empiricism' and 'continental rationalism' were applied retrospectively, as a convenient way to distinguish the two schools of thought.
TRUE / FALSE

2 Descartes rejected the principle of a scientific method of enquiry, claiming instead that truths about the world can be deduced from observation by rational thought alone.
TRUE / FALSE

3 The only 'adequate' knowledge we can have, according to Spinoza, is through rational thought. Sensory experience and mere intuition are 'inadequate'.
TRUE / FALSE

4 Locke and Leibniz are polar opposites on the empiricist–rationalist spectrum: Locke denied the existence of innate ideas, and Leibniz denied the possibility of empirical knowledge.
TRUE / FALSE

5 What Leibniz called monads are 'windowless'; information cannot enter them from outside.
TRUE / FALSE

TEN THINGS A GENIUS KNOWS

1 Modern science and modern philosophy
The year 1543 is often cited as the beginning of the so-called scientific revolution, the year that Copernicus published his explanation of a heliocentric Universe, and Vesalius published his textbook of anatomy. The authority of the Church was increasingly undermined by science, and philosophy no longer had to confirm or conform to Christian doctrine. Philosophers were not only liberated, but inspired by modern science, and sought to put their theories on a scientific footing. In epistemology, some took this to mean that knowledge of the world could be acquired by rational thought, while others that knowledge comes primarily from empirical observation.

2 Continental rationalism and British empiricism
The two distinct schools of thought in epistemology evolved from the ideas of two very different thinkers: an Englishman, Francis Bacon, and a Frenchman, René Descartes. As a consequence, English-speaking philosophers tended towards empiricism, with its connection to the natural sciences, while philosophers in Europe tended towards rationalism, and the great rationalists Descartes, Spinoza and Leibniz were mathematicians as well as philosophers. The distinction is not as sharp as is sometimes assumed, however. British empiricists did not deny that we have an innate capacity for reasoning, nor the value of reasoning to draw conclusions from sensory information. Likewise, most rationalists accepted the value of empirical knowledge, especially in the sciences, but not as a foundation for certain knowledge.

3 The British empirical tradition
Although the major discoveries in the natural sciences were being made in continental Europe by the likes of Copernicus, Vesalius and Galileo, the implicit empiricism of their methods found its greatest adherents in Britain. The first of these was Francis Bacon, a pioneer of scientific method, starting with observation of phenomena and then following a systematic procedure to establish a theory. His rejection of what he saw as introspective rationalism marked the beginning of a succession of British empiricist philosophers that includes Thomas Hobbes, John Locke and David Hume.

4 Descartes's three kinds of knowledge
Meanwhile, in France, Descartes took a very different interpretation of the way that we gain our scientific knowledge. For him, more important than the empirical observation is the reasoning that is applied to it and, besides, there are some ideas that are not discoverable by empirical means. He argued that there are three kinds of ideas: some are simple sensory experiences, such as our idea of the Sun as we see and feel its warmth; then there are ideas of reasoning, such as that the Sun is a star composed of burning gases; and, lastly, there are ideas that are neither sensory experiences nor reasoned conclusions, but universal unchanging truths, such as that the sum of the angles of a triangle equals two right angles. Such ideas, he claimed, are innate: our minds have an innate ability to form this idea by reasoning alone.

5 Benedict Spinoza
While Spinoza agreed with Descartes that scientific knowledge should be built from undoubtable premises by a method of rational thought, his rationalism is quite different from Descartes. He describes three different kinds of knowledge. The first, which he calls opinion or imagination, is the knowledge we have through our encounters with the external world, or from reading or hearing of things. Ideas conceived in this way are 'inadequate'. 'Adequate' ideas are those of the second and third kinds of knowledge, which are ideas provided by the mind rather than the senses: either reason, knowledge gained through the intellect, or

intuitive knowledge of the essence of things. We have these intuitive ideas because, according to Spinoza, along with everything else in the Universe we are a part of the single substance that constitutes reality.

6 John Locke

Locke was not the first of the British empiricists, but in *An Essay Concerning Human Understanding*, he was the first to set out explicitly the basic principle of empiricism – that at birth the human mind is a blank slate, with no innate ideas. Ideas, he explains, are 'the Object of the Understanding, when a man thinks', and are the building blocks of knowledge. Because they are not innate, they must come from experience, which he says is of two kinds: either 'sensitive' ideas, our sensory experience of the external world; or 'reflective' ideas, the experience we have of reflecting on and thinking about those sensitive ideas, our reasoning.

7 Gottfried Leibniz

Leibniz, an out-and-out rationalist, was incensed by Locke's essay, and wrote his own point-by-point refutation of it, the *New Essays on Human Understanding*. In it he argued that all ideas are innate, and that we acquire no knowledge from sensory experience. He explains his view by reference to his theory of individual substances, the 'monads', in which 'each substance is a world apart, independent of everything outside of itself except for God'. Each person's mind is a monad, and as monads are independent of one another, we cannot have access via our senses to any other monads; but because each monad is a microcosm reflecting the entire Universe, all our knowledge can come from within.

8 Kant: reconciling rationalism and empiricism

Immanuel Kant is often credited with reconciling the two sides of the debate. He argued that we have a 'sensibility' enabling us to perceive objects in the phenomenal world of space and time, but also an understanding of the concepts of space and time, what he called the 'categories of understanding' (including substance, quantity, quality, relation and modality). We must have knowledge of these concepts in order to understand the objects we perceive empirically, so they must be *a priori* and innate; we get to know things empirically through sense experience, but we also have an innate understanding of the parameters that define them.

9 Nature vs nurture

Although the rationalist–empiricist debate in epistemology died down after Kant, the argument of what is innate and what is learnt by experience resurfaced during the 19th century – not so much among philosophers, however, but scientists. Charles Darwin's theory of evolution by natural selection, and Gregor Mendel's discovery of the rules of heredity sparked the 'nature versus nurture' debate. This centred on the question of whether our behaviour and mental make-up, like physical traits, are a matter of heredity and therefore innate, or whether they are the product of our environment and our experience of it.

10 Noam Chomsky: universal grammar

The nature–nurture debate continued into the 20th century with the new science of psychology. The predominant school of thought in the first half of the century, behaviourism, took the empiricist view that we are born a 'blank slate' and all our behaviour is learned or 'conditioned' by our environment. But in the late 1950s, Noam Chomsky revived the rationalist view that there are innate ideas, with his theory of language learning. He had observed that children everywhere learn language more quickly and easily than should be expected of such a complex task, and he developed the idea that there is an underlying structure to all languages, a 'universal grammar' determined by the structure of our brains, which is genetically transmitted and therefore innate.

TALK LIKE A GENIUS

❛ Possibly because of a difference of temperament, reinforced by geographical separation, British philosophy developed along quite different lines from that in mainland Europe from the medieval period onwards – and the difference is as noticeable as ever today. ❜

❛ It's interesting that the period of history following the "founding fathers" of rationalism and empiricism, Descartes and Locke, is known as the Enlightenment, as if there had been some revelation. It's also known, perhaps more appropriately, as the Age of Reason. ❜

❛ Although Chomsky's theory of universal grammar appears at first to support the rationalist idea of innate knowledge, he doesn't say we are born knowing a language, but that we have an innate understanding of the underlying rules of language. This is more in line with Kant's idea that we have *a priori* understanding of such things as the physical laws of space and time. ❜

WERE YOU A GENIUS?

❙ TRUE – Philosophers in the two traditions placed more importance on their philosophical than on their geographical differences.

❷ FALSE – The *Discourse on the Method* advocated a strictly scientific approach, but emphasized that not all knowledge can be acquired empirically.

❸ FALSE – Spinoza calls empirical knowledge 'inadequate', but both reason and intuition can provide 'adequate' knowledge.

❹ TRUE – But while Leibniz rejected empiricism outright, Locke did not entirely rule out the role of rational thought in acquiring knowledge.

❺ TRUE – Monads only appear to interact with one another because of their 'pre-established harmony'.

THE BLUFFER'S SUMMARY

The beginnings of modern philosophy were characterized by the debate between rationalism and empiricism, echoing the classical divide between Plato and Aristotle.

Different kinds of truth

'All objects of human reason or enquiry may naturally be divided into two kinds, to wit, Relations of Ideas and Matters of Fact.'

DAVID HUME

Definitions of what knowledge is typically involve notions of truth and justification, so the concept of truth is an important concern of epistemology. Not just whether a proposition is true or not, but also how we know that it is true and what justification we have for believing it. The truth, however, is far from simple. A proposition can be verified in different ways: for example, by comparing it with the facts – what is actually the case – or by logical argument. Philosophers on both sides of the rationalist–empiricist debate, notably Leibniz and Hume, recognized that just as there are different methods of verification, there are also different kinds of truth.

There's more than one kind of truth, but can you tell what stands to reason, and what are the facts of the matter?

1 For Leibniz, whereas truths of reason are incontrovertible, truths of fact, being contingent on whatever is the case, are simply a matter of belief.

TRUE / FALSE

2 'This cow is female' is an analytic proposition, as the subject implies the predicate.

TRUE / FALSE

3 The phrase 'relation of ideas' is used by Hume to refer to the rational process of logic, inferring a conclusion from the connection of premises.

TRUE / FALSE

4 According to Kant, all *a priori* knowledge is necessary and therefore universal, while all *a posteriori* knowledge is contingent and particular.

TRUE / FALSE

5 The American pragmatists maintained that we can make beliefs become true by acting as if they are.

TRUE / FALSE

TEN THINGS A GENIUS KNOWS

1. What truth is

The words 'true' and 'false' are used a great deal in logic. It could be said that the purpose of logic is to distinguish what is true from what is false. Logical arguments can be analysed to assess whether one thing follows from another, and if an argument is valid, and the premises are true, the conclusion must also be true. But, of course, the premises have to be shown to be true – there must be a firm foundation for that argument. And there other ways than logic for establishing the truth or falsity of a statement: we can, for example, check whether it is true that it is raining by looking out of the window; or we can accept something as true because of the authority from which the information comes.

2. Truth and belief

One of the fundamental differences between philosophy and religion is that where religion demands certain things be accepted as a matter of faith, philosophy requires rational grounds for believing something to be true. While a devout Christian, for example, firmly believes that God exists, and for him or her that is true, belief alone is not enough to satisfy a philosopher.

3. Truth and facts

A commonsense answer to the question 'What is truth?' is to say that a statement is true if it matches what is actually the case, the facts of the matter. If I say 'There are two apples on the table', you can check whether that's true by looking on the table, verifying it empirically. Similarly, if I say 'If I put two more apples on the table, there will be four apples', you can check this either empirically by putting them there and counting, or by doing the calculation in your head.

4. Different kinds of truth

Although the commonsense answer would appear to distinguish between what is true from what is just belief, it doesn't go the whole way in explaining the nature of truth. The mathematician and philosopher Gottfried Leibniz realized that there is a difference between what he called truths of fact (things that are verified by reference to what is the case in the world) and truths of reasoning (things that we can verify by rational thought). For example, a statement such as 'Socrates was Greek' may or may not be true, but can be checked against the facts, but it stands to reason that the statement '2 + 2 = 4' is true. A truth of reasoning cannot be denied without contradiction; it would make no sense to say that 2 + 2 does not equal 4, but it is not logically contradictory to say that Socrates was not Greek.

5. Hume's fork

David Hume came to very much the same conclusion as Leibniz, that there are two different kinds of truth, either a 'relation of ideas' or a 'matter of fact'. However, he saw a deeper significance in this distinction: true statements about matters of fact provide us with knowledge, they tell us something about the world, but are contingent – they are verified empirically by observation of what is the case. True statements about relations of ideas, on the other hand, are necessary truths: they cannot be contradicted, but they tell us nothing about the world. Like two prongs of a fork, the types of truth are distinct and separate. And what's more, Hume asserts, you cannot use a relation of ideas to prove a matter of fact: we cannot get knowledge of facts in the world by reason alone.

6. Analytic and synthetic statements

Some truths are necessary truths, meaning that they cannot be denied without contradiction, and that it is impossible to be otherwise. Others are contingent truths, as their truth depends on whether or not it is the case, and they can be denied without logical contradiction. A similar (but subtly different) distinction is made between two types of statement: analytic and synthetic. A proposition such as 'All bachelors are unmarried' is analytic, as the predicate 'unmarried' is implicit in the subject 'bachelor' (the definition of the word 'bachelor' is an unmarried man), and although a necessary truth, tells us nothing new. The proposition 'All bachelors are happy', however, is synthetic, in that the predicate is a different concept from the subject, and so, unlike an analytic proposition, tells us something about the world.

7 A priori and a posteriori

A further distinction between different kinds of truth and propositions, and one that is more relevant to the epistemological debate between rationalism and empiricism, is between the concepts *a priori* and *a posteriori* – how we come to know the truth of a proposition. *A priori* knowledge is that which we have independent of experience, and includes the sort of analytic statement 'All bachelors are unmarried', but also truths such as mathematical propositions (for example, $2 + 2 = 4$), and deductions from logical reasoning. Knowledge, on the other hand, depends on empirical evidence or experience.

8 A priori and synthetic

Hume's fork was a good metaphor for the rift between British empiricism and continental rationalism, and it seemed that never the twain would meet. But Immanuel Kant challenged one of the assumptions underlying that difference of opinion, that all *a priori* knowledge must be analytic. Instead, he argued in his *Critique of Pure Reason* that knowledge of mathematics and science, and even of metaphysics, is not only *a priori* but also synthetic: it is known independently of experience, but can still tell us something new about the world – we perceive the world by experience, but comprehend it with our reason.

9 American pragmatism

A radically different attitude to the meaning of truth emerged with the establishment of the first distinctively American school of philosophy in the United States – the American pragmatists. Founded by Charles Sanders Peirce in the 1870s, the pragmatist school considered philosophy and reasoning in terms of its use in achieving practical ends. As Peirce put it, 'To ascertain the meaning of an intellectual conception one should consider what practical consequences might result from the truth of that conception.' Truth, they maintained, is confirmed by the result of putting a conception into practice; something is not simply true, but becomes true by acting upon it.

10 William James: useful truth

Peirce's colleague and friend William James expounded on the pragmatist concept of truth, arguing that it is not an absolute, but an expedient in the way we think, and only has a value in so far as it is useful. Differentiating between truth and facts, he explains that facts are not true, but simply are; while truths emerge from them, they also add to the facts, which then reveal new truths. For ancient people, the truth of a flat Earth emerged from the facts available to them, and it was an expedient way of thinking until new facts emerged, changing what they considered to be the truth.

TALK LIKE A GENIUS

❝ Leibniz and Hume both recognized that you can tell if some things are true just by thinking about them, but others require fact-checking. The difference between the two is what distinguishes mathematics from the natural sciences, and what distinguishes rationalism from empiricism. ❞

❝ It's obvious from Hume's description of necessary and contingent truths which side of the rationalist–empiricist debate he takes. He says that truths of reason can't be contradicted, but they don't tell us anything. Truths of fact may need verifying, but at least they tell us something we didn't already know. ❞

❝ William James illustrated his idea of something becoming true with a story of someone lost in a forest. He finds a path, and has a choice of following in the belief that it will lead him out of the forest to safety, or staying where he is and dying of cold and starvation. Whichever choice he makes, it becomes true by his action or inaction. ❞

THE BLUFFER'S SUMMARY

Truth, and how we know something is true, can be either a matter of reasoning, or a matter of fact.

Good and evil

'There is nothing either good or
bad, but thinking makes it so.'

WILLIAM SHAKESPEARE (*HAMLET*, ACT 2, SCENE 2)

When the city-state of Athens adopted a form of
democracy in 508 BCE, there was a sea change in
philosophical thought. Where previously philosophers
speculated about the nature of the Universe around
us, the Athenian philosophers, led by the example of
Socrates, examined human life and how it should be
lived, how we decide between right and wrong, good
and bad. Moral philosophy (also known as ethics) has
its roots in Socrates's exploration of notions of virtue
and correct behaviour and, no doubt because of its
relevance to our everyday lives, has become a central
concern of philosophy ever since.

**How's your moral compass – good, bad or
indifferent?**

1 Moral philosophy is concerned with
concepts of good and bad, while ethics
is concerned with morally correct conduct.
TRUE / FALSE

2 Socrates was the first of the Greek
philosophers to consider questions
of what we now call moral philosophy,
examining ideas of personal morality
without reference to the law or the gods.
TRUE / FALSE

3 According to Plato, we have an innate
sense of morality: we are born with a
knowledge of what is right and wrong, but
must use reason to access that knowledge.
TRUE / FALSE

4 Moral philosophy is concerned
primarily with human behaviour
and is not generally considered to apply to
other animals or inanimate objects.
TRUE / FALSE

5 To reach an objective judgement
of the ethical correctness of any
course of action, it is necessary to ignore
the morality of the agent, the person
performing the action.
TRUE / FALSE

TEN THINGS A GENIUS KNOWS

1 What moral philosophy is

Moral philosophy, also known as ethics, is the branch of philosophy that deals with questions of good and bad, right and wrong behaviour. Moral philosophers examine our understanding of the abstract notions of good and bad, how we learn those notions, and how we apply them in judging the morality of our actions and making decisions about how we live our lives.

2 Living virtuously

As well as exploring the notions of good and bad, and criteria for judging the morality of a course of action, moral philosophy examines these in the context of the way we live our lives. For the Greeks, this meant living a 'good life' (see pages 100–103), one that balances virtue and personal satisfaction. Others have suggested that a morally correct life is one that follows a particular moral code, such as that of a religion. The way we live our lives then raises another concern of moral philosophy: what the purpose or meaning of our existence is.

3 The nature of virtue

A central concern of the classical Greek philosophers was to attempt to define abstract concepts. The key question in moral philosophy was 'What is virtue?' – what makes an action, or a person, good or bad? What is the nature of virtue? The various answers to this question laid the foundations for different schools of thought in moral philosophy. Some considered virtue as a quality or property that is inherent in an action: philanthropy, for example, is inherently good, while theft is inherently bad. Some argued that there were universal criteria for judging virtue, others that there are degrees of virtue, or that virtue was a human construct liable to change.

4 Virtue is knowledge

One of the first philosophers to address questions of morality was Socrates, who challenged assumptions about the idea of virtue. In debates with his fellow Athenians, he showed that they thought they knew what virtue is, and could recognize it when they saw it, but were unable to pin down a precise definition. He suggested that in order to do good, one has to know what is right, and the harmful consequences of not acting virtuously. Virtue, then, is a matter of knowledge. People naturally want to do good, and will do so, if they know what is right; no one will knowingly do wrong.

5 Happiness and morality

Socrates went one step further in his description of virtue. Having explained that knowledge leads to virtue, that a person who knows what is morally correct will do good, he went on to say that that person will, therefore, be happy. Happiness, for Socrates, is an inevitable consequence of virtue. Like virtue, however, happiness is not easily defined, and there are many different aspects to it, such as pleasure, contentment and joy. And while acting virtuously may bring happiness, it does not follow that doing what makes us happy is necessarily virtuous.

6 Plato's perfect virtue

According to Plato, the world we live in is only an imperfect 'shadow' of the real world, the world of Forms (see page 81). In this ideal world are the perfect Forms or Ideas of such things as virtue, and what we see as virtue in our earthly world is merely an imitation of that perfect virtue. To act virtuously, we must emulate that perfect virtue, but first we need to access our innate knowledge of it, which can only be done by philosophical reasoning.

7 The golden mean
Aristotle, as so often, fundamentally disagreed with Plato. He believed that we learn what virtue and morality are from our experience of individual instances that we recognize as morally correct in the world, not some perfect Platonic Form. There is no such thing as perfect virtue (or, for that matter, perfect evil) in this world or any world of Forms, but there are degrees of virtue. To act in an optimally virtuous way we should find the 'golden mean' between extremes of virtue, and behave with moderation. As an example, he points out that while courage is rightly considered a virtue, too much courage is recklessness, and too little courage is timidity.

8 Actions and agents
During the so-called Age of Reason, there was renewed interest in moral philosophy. But instead of the classical preoccupation with the 'good life' and the nature of virtue, or medieval ideas of morality prescribed by divine command, the emphasis shifted to an examination of how we can judge the morality of an action. For example, are there any universal, objective criteria for morality, moral facts or moral laws? Or is morality subjective? And should an action be judged by its consequences, or the intentions, motives or even virtue of the agent performing it?

9 Moral luck
You'd be forgiven for assuming that factors outside our control have no bearing on the morality of our actions. But in the 1970s, Bernard Williams pointed out that what he called 'moral luck' can influence our judgement of morality. For example, a driver convicted of dangerous driving in most countries would be fined and banned from driving, at least temporarily. But if a child had stepped into the road and been killed, that same driver would face more serious charges and maybe a prison sentence. In the first instance, the driver was just lucky nobody was killed, yet we judge the second instance more harshly.

10 Practical ethics
Perhaps more than other branches of philosophy, moral philosophy has obvious practical applications. Unlike religion, or governments, however, it does not offer specific ethical rulings, and it may appear too abstract to offer practical guidance, but the arguments of moral philosophers provide a framework for ethical decision-making. This is especially relevant today, with advances in science and technology posing new ethical problems. Decisions in the fields of government and the law, science, medicine and business are all held up to ethical scrutiny, and philosophers have a part to play in ensuring they are morally correct.

TALK LIKE A GENIUS

🍂 We all like to think that we have a sense of morality, that we know broadly the difference between right and wrong, but it is not so easy to justify our gut reactions rationally, to say exactly what it is that makes something good or bad. 🍂

🍂 It's often said that ignorance of the law is no excuse. Applying the same principle to morality then, you are considered morally culpable even if you didn't know what you were doing was morally wrong." 🍂

🍂 If somebody does something bad, that doesn't make him a bad person. Good people sometimes do bad things – and bad people sometimes do good things. Nevertheless, the fact that someone is good doesn't excuse any morally wrong behaviour. 🍂

🍂 If I notice I've left the stove on before going to bed, it's seen as careless. But if I don't notice, and the house burns down and somebody dies, it's criminally negligent. Does that mean it's morally bad to be unlucky? 🍂

1 FALSE – In philosophy, the terms 'ethics' and 'moral philosophy' are practically interchangeable; both refer to the branch of philosophy involving concepts of morality.

2 TRUE – Before Socrates, Greek philosophy was concerned predominantly with metaphysics; Socrates shifted the emphasis to human life and how it should be lived.

3 TRUE – Plato argued that knowledge of morality is innate; Aristotle argued that, on the contrary, we acquire a sense of morality through experience.

4 TRUE – But it is a moot point whether at least some animals have a sense of right and wrong, or 'acts of God' have a moral dimension.

5 FALSE – In many schools of thought in moral philosophy, the intentions and motives of the agent are taken into consideration.

THE BLUFFER'S SUMMARY

Moral philosophy, aka ethics, examines the concepts of good and bad, and how we judge what is morally right and wrong.

The good life

'The unexamined life
is not worth living.'

SOCRATES

For most people today, the phrase the 'good life' conjures up ideas of luxurious leisure, or escaping from the rat race and living off the land. For ancient Greek philosophers, however, it was a central concept of moral philosophy: the way we should best live our lives, achieving an ideal combination of virtue and personal happiness. There have been, of course, differing opinions of what that balance should be, ranging from austere asceticism, through religious devotion, to hedonism. In the modern world, the question of the aim or purpose of life has been revived by existentialist philosophers.

How good is your knowledge of what makes a good life?

1 The Greek concept of *eudaemonia* was of a life of physical, intellectual, emotional and spiritual fulfilment, achieved by pursuit of excellence in all things.

TRUE / FALSE

2 Diogenes the Cynic chose to live on the street, rejecting the comforts of civilization. The term 'cynicism' was later used to describe the philosophical stance he and others adopted.

TRUE / FALSE

3 For the Epicureans, all forms of sensual enjoyment are superior to pleasures of the soul, such as intellectual pursuits and living virtuously.

TRUE / FALSE

4 In Daoism and Confucianism, a 'good life' is defined as one that is in accord with the ordained 'way of heaven'. Its goal is to ensure eternal peace for the soul.

TRUE / FALSE

5 Believing that traditional ideas of morality and virtue prevent us from living life to the full, Nietzsche urged us to re-evaluate notions of good and bad to discover more life-affirming ways of being.

TRUE / FALSE

TEN THINGS A GENIUS KNOWS

1 What a 'good life' is

As well as examining the nature of virtue, and attempting to define abstract concepts such as good and bad, moral philosophy is concerned with the broader notion of the best way to live one's life. The classical Greek idea of a 'good life' and the various interpretations of it set the parameters for this debate: it is not just about living in accord with what is considered morally correct, but also finding personal happiness and satisfaction. At various times and to various degrees, religion, society and even governments have prescribed the elements of what constitutes a good life. In recent times the emphasis has shifted to a more personal individual interpretation.

2 Eudaemonia

As always, the ancient Greeks had a word for it. *Eudaemonia*, which carries the meanings of well-being, flourishing, happiness and welfare, was at the centre of their idea of a good life. And this *eudaemonia*, 'living well', could be found by pursuing what they called *arete*, a complex notion that included moral virtue, but also excellence, ability and achieving one's potential. 'Good', in the context of a good life, was as much about fulfilment as virtue. Socrates, who was in the vanguard of moral philosophy, believed that we should constantly be examining our lives to ensure we lived up to the standards of *arete* and, in doing so, would find satisfaction and happiness.

3 Aristotle and self-realization

Aristotle took things a step further in his notion of living well. He believed that by realizing one's full potential, one will both act morally correctly and find contentment. First, he suggested, we must recognize the three elements of our nature: the physical, emotional and rational. We can achieve fulfilment by living in accord with

our nature, and thus avoid the frustration and unhappiness caused by unrealized potential. Just as physical and emotional needs can be satisfied in moderation, rather than indulgence, so too are our rational needs, which can be satisfied by acting with moderate virtue, avoiding extremes.

4 Epicureans

After Aristotle, there were conflicting opinions of what the good life meant. On the one hand there were those (the cynics and stoics) who thought *eudaemonia* came from virtuous living; on the other, were those (the Epicureans) who thought that pleasure and a pleasant life were an indication of living wisely and virtuously. The thinker behind this movement, Epicurus, wasn't advocating a life of sensual pleasure, but rather that happiness, or contentment, should be our aim. This comes, he said, from peace of mind, and freedom from fear, especially the fear of death, which he saw as simply non-existence and therefore, literally nothing to fear. Knowing this is the only life we have, we can then enjoy pleasures in moderation, and discover that it is impossible to live a pleasant life without living justly, and it is impossible to live justly without living a pleasant life.

5 Cynics

The Epicurean philosophy was almost the polar opposite of that adopted by Diogenes of Sinope, who was given the epithet 'the Cynic' (meaning doglike) because of his decision to live on the street, like a stray dog. He and his followers, later dubbed the cynics, believed that the only guide to the good life was virtue – not pleasure nor social conventions, or worldly values, but a good and simple life totally in accord with nature. And Diogenes didn't just talk the talk; he lived in an urn, went without clothes or washing, ate, drank and relieved himself whenever and wherever he needed to, forgoing the wealth, status and comfort sought by most Athenians.

6 Stoics

The cynics' idea that we should live in harmony with nature was also taken up by Zeno of Citium, founder of stoicism. He approached the subject from a slightly different angle, however, arguing that we are a part of Nature. Nature is governed by reason, so there is nothing we can do to change it. Faced with this, we should accept everything that Nature puts in our path, including our mortality, with equanimity, tempering our emotions with reason. Worrying about the things we can't do anything about is what gets in the way of the good life, as does yearning for wealth, power and worldly pleasure. Living a noble and virtuous life in accord with nature is both sufficient and necessary for a good life.

7 The afterlife

Stoicism became the predominant philosophy of the Roman empire as Greek influence waned and, as such, influenced much of early Christian thinking too. But as the Christian Church evolved, its moral philosophy (like that of Judaism, Islam and other religions) was steadfastly prescribed by divine commandments – albeit supported by neo-Platonic and neo-Aristotelian arguments. And implicit in these commands was the idea that a virtuous life is not so much about a good life here on Earth, as ensuring the salvation of the immortal soul in the afterlife.

8 Non-Western ideas of the good life

At roughly the same time as the Athenians, philosophers in India and China were also developing comprehensive systems of moral philosophy and distinctive ideas of a 'good life' (see pages 124–131). There are some parallels with Greek thinking; for example, Laozi advocated living according to *Dao*, 'the way', to a achieve a life in tune with the natural world and not upsetting the harmonious balance of the Universe. Confucius, however, saw the 'way of heaven' as living with respect for other people, being a good member of society. For Buddha, the emphasis was on personal development, living in harmony with the Universe to ensure an eventual freedom from the cycle of death and rebirth.

9 Nietzsche's Superman

Nietzsche's infamous pronouncement that 'God is dead' was a dismissal not only of religion, but also of the morality associated with it. He saw traditional moral laws as 'slave morality,' restricting our ability to live life to the full. Rather than living by ethics imposed on us, we should find our own personal morality that allows us to act in a life-affirming way. Once we do that, we have the possibility of surpassing those limitations and becoming an *Übermensch*, or Superman, and living a life that is fulfilling on its own terms.

10 The experience machine

A thought experiment by Robert Nozick helps us to challenge some assumptions about ideas of the good life. Imagine, he says, a machine that can stimulate your brain and nervous system so that you can experience anything you desire, as if it is actually happening to you. You could plug into the machine for a lifetime, avoiding all the suffering of real life – but would you want to? Most of us would say no, preferring an 'authentic' experience to an illusion. We would undoubtedly experience more pleasure by plugging in, but maybe there is, after all, more to our happiness, and what we consider a good life.

TALK LIKE A GENIUS

❝ When we look back on someone's life – in an obituary or eulogy, for example – we assess that life in terms of what we consider to be a "good life". And, most often, that means his or her personal achievements just as much as the altruistic things he or she may have done. ❞

❝ Increasing awareness of environmental issues has meant that, after centuries of defining the good life in terms of religious, social or personal morality, we're forced to re-examine the cynic, stoic and Daoist idea that we should live in accord with nature. ❞

❝ It's our attitude to what happens to us when we die that motivates the way many of us live our lives. We either do good to protect our immortal souls, or live life to the full, knowing it's the only one we've got. ❞

❝ Ludwig Wittgenstein summed up modern attitudes to the good life when he said, "I don't know why we are here, but I'm pretty sure that it is not in order to enjoy ourselves." ❞

WERE YOU A GENIUS?

1 TRUE – The ancient Greeks believed the goal in life is to achieve one's full potential in everything one does.

2 TRUE – Diogenes lived strictly according to his cynic principles, eschewing anything that was not virtuous and in harmony with nature.

3 FALSE – Epicurus held that a contented soul is paramount in achieving a pleasant life, and more lasting than physical welfare.

4 FALSE – In Daoism, the aim of a good life is to follow the natural order of the Universe and, in Confucianism, to follow the natural order of human society.

5 TRUE – According to Nietzsche, living according to ideals of virtue in the hope of a better life after death restricts our ability to achieve our true potential.

THE BLUFFER'S SUMMARY

Philosophers have identified several ingredients for a 'good life', including morality, well-being, happiness and achievement, but disagree about the exact recipe.

Relativism

'In argument about moral problems, relativism is the first refuge of the scoundrel.'

ROGER SCRUTON

Ideas of what is morally right or wrong are so deeply ingrained in our culture that we often assume they are based on absolute ethical truths. Different cultures, however, have different moral standards. Slavery, for example, although universally condemned today, has been considered acceptable in many societies, including the Athenian city-state that was the birthplace of Western moral philosophy. But among the ancient Greek philosophers were some, the relativists, who challenged the assumption that moral values are universal and unchanging: the ethical standards of a particular social group at a particular time determine what is morally right and wrong.

It's relatively simple to find out if you're absolutely *au fait* with relativism...

1 Just as the sceptic would argue that no statement can be shown to be true or false, the relativist argues that nothing can be shown to be morally right or wrong.

TRUE / FALSE

2 The 'hardline' relativist view is that legislation, such as that protecting universal human rights, an unjustified imposition of the moral values of one culture on others.

TRUE / FALSE

3 The sophists of ancient Greece were so-called because of their use of sophistry, using deliberately misleading arguments to win legal cases.

TRUE / FALSE

4 Moral relativism assumes that moral values are human constructs. Relativism is, therefore, considered to be incompatible with religious faiths.

TRUE / FALSE

5 Plato's *Protagoras* exposes a flaw in the relativist's argument by forcing the eponymous character to admit his claim that all claims are relative is itself a relative claim, so has no absolute validity.

TRUE / FALSE

TEN THINGS A GENIUS KNOWS

1 What relativism is
The term relativism is generally applied to a view in moral philosophy that moral values have no absolute validity, but are relative to a particular context. There are, however, several forms of relativism, including truth relativism, the view that there are no absolute truths, only points of view dependent on a particular perspective. At the heart of moral relativism is the belief that it is not possible for us to see the world objectively, to get a 'God's-eye-view' of things as they actually are. Our knowledge of the world is shaped by our particular perspective, which is itself determined by such things as culture, religion and history. Our moral values are based on this knowledge, and so may differ from place to place and time to time, and are, therefore, relative rather than absolute truths.

2 The sophists
The first advocates of a form of relativism appeared in Athens in the fifth century BCE. The newly formed democratic city-state spawned a group of teachers – the sophists – who offered tuition in philosophy, law and the art of rhetoric – especially to clients who wanted to argue their cases in the courts. Among the sophists was Protagoras, who turned his lawyer's mind to philosophy, and concluded that there was more than one side to every argument, and that opinions depend on perspective. In his famous phrase 'Man is the measure of all things', he dismissed the prevailing view that there are absolute and universal moral truths, but only what an individual considers, from his perspective, to be the truth.

3 Truth relativism
The school of philosophy that Protagoras inspired, known as sophism, was not restricted to moral philosophy, but covered the broader area of truth relativism – the view that there is no absolute truth, it is dependent on perspective, and points of view have no absolute validity. Plato, like his mentor Socrates, was highly critical of the sophists, whom he thought were merely paid orators and shysters, not philosophers. He pointed out the flaw in the sophists' argument: self-contradiction. Relativism holds that no statement is absolutely true – but then the statement 'no statement is absolutely true' itself has no absolute validity.

4 Individual relativism
Protagoras's relativism was centred mainly on the notion that, as in a court of law, there are two sides to every argument. Specifically, it was about the perspective of the individuals concerned. Instead of an absolute truth, there is what is true for each individual; and instead of absolute moral values individual people create their own ethical standards, and each individual's moral stance is right for that individual. And as individuals' perspectives change throughout their life, so too do their moral values, in line with their experiences.

5 Cultural relativism
Despite Plato's refutation of relativism, the idea gained considerable popular acceptance. Particularly influential was the notion that moral attitudes are not simply the preferences of individuals, but are moulded by the social group in which an individual lives, expressed in Athens at the time by the poet Pindar's line 'Custom is king of all'. Cultural relativism maintains that moral values are not only shaped by social context, but apply only in that context – they do not have universal validity.

6 Objectivism
Of course, not all philosophers agree that there are no absolute, universal moral values, just as there are those who reject the sceptics' claim

that there are no objective, verifiable truths. Moral objectivism, the direct opposite of moral relativism, is the view that there are some absolute, objective moral truths. And although the evidence for moral relativism (in the form of differing ethical standards from place to place and time to time) is strong, even a hardline relativist would have difficulty arguing that such things as genocide and torture of innocent people is morally right in a society where they are considered acceptable.

7 Religious commandments

Moral relativism's basic tenet, that ethical values are dependent on context, implies that they are determined by humans' perspectives of the world. The moral standards espoused by most religions, however, are based on divine commandments, which are necessarily absolute and eternal moral truths. It would seem, then, that these religions contradict the very idea of moral relativism. However, although adherents argue these are absolute moral values, they differ from one religion to another, and even within a single religion attitudes to sexual and dietary taboos, for example, have changed dramatically over time.

8 Are morals a matter of taste?

Both individual and cultural relativism have been likened to the view in aesthetics that, in matters of taste, there can be no right or wrong. If I say that I find a painting beautiful, it is beautiful to me, and you cannot say that I am wrong. Similarly, if a society considers polygamy morally desirable, it cannot be refuted – that is what that society thinks. Because moral values are often strongly believed and hotly debated, the idea that morality is simply a mater of taste is difficult to accept, and we are more inclined to take an objectivist stance, at least on some ethical issues.

9 Morals of the majority

If we accept the argument of cultural relativism that moral values are determined within the context of specific social groups, then the morality of a society is presumably a broad consensus of its members' moral attitudes. In other words, morality, far from being absolute, is just what the majority believe is right, or at least what the majority happen to consider is acceptable in any given time or place. That, however, raises the question of whether something is good because the majority think it is good, or whether the majority think it is good because it is good (see page 110).

10 Isaiah Berlin's commonsense answer

It would seem that relativism and objectivism were irreconcilably opposed, but in discussion about practical ethical problems, both sides have their merits: we intuitively feel that there are some things that are absolutely morally unjustifiable, yet we accept there are widely different moral values from culture to culture. By looking at moral attitudes in the 'real world', rather than the abstract world of philosophizing, Isaiah Berlin proposed a down-to-earth middle way, dismissing both out-and-out relativism and absolutism. There are, he suggested, some things that are, and always have been, universally considered morally wrong: such things as murder and theft. These can be treated as if they are universal, objective moral truths, and not as a matter of relativism; those moral values that differ from culture to culture should have no absolute validity.

TALK LIKE A GENIUS

❛ It's true that not so very long ago, child labour was considered quite acceptable even in Europe and America, but that does not necessarily mean that the exploitation of children in sweatshops should not be denounced as morally wrong. ❜

❛ Societies around the world are becoming increasingly multicultural, and it's important that we are tolerant of practices that differ from our own. But are we unfairly imposing our values on others if we insist on adherence to our moral codes? ❜

❛ Of course, different attitudes to moral questions have evolved in different societies, but there is a general consistency of opinion on the most important fundamentals of morality across all cultures, suggesting there are some absolute moral rights and wrongs. ❜

❛ The tolerant, liberal relativist may often find herself in the strange position of arguing for the validity of a cultural or religious moral stance that is totally opposed to the very idea of relativism. ❜

1 FALSE – The relativist argument is that actions can be considered morally right or wrong, but this is dependent on context – it is not absolute or universal.

2 TRUE – Even though a majority of countries may agree with those laws, there are some societies that reject, for example, prohibition of the death penalty.

3 FALSE – The name 'sophist' comes from the Greek *sophós*, 'wise', which is also the root of the pejorative word 'sophistry' and sophism, a school of philosophy

4 TRUE – Theistic religions almost invariably hold that moral values are divine in origin; even non-theistic religions, such as Buddhism, hold that there are absolute moral truths.

5 TRUE – Plato had no time for Protagoras's relativism, and showed that it was self-contradictory.

THE BLUFFER'S SUMMARY

Moral relativism is the view that there are no absolute, universal moral rules; what is considered morally correct depends on context.

Is and ought

'Morals excite passions, and produce or prevent actions. Reason of itself is utterly impotent in this particular. The rules of morality, therefore, are not conclusions of our reason.'

DAVID HUME

David Hume cast a sceptical empiricist's eye over how rational thinking shapes what we know and how we make decisions, and concluded that reasoning has its shortcomings. He argued that we cannot discover meaningful facts about the world by reasoning alone (see pages 84–87), and when he turned his attention to questions of morality, concluded that reason cannot provide a basis for moral actions either, but instead these result from our 'passions'. In his view, there is no rational basis for ethical statements, and it is a mistake to move from a descriptive statement of fact to a prescriptive moral rule, to go from an 'is' to an 'ought'.

It is good to have all the facts, so you ought to see if there's anything you're missing...

1 When Hume talks about 'passions', he refers to emotions of all kinds – the things that motivate our actions without conscious thought.

TRUE / FALSE

2 According to the subjectivists, all ethical statements and moral rules are untrue.

TRUE / FALSE

3 The 'naturalistic fallacy' described by G.E. Moore is the false assumption that anything that occurs in the natural world is good, and anything that doesn't occur naturally is bad.

TRUE / FALSE

4 The main objection to subjectivism is that it doesn't tally with ethics in the 'real world' of practice. Ethics are judged by objective moral values, which subjectivists say do not exist.

TRUE / FALSE

5 Kant challenged the subjectivist notion that there are no objective moral facts by arguing that Hume was wrong: moral rules are arrived at by reasoning, not the 'passions'.

TRUE / FALSE

TEN THINGS A GENIUS KNOWS

1 Facts and values
We derive our explanations of the physical world around us by rational thought based on the information available to us, in the form of objective statements of fact that say something true about the world. Statements about morality, however, are not statements of fact, but of value; 'humans are mortal', for example, is a statement of fact, whereas 'theft is bad' is a statement of value. As well as such descriptive moral statements, there are prescriptive moral rules, such as 'it is morally wrong to steal' (meaning 'you ought not to steal'), which are also value statements.

2 Hume's guillotine
Just as Hume made a distinction between two kinds of true statement (see pages 92–5), he also recognized the fundamental difference between statements of fact and statements of value. The problem with moral philosophy, he noted, is that in arguing the case for a moral judgement or rule, we invariably move from an objective description to a subjective prescription without explanation – as he puts it, there is an unjustified shift from 'is' to 'ought'. Using what has become known as 'Hume's guillotine' he separates the realm of facts from that of values: it is not possible, logically, to derive an 'ought' from an 'is'.

3 The slave of the passions
Taking a characteristically empiricist stance, Hume said that reasoning alone can tell us nothing certain about the world. But more than that, he said that what he called moral actions, the things we do that can be judged as morally right or wrong, are not motivated by rational thought. Instead, he argued that 'Morals excite passions, and produce or prevent actions. Reason of itself is utterly impotent in this particular. The rules of morality, therefore, are not conclusions of our reason.' Although we may use reason to explain or justify our actions, it does not drive us to action, but is 'the slave of the passions'.

4 The naturalistic fallacy
It's not just *is* and *ought* that need to be separated, according to G.E. Moore. Many moral arguments are, he said, based on what he calls the naturalistic fallacy, that ethical concepts, such as 'good' and 'bad', are assumed to be the same thing as natural concepts, such as 'pleasurable' and 'painful'. There are no grounds for us to assume that, for example, because something causes pleasure it is necessarily morally good. Moore argued that, unlike natural properties, ethical properties are not identified and analysed with our senses and reason, but with an intuitive moral sense.

5 Subjectivism
In arguing that the 'passions', rather than reason, motivate our moral actions, Hume makes a persuasive case for 'subjectivism', the view that value, and hence morality, is based on our subjective beliefs or emotional reactions, rather than objective external fact. He gives the example of a wilful murder: it is impossible to find in it 'that matter of fact, or real existence, which you call vice', but only 'passions, motives, volitions and thoughts'. If, however, you examine yourself, rather than the murder, you will find that the 'vice' arises from your disapproval of the action, and it is 'passions', not reason, that provoke the reaction.

6 An absence of objective moral facts
At the core of moral subjectivism is the idea that morality is not derived from objective external reality. So-called naive subjectivism denies the existence of objective ethical facts (or that they are not objectively true or false), and argues that moral values are expressions

of our beliefs, attitudes or emotions. Because a moral statement is simply a description of our feelings about an action, not an objective fact, it is not a basis for a rational argument. If I say 'killing is bad', I'm describing my feelings about killing, stating an opinion, much as I might say 'broccoli is disgusting' – and nobody can tell me that is not how I feel.

7 The boo/hurrah theory
In the 20th century, A.J. Ayer and others popularized a subtly different form of subjectivism: 'emotivism'. Also known as the 'boo/hurrah' theory, emotivism is also based on the idea that there are no objective ethical facts, and our moral statements are expressions of our preferences. But they are not merely descriptions of our feelings; they also express our approbation or disapprobation. So that when I say, for example, 'murder is wrong', I mean 'I disapprove of murder – boo!', and if I say that philanthropy is good, what I mean is 'I approve of philanthropy – hurrah!'

8 Subjectivism in practice
Although it is difficult to refute the argument that there are no objective moral facts, subjectivism and emotivism present problems when applied to practical ethical situations. If morality is subjective, and moral statements merely expressions of emotions or attitudes, then there can be no meaningful rational argument about the morality of an action. For instance, if you say that genocide is morally wrong, according to the subjectivist all you are really saying is that you don't like it or disapprove of it. And that goes against the grain for most of us, as we feel intuitively that genocide is morally wrong – the problem is finding a rational argument that isn't based on subjective values.

9 Prescriptivism
The criticism that subjectivism provides no rational, logical basis for a particular moral stance led to a slightly different interpretation of the subjectivist argument – 'prescriptivism' – which to some extent bridges the is/ought divide. As proposed by R.M. Hare, the prescriptivist argument is that moral statements have a prescriptive element, they are in effect commands, and not just expressions of attitudes; the statement 'killing is bad' is an order not to kill. Because this is a universal command (everybody must not kill) and not a personal statement of preference, it is more capable of rational debate, and disagreements over ethical values can be seen as conflicting moral commands.

10 Kant's counterargument
Immanuel Kant famously said that he had been 'woken from his dogmatic slumber' by reading Hume, but this awakening prompted his mission to build a comprehensive system of philosophy fundamentally opposed to Hume's. In terms of moral philosophy, Kant completely rejected Hume's subjectivist arguments, instead arguing that, since only rational beings have a sense of morality, moral judgements must be the result of rational thought. There are therefore, he concluded, objective ethical facts.

TALK LIKE A GENIUS

❝ Certain moral laws are so universally accepted that we tend to take it for granted that they are based on facts. But a rule such as "do not steal" is based on the notion that theft is bad – which is a statement of value, not a verifiable fact. ❞

❝ If moral values are subjective, rather than based on objective facts – and it's difficult to show that isn't the case – then isn't your only reason for considering slavery morally wrong is that you disapprove of it? ❞

❝ You can have no argument with a person who finds same-sex marriage morally repugnant, because it's a true description of her feelings. You can argue, though, when she infers that it is, therefore, morally wrong. ❞

THE
BLUFFER'S
SUMMARY

Prescriptive moral rules are not statements of fact, and cannot be derived from descriptive statements of fact.

Kant's categorical imperative

'Act only according to that maxim whereby you can, at the same time, will that it should become a universal law.'

IMMANUEL KANT

For many people, behaving morally consists of adhering to a set of rules laid down for them by some authority, such as the laws of the land or religious commandments. Many philosophers, however, have tried to find some criteria for assessing the morality of actions, rather than blindly following these rules. One method, 'consequentialism', is to judge an action by its outcomes. But some, notably Immanuel Kant, believed we have a duty to do what is morally correct: the outcome doesn't change the morality of the action. There are some things that are simply either good or bad, no matter what the consequences.

Kant believed we can tell the difference between right and wrong; let's see if you can.

ARE YOU A GENIUS

1 Only with the emergence of thinkers like Machiavelli did the idea 'the end justifies the means' begin to take hold.

TRUE / FALSE

2 If a person unknowingly murdered a terrorist for personal gain, but saved innocent lives as an unforeseen consequence, a consequentialist would say that the killing was morally good.

TRUE / FALSE

3 Kant's 'hypothetical imperative' describes how to act in order to achieve specific ends, but not which ends are morally good. His 'categorical imperative', is an absolute rule to be universally obeyed, and is justified as an end in itself.

TRUE / FALSE

4 Kant described his categorical imperative as a paraphrase of the so-called Golden Rule: 'Treat others as you would wish them to treat you'.

TRUE / FALSE

5 Schopenhauer was deeply influenced by Kant's transcendental idealism, and built his own moral philosophy on the principles of the categorical imperative.

TRUE / FALSE

TEN THINGS A GENIUS KNOWS

1 Moral authority
What is considered to be morally good or bad behaviour in any society is almost invariably enshrined in laws, a moral code dictated by some form of authority. This may take the form of a religious authority enforcing divine commands, or a government enacting civil laws. But these moral codes are specific about which actions are bad or good, and the morality of an action is judged by whether or not it conforms to those rules, rather than general guidelines of what constitutes ethical behaviour. While many of these laws, such as forbidding theft, are universal, there are others that are specific to particular societies. This raises the question of moral relativism (see pages 104–7), which challenges the authority of such moral codes.

2 Divine commands
Among the first to question the authority of especially religious moral laws were the Athenian philosophers. Plato summed it up by asking, 'Is the pious loved by the gods because it is pious, or is it pious because they love it?' In other words, does religion simply endorse an existing universal moral law, or is it religion that decrees what constitutes morality? For much of history, religion has been the arbiter of morality, and the question still has some relevance, even when the authority is a secular one. Perhaps, as Isaiah Berlin suggested, we are confusing 'our own constructions and inventions with eternal laws or divine decrees'.

3 Consequentialism
In Europe, religious authority was increasingly undermined by a rising tide of humanist thinking during the Renaissance. In place of blind acceptance of the dogmas of the Christian Church, philosophers returned to the idea of examining the nature of morality, what makes an action good or bad. In the vanguard of this shift in thinking was Niccolò

Machiavelli, whose dictum 'the end justifies the means' heralded a move towards judging the morality of a course of action by its outcomes or consequences, rather than rigid adherence to any set of moral rules. 'Consequentialism', as this idea is known, became the predominant basis for moral philosophy in the Enlightenment period.

4 Deontology
In sharp contrast to the consequentialism of mainstream moral philosophy in Europe, the Christian Church (and other religions) continued to advocate a moral code in which morality is determined by the action and whether that action conforms to specific rules, rather than its outcomes. Because it is characterized by a duty to follow laws, such as divine commandments, religious or civil laws, or simply social or cultural norms, this is known as 'deontology' (from the Greek *deon*, meaning 'duty' or 'necessity').

5 Motives and intentions
It is not only consequences, or a duty to adhere to rules, that need to be considered in determining morality: the motives and intentions of the agent – the person doing it – should also be taken into account, and a distinction made between the morality of the action and the morality of the agent. Consequentialists such as J.S. Mill argued that morality depends on intention to cause a good outcome, even if the motive was self-interest or dutiful following of a moral code. Immanuel Kant, however, dismissed the whole idea of consequentialism. There is only one wholly good thing, he argued, and that is good will; so, it is the will, or motive (rather than the intention), of the agent that determines the morality of an action.

6 Free will and autonomy
Kant presented a carefully reasoned argument for his unfashionable deontological stance. In defence of the idea of duty, he argued that we have a duty to act in a morally correct way, and

choosing to follow this duty, the motive for doing something, determines its morality. A necessary factor here is free will – without the freedom to choose a particular course of action, there is no morality, as we could not do otherwise. Kant also emphasized that, in exercising our free will, we can act autonomously, not simply obeying rules imposed by an outside authority, but according to moral laws we have deduced for ourselves, and that we have a moral duty to adhere to.

7 The noumenal world

Kant's transcendental idealism (see pages 24–7) is a comprehensive system of philosophy, linking all aspects of his philosophical thinking. He explained that the phenomenal world – the world that we experience – exists in time and space and is, therefore, governed by scientific laws, and so are our physical actions in that world. Free will and moral choice are not determined by those scientific laws, however, and take place in the noumenal world – the world of things-in-themselves. Morality, Kant explains, is subject to the laws that govern the noumenal world.

8 Universal moral laws

It is Kant's argument that the noumenal world is subject to laws that leads to his outright rejection of consequentialism. We have free will and autonomy, but in addition, we have the faculty of rationality, of using reasoning to make decisions. Only rational beings are able to make moral choices; so morality is based on reason. And if a rational argument is valid, Kant continues, it is universally valid; therefore, if something is shown by rational argument to be morally correct, it is always correct. In that sense, the laws of morality are as eternal and universal as the laws of physics. An action in accordance with such a universal law will always be morally good, and so we have a duty to follow these laws.

9 The categorical imperative

Rather than specify what actions are and are not morally good, Kant offered a way that each one of us can judge the morality of any of our ethical choices. In contrast to what he called the 'hypothetical imperative' of consequentialism – if I do X, then Y will result – he proposed the 'categorical imperative': an action is only morally permissible if it accords with a rule you can consistently and universally apply to yourself and others. By universalizing a moral proposition, we can see if this results in irrationality or logical contradiction. His example was the proposition 'it is permissible to lie': this would be irrational if everybody lied, as nobody could believe anybody; and the idea of lying implies that there is also truth-telling, a logical contradiction if lying were universally acceptable.

10 The second formulation

In the first formulation of the categorical imperative, Kant neatly summed up the idea of moral rules that are universal, and so analogous to the scientific laws governing the physical world. From this, he went on to refine his reasoning in further formulations of the idea. He realized, for example, that a self-serving proposition, such as 'always look after number one', could be universalized without logical contradiction, but is not morally justifiable. To overcome this, his second formulation states: act in such a way that you always treat humanity, whether in your own person or in the person of any other, never merely as a means to an end, but always at the same time as an end.

TALK LIKE A GENIUS

❛ Although he says that we have a duty to act according to moral rules, Kant doesn't actually tell us what those rules are, what is morally good or bad, just how we should decide on them. ❜

❛ Religion has traditionally been the source of our moral codes. But the secularization of society in the modern world hasn't produced the moral vacuum that some religious people predicted, because our morality is actually based on rational thought rather than divine command. ❜

❛ On the face of it, judging an action by the outcome is a good practical rule of thumb, but it doesn't really tackle the issue of whether an action is good or bad in itself. It's difficult to justify the morality of allowing a sadistic thug to torture and kill a petty criminal for fun, just because it happens to bring about a greater good. ❜

❛ It's all very well having a system of ethics based on very specific rules, but then people end up doing things out of duty, without really thinking about the morality of their actions. Kant's categorical imperative forces us to consider the morality of those rules. ❜

WERE YOU A GENIUS?

1 FALSE – As early as the fifth century BCE, some moral and political philosophers in Greece and China argued that the ends justify the means.

2 FALSE – Although consequentialism judges morality by outcomes, many consequentialists take into account the intentions and motives of the agent, and make a distinction between the morality of the act and that of the agent.

3 TRUE – Kant criticized consequentialism for not being able to rise above the level of hypothetical imperative, which is based on subjective considerations rather than absolute, universal demands.

4 FALSE – Kant recognized the similarity, but insisted the Golden Rule is a hypothetical imperative ('if you want to be treated this way, do this'), whereas the categorical imperative is absolute and universally binding..

5 FALSE – Schopenhauer revered Kant, but found his moral philosophy overly abstract and impractical, with no understanding of what motivates human actions.

THE BLUFFER'S SUMMARY

Kant rejected the mainstream idea of consequentialism, proposing instead that something is only morally justifiable if it can be considered a universally applicable rule.

Utilitarianism

'The greatest happiness of the greatest number is the foundation of morals and legislation.'

JEREMY BENTHAM

At the end of the 18th century, British philosophy continued to follow its own distinctive course. While in mainland Europe Kant's transcendental idealism dominated the scene, in Britain Jeremy Bentham (1748–1832) developed a moral philosophy in the British empiricist tradition, but influenced by continental revolutionary political philosophy: , utilitarianism. In contrast to Kant's stern, rule-based categorical imperative, utilitarianism was based on the principle that what causes pleasure is morally good. Bentham saw this as a basis not just for personal ethics, but also for public morality, and with the advocacy of his protégé John Stuart Mill, utilitarianism influenced much of the social and political reform in Britain in the 19th century.

Do you have the great pleasure of knowing about utilitarianism, or is it just a pain?

1 Bentham's formula for calculating the 'utility' of an action included variables such as the intensity, duration, certainty, purity and extent of the pleasure caused.

TRUE / FALSE

2 Utilitarianism was a significant influence on Marx's vision of a socialist state described in *The Communist Manifesto*.

TRUE / FALSE

3 Mill's concept of utilitarianism, incorporating the 'harm principle', can be seen in practice today, for example, in legislation decriminalizing recreational drug use or legalizing same-sex marriage.

TRUE / FALSE

4 Robert Owen set up a textile factory in Scotland, and later founded a utopian socialist commune, 'New Harmony', in the US, based on the principles of utilitarianism.

TRUE / FALSE

5 The phrase 'the greatest happiness for the greatest numbers' was coined 20 years before Bentham was born.

TRUE / FALSE

TEN THINGS A GENIUS KNOWS

1 Morality and happiness

Utilitarianism emerged from two distinct strands of Enlightenment thought: the British tradition of moral philosophy connected to the empiricism of Hobbes, Locke and Hume, and the revolutionary social and political philosophy of French thinkers such as Jean-Jacques Rousseau. Above all, it built on the idea of consequentialism: that the morality of actions should be judged by their outcomes, which had been gaining ground since the Renaissance. It also, however, harked back to the ancient idea of the 'good life', defining whether consequences are good or bad in terms of happiness and well-being, and more specifically, the welfare of society as a whole: the common good.

2 Utility

The term 'utilitarianism' derives from Jeremy Bentham's use of the word 'utility' to describe the usefulness of a course of action in bringing about an outcome of happiness or well-being. To assess an action's utility, however, we have to consider what constitutes happiness. Bentham, like Epicurus long before him, worked from the premise that happiness is defined in terms of what gives pleasure, and unhappiness by what causes pain. What he called the 'two sovereign masters' – pain and pleasure – are the yardsticks we can use to measure happiness, but moreover they define the morality of an action: what gives pleasure is morally good, what causes pain is morally bad.

3 Pleasure and pain

If whatever brings about happiness is morally good, then we can judge the morality of an action – and decide on a morally correct course of action – by the amount of pleasure (or pain) it causes. Hence, Bentham's dictum of 'the greatest happiness of the greatest number', or more precisely that an action is morally justified to the extent that it maximizes the amount of pleasure, and minimizes the amount of pain. The inclusion of the phrase 'greatest number' is significant: Bentham saw the principle applying not only to personal morality, but also to 'the business of government … to promote the happiness of the society', and so 'pleasures then, and the avoidance of pains, are the ends that the legislator has in view'.

4 The felicific calculus

Bentham's utilitarianism was very much a product of the Age of Enlightenment, and, like other Enlightenment philosophers, he was keen to ensure it had some degree of scientific credibility. Therefore, he devised a 'calculus of felicity', a systematic method of measuring the utility of any course of action, exactly how much pleasure or pain it would cause. He proposed units of measurement of pleasure and pain (sometimes known as *hedons* and *dolors*), and a formula that calculated utility – the sum of all pleasure that results from an action, minus the sum of all pain. The excess of pleasure over pain is the measure of the morality of the action.

5 J.S. Mill's harm principle

While Bentham formulated the concept of utilitarianism, it was his godson J.S. Mill who refined and popularized it. He regarded utilitarianism as an embodiment of the so-called Golden Rule 'do as you would be done by', but also suggested that its converse 'don't do to others what you wouldn't want done to you' also applies. He proposed what became known as the 'harm principle' – that every individual should be free to do whatever gives them happiness, so long as that doesn't impinge upon the happiness of others.

6 Impact on society and politics

Of course, utilitarianism had significant political implications. Bentham saw it as a guide for legislators, but more importantly explicitly stated that in calculating utility 'everybody is to count for one, and nobody for more than one'. As well as this radically egalitarian stance, utilitarianism challenged many of the contemporary social mores, especially regarding sexual behaviour: the idea that if your pleasures aren't harming anybody, they're morally acceptable was a tough one to sell in strait-laced Britain. Just as controversial was the notion that many businesses and industries caused their workers unnecessary suffering. Much social reform in 19th-century Britain was inspired by utilitarian principles, and especially thanks to Mill's advocacy of utilitarianism.

7 Higher and lower pleasures

Mill campaigned tirelessly to see the principles of utilitarianism practically applied and adopted in legislation. However, despite his espousal of the idea of equality (he was the first member of parliament to propose that women should have the vote), he believed that pleasures are not all equal. While Bentham argued vehemently that there is no 'hierarchy of pleasures', Mill maintained that moral and intellectual pleasures, 'higher pleasures', are superior to the 'lower' physical and sensual pleasures, and should count for more in the reckoning of happiness and morality; and with more than a whiff of snobbery stated, 'It is better to be a human being dissatisfied than a pig satisfied; better to be Socrates dissatisfied than a fool satisfied'.

8 Rule utilitarianism

The 'classical' utilitarianism of Bentham and Mill is a consequentialist moral philosophy: it judges morality by consequences, and advocates choosing actions by their probable outcomes. Every action is assessed on its own merits; there are no hard and fast rules. But later philosophers have argued that it is often difficult to weigh up all the consequences of an action, and make a quick decision. Instead of this 'act utilitarianism', they suggested a 'rule utilitarianism': some rules of thumb that have been shown by experience to maximize utility, analogous to the sort of legislation Bentham had proposed.

9 The trolley problem

Philippa Foot challenged the utilitarian idea of 'the greatest happiness of the greatest number' with her 'trolley problem': five people are tied to the tracks in the path of a runaway trolley; you can prevent them from being killed by pulling a lever to divert the trolley onto a side track, but then the trolley will inevitably kill another person on that branch. Should you deliberately kill one person to save the other five? Is the harm done justifiable? What if the one person is your daughter? Does everybody 'count for one, and nobody for more than one'?

10 Utilitarianism and animal rights

Others have taken utilitarian principles still further. Bentham himself had suggested that we should consider the happiness of non-human as well as human animals when deciding the utility of an action, famously stating: 'the question is not, Can they reason? nor, Can they talk? but, Can they suffer?' His argument was taken up again in the 20th century (to a more receptive audience) by Peter Singer. Singer argued that if animals are capable of experiencing pleasure and pain, then the principles of utilitarianism apply to them and, indeed, equally to all sentient beings.

TALK LIKE A GENIUS

❝ Machiavelli and Bentham make strange bedfellows, but they both agree that, in the final analysis, it is the consequences of our actions that determine whether they were morally justified. ❞

❝ Does the football fan derive more pleasure from the Cup Final than an opera buff gets from Tosca? Possibly... but perhaps there's a qualitative difference in the pleasure they each get ❞

❝ One of the strengths of utilitarianism is that it is egalitarian: nobody's well-being is valued above anybody else's. In practice though, how many of us would consciously inflict suffering on someone we love for the greater good? ❞

❝ If we're talking about the greatest good for the greatest number, do we mean the grand total of happiness of the population, or the highest average happiness, the maximum good per person? ❞

THE
BLUFFER'S
SUMMARY

A morally correct action is one that maximizes the excess of pleasure over pain, or minimizes the excess of pain over pleasure.

Existentialism

'Existentialism does not offer ... the consolations of an abstract evasion: existentialism proposes no evasion.'

SIMONE DE BEAUVOIR

As much a cultural movement as a philosophy, existentialism was popularized by Jean-Paul Sartre in the 1940s, inspiring the 'Beat Generation' of the 1950s and anti-establishment student demonstrations in the 1960s. But its roots lay a century earlier, in the work of Søren Kierkegaard, which paved the way for FriedrichNietzsche, and others, to explore a subjective approach to the understanding of human existence. Disaffection with religion and the increasingly alienating effect of modernization prompted a search for the meaning of life, rather than an abstract ontological theory of existence.

Find out if you know more than the beatniks did about existentialist philosophy.

1 It was Søren Kierkegaard who first described existential crisis and the angst caused by it.

TRUE / FALSE

2 Existentialist philosophy denies the existence of God.

TRUE / FALSE

3 The key concern of existentialism is the 'human condition', examined in the light of the purposelessness of human existence. Rather than offering an ontological explanation, it advocates a subjective approach to finding meaning in life.

TRUE / FALSE

4 Existentialism regards rationality as an inappropriate way of making existential decisions, which ignores the possibility of finding a subjective meaning in life.

TRUE / FALSE

5 For Albert Camus, the only conceivable response to the futility of human existence is suicide.

TRUE / FALSE

TEN THINGS A GENIUS KNOWS

1 The subjective experience

The term existentialism to describe a distinct branch of philosophy was first adopted by Jean-Paul Sartre, and strictly only refers to the movement he spearheaded in the 1940s. However, it is more loosely used to refer to a subjective approach to philosophical enquiry that emerged in the mid-19th century. As traditional cultural and religious tenets were eroded, there was a gradual recognition that neither philosophy nor science could adequately explain human existence, nor more specifically the purpose of our existence. This, according to the existentialist, is experienced subjectively by each individual, and cannot be governed by objective moral philosophy or scientific thinking. At the centre of existentialism is the human subject who, given the freedom to choose, can live life 'authentically'.

2 Existential angst

Generally regarded as the prototypical existentialist, Søren Kierkegaard used his own subjective feelings as the starting point of his philosophical thinking. When we face extremes in our lives, he noticed, we find ourselves alone, and experience feelings of anxiety and dread as we have to decide which way our lives should take. He likened this to the dizzy sensation of standing on a cliff edge, overwhelmed by the idea that we can choose to jump off, or not. The angst we feel at these moments of 'existential crisis' is, he explains, the sudden realization that we have the freedom to choose between hope and despair.

3 Living authentically

Kierkegaard pointed out that each individual has to make the choices when faced with such a crisis; the decisions cannot be prescribed by cultural norms, philosophy or even religion. It is the individual who undergoes the crisis, and who makes the choice, so it is up to the individual to take responsibility, and to find for him- or herself a purpose in life. 'The crucial thing', according to Kierkegaard, 'is to find a truth which is truth for me, to find the idea for which I am willing to live and die'. In this way, we can live life with sincerity and passion, and what existentialists call 'authenticity'.

4 A Godless Universe

Another precursor of existentialism was Friedrich Nietzsche, whose famous proclamation that 'God is dead' formed the basis for his philosophy based on a subjective, individualistic perspective. The demise of traditional morality that came with collective religion led inevitably to the kind of existential crisis Kierkegaard described, but across the whole of society. We all have to come to terms with the realization that we live in a Godless Universe, and decide for ourselves the kind of life we want to lead. For Nietzsche, this meant daring to become who you really are, the alternative being to submit to conventions imposed on you by others.

5 Martin Heidegger

The early 20th century saw a rejection of the abstraction of metaphysical speculation, especially in Husserl's phenomenology (see page 33). Influenced by Husserl's ideas, Martin Heidegger set about exploring the nature of existence, but instead of just examining the physical world, the objects of human experience, he pointed out that we also exist as objects of our experience, and so 'We are ourselves the entities to be analysed'. In *Being and Time*, he explains that we experience our being as a past, present and future, and also that our being has an end. In light of our awareness of mortality, it is our responsibility to find significance in our lives and live authentically.

6 Self-awareness

Like Heidegger, Maurice Merleau-Ponty rejected the label 'existentialist', but certain elements of his thinking were influential on the emerging existentialist movement. He took Heidegger's idea that we are the object of our own experience, but added that we are both subject and object of that experience – we are self-aware. Each individual has a unique existence, a unique experience of the world, and most importantly a unique experience of being. We can only understand the world from our own subjective individual perspective, and our lives can only be lived subjectively.,

7 Jean-Paul Sartre

Existentialism per se came to fruition in the philosophical writings (and plays and novels) of Jean-Paul Sartre. Starting from the standpoint of a subjective approach to philosophical thinking, and an atheist's perspective of morality, Sartre turned traditional thinking on its head. For much of history, it had been assumed that we were created, we exist, for a purpose; as Thomas Aquinas put it, 'essence precedes existence'. Sartre refuted this, saying that humans appear in the world without purpose, and can only define themselves through their experience of the world, their existence precedes their essence. What is essential to being a human, what defines them as an individual, is determined by what they decide to become.

8 Freedom from convention

Sartre depicts the Universe as Godless and indifferent to our existence. It does not provide our lives with any purpose or meaning. So individual humans are free to choose what kind of life they want to lead; it is not determined by nature. But neither should it be determined by the culture into which a person is born. Sartre and his followers regarded conformity to social mores as 'bad faith', a form of bourgeois oppression. Instead, they advocated breaking free from convention and adopting an authentic way of being.

9 Albert Camus

Sartre's one-time colleague Albert Camus (they fell out over Camus's condemnation of totalitarian communism) is widely regarded as an existentialist philosopher, but he himself denied being an existentialist or, indeed, a philosopher. Nevertheless, in his writing he examined a central existentialist question: if life is meaningless, is it worth living at all? Once we realize that our existence has no purpose, and that we are mortal, wouldn't suicide be the sensible option? From this pessimistic viewpoint, however, he suggests that once we can accept both the futility of life, and the inevitability of death, we can appreciate life itself and the fleeting happiness it can bring us.

10 The absurd

It is the crux of the human condition, Camus says, that faced with an incomprehensible Universe, a purposeless existence and our own mortality, we continue to have what he describes as an absurd demand for significance. In his essay, 'The Myth of Sisyphus', he likens Sisyphus's meaningless task of repeatedly pushing a rock up a mountain, and see it roll back down again, to the futility of human existence. Rather than give up, Sisyphus continues with renewed resolve, in a futile, absurd attempt to give his efforts meaning. But it is the struggle itself that ultimately gives Sisyphus a purpose – and living life, despite its absurdity, that gives our lives meaning.

TALK LIKE A GENIUS

❝ There are no dos and don'ts in existentialism; it's not about what is morally right and wrong. To use Nietzsche's phrase, it's "beyond good and evil", and describes a way of being, how you should live your life, rather than what you should do. ❞

❝ Sartre's existentialism offers us the freedom to live as we choose. But that freedom isn't a blank cheque – we have to live with the consequences of our choices, so have a responsibility to do something worthwhile with our lives. ❞

❝ If you believe that existence is devoid of any purpose, you have to wonder what point there is in going on with it. But even Camus recognized that putting an end to it is just as absurd and pointless, so we might as well carry on with our lives. ❞

❝ Interest in existentialism and its left-leaning, anti-establishment connotations had dwindled by the time Sartre died in 1980. Since then, no comparable philosophical movement has captured the public imagination in quite the same way. ❞

THE BLUFFER'S SUMMARY

In an indifferent Universe, with no purpose to our existence, we have to find meaning in life for ourselves.

Chinese philosophy

> 'What the great learning teaches, is to illustrate illustrious virtue; to renovate the people; and to rest in the highest excellence'

KONG FUZI (CONFUCIUS)

Unlike the first Greek philosophers, thinkers in ancient China had little time for metaphysics, which they saw as the remit of religion, and instead focused their attention on questions of moral philosophy. The sixth century BCE was a time of political upheaval and internal conflict in China, and philosophers, who mainly came from an emerging class of administrators, sought social and moral codes that would bring some stability. Common to them all was the idea of living virtuously, but there were several different theories of how this could be achieved, including the four main Chinese philosophical schools of thought: Daoism, Confucianism, Mohism and legalism.

Can you tell the difference between Laozi, Mozi, Kongzi and Zhuangzi?

1 The Chinese philosophers Laozi and Kong Fuzi, the founders of Daoism and Confucianism, predate the earliest Greek philosophers.

TRUE / FALSE

2 From the sixth to the third century BCE, a 'golden age' of Chinese philosophy saw numerous thinkers suggest different ways of organizing Chinese society; it became known as the 'Hundred Schools of Thought'.

TRUE / FALSE

3 Kong Fuzi avoids any mention of the gods in his philosophy, instead referring to *tian*, or heaven, as the source of moral authority and moral order.

TRUE / FALSE

4 Mao Zedong adopted legalism as a model for a strict authoritarian communist society, but also admired Mozi's idea that everyone should be treated equally regardless of their origins.

TRUE / FALSE

5 The works of Kong Fuzi were required reading for students taking Chinese civil service exams until the 19th century.

TRUE / FALSE

1 Daoism

One of the first of the so-called 'Hundred Schools of Thought' of ancient China, Daoism was based on the teachings of Laozi, collected in a book titled the *Dao de jing* (*The book of the way of virtue*). In it, Laozi describes the harmonious balance of the natural world, and explains that this is a manifestation of *dao*, 'the way', and that because of our free will, we humans have strayed from this path. To resolve social unrest, as well as to achieve individual fulfilment in life, Laozi says that we must reject social conventions and live with a natural spontaneity, in harmony with *dao*, the way of the cosmos.

2 Zhuangzi

The *Dao de jing* was considered one of the classic Chinese texts, and Daoism became established as a major school of Chinese philosophical thought. Among the many Daoist philosophers was Zhuangzi, who in the fourth century BCE wrote a collection of allegories and fables, known as the Zhuangzi, seen as a companion volume to Laozi's book. As well as reinforcing Daoism's core message, Zhuangzi attempted to show the illusory nature of the world we live in and the mistaken conceptions we have of it. In one famous anecdote, for example, he describes dreaming that he was a butterfly, and on waking, wondering how he could tell if he was Zhuangzi who had dreamt of being a butterfly, or a butterfly now dreaming of being Zhuangzi.

3 Confucius

According to legend, Laozi was working as an archivist in the court of the Zhou emperors, and was periodically consulted by a young administrator, Kong Qiu. Kong, as an advisor to the court, was keen to introduce social reforms to bring stability and order. His ideas were well received, earning him the title Kong Fuzi, Latinized to Confucius, or simply Kongzi, the Master Kong. Like many civil servants, Kong was conservative in his ways, and proposed a moral philosophy based on traditional values and conventional ideas of virtue, which would form the basis for a structure of effective and just government.

4 The mandate of heaven

While the emphasis in Daoism was on the individual and his or her relationship with the natural cosmic order, Confucianism focused on the more practical business of the structure of society and the individual's place in it. Kong Fuzi deliberately avoided reference to the mystical *dao*, or indeed any supernatural forces, other than what he called *tian*, or heaven, the source of natural moral order. Good deeds have the approval of *tian*; bad deeds are punished by *tian*. Importantly, he suggested that rulers, such as the emperors of China, do not have a divine right to rule, but are given a mandate by heaven, which can be withdrawn if they rule unwisely or unjustly.

5 Cultivating virtue

In the same way that he believed there was no divine right to rule, Kong Fuzi believed that virtue was not a god-given quality of certain classes of society. Heaven is the source of moral order, but rather than bestowing it upon people, it is made available to all, so that virtue can, and should, be cultivated in everyone, from all social classes. Chinese society in Kong Fuzi's time was rigidly hierarchical, and there was little or no social mobility, but what he suggested was that even the humblest members of it could earn the approval of *tian*.

6 *Junzi*, the superior man

Kong Fuzi argued that virtue can be learnt, and that the best way to learn is by example. A ruler, for example, can inspire his subjects to behave correctly by his own virtuous actions, just as a child learns its morality from observing the behaviour of its parents. For Kong Fuzi, the ideal model of virtue was the sage or scholar, whose behaviour is guided by wisdom. Not everyone has the ability to achieve that level of learning, but we can all aspire to becoming what he called *junzi* – the 'gentleman' or superior man.

7. The five constant relationships

With its emphasis on traditional values, Confucianism endorses the hierarchical structure of society, and suggests that correct behaviour is that which is appropriate to social status. Nevertheless, the idea of providing an example of virtuous behaviour is a two-way process; we should not only show deference to our superiors, but also benevolence to those of lower status. There is a natural order of superior and inferior, shown in what Kong Fuzi identifies as the five constant relationships: sovereign and subject; father and son; husband and wife; elder and younger brothers; and older and younger friends.

8. Ritual and ceremony in Confucianism

To reinforce the notion of respect for one another, and to give form to the examples of correct behaviour, Kong Fuzi advocated a strict adherence to social niceties and conventions. In addition, he suggested that traditional religious ceremonies, especially those involving worship of ancestors, served a purpose in exemplifying the notion of respect and correctness. Confucianism, while not itself a religion, developed the practice of various rituals symbolizing the values of loyalty, respect and propriety.

9. Mohism

Mozi, a fifth-century BCE thinker, disagreed strongly with the principles of both Daoism and Confucianism. The school he founded, Mohism, was based on logical argument and reasoning, rather than mysticism or tradition, and encouraged thinking rather than obedience to moral rules or social conventions. Above all, he objected to the class-ridden structure of Confucianism and its insistence on ritual. Mohism was based on the ideas of equality and impartiality, that we should care for one another regardless of status or relationship, and also on the principle of reciprocity, that we should treat everyone as we would like to be treated ourselves.

10. Legalism

Mozi's rational approach to moral and political philosophy was in stark contrast to the quasi-religious ethical ideas of other schools of Chinese philosophy. In practice, these had not brought about the political stability that was necessary as warring factions fought for control of the Chinese empire, and from Mohism a more practical movement, legalism, evolved, based on evidence and reason. Central to Legalist thought was the idea that people are, by nature, inclined to be bad, and it is the job of the state to ensure they behave correctly. The three cornerstones of this authoritarian philosophy, described by Han Feizi in the third century BCE, are *fa*, the law, which is applicable to everyone equally; *shu*, the methods by which the law is enforced; and *shi*, the legitimate power of the ruler.

❝ Because of its mystical element of following "the Way", Daoism lends itself easily to a religious interpretation and practice. Confucianism is less spiritual, but with its emphasis on ceremony and ritual has also been considered a humanistic or rationalist religion. ❞

❝ Although Chinese legalism is sometimes compared to Machiavelli's realpolitik, it bears a stronger resemblance to Hobbes's view that law and order need to be imposed to counteract the selfishness of human nature. ❞

❝ Zhuangzi's literary anecdotes contain references to questions of philosophy of the mind – such as concepts of self and identity, the problem of other minds, and the unreliability of our senses – to emphasize the importance of following the *dao*. ❞

❙ FALSE – Laozi and Kong Fuzi were approximately contemporary with Pythagoras, shortly after the emergence of philosophy in Miletus.

❷ TRUE – The turbulent political scene in China during this period inspired administrators and lawmakers to seek solutions that would bring stability.

❸ TRUE – Confucianism is fundamentally a humanistic philosophy, with *Tian* as a guiding principle.

❹ TRUE – Mao agreed with Mohism's principles of equality, but believed that the rule of the state should be strictly enforced.

❺ TRUE – The Han dynasty's Emperor Wu promoted Confucianism as the official imperial philosophy, and it remained a central pillar of government for successive emperors.

THE BLUFFER'S SUMMARY

The many schools of classical Chinese philosophy offered various interpretations of virtuous living, and models for an ideal society.

Buddhism

'To cease from evil, to do good, and to purify the mind yourself, this is the teaching of all the Buddhas.'

SIDDHARTHA GAUTAMA (THE BUDDHA)

Although considered by many people to be a non-theistic religion, Buddhism can also be seen as a system of moral philosophy. It has its roots in the Vedic religions of ancient India, but the distinguishing features of Buddhism are beliefs based on the rational arguments of a single man, Siddhartha Gautama, in the sixth century BCE. Gautama spent many years in meditation before he reached what he called 'enlightenment', the conclusion of his thought process, on which he could base a comprehensive system of philosophy. As the Buddha or 'enlightened one', he and his ideas gained a considerable following across Asia, and today more than 500 million people identify themselves as Buddhist.

How enlightened are you about the principles of Buddhism?

1 Siddhartha Gautama only became aware of human suffering when, aged 29, he ventured from his palace and came across old, sick and poor people for the first time.

TRUE / FALSE

2 The Eightfold Path is a practical guide to eliminating desire and attachments, and so living a life free from suffering.

TRUE / FALSE

3 Gautama rejected the idea of *atman* – an eternal soul – and instead said that human existence is characterized by impermanence, 'not-self' and suffering.

TRUE / FALSE

4 Gautama attained enlightenment in a moment of divine inspiration while meditating under the Bodhi tree.

TRUE / FALSE

5 The ultimate aim of life in Buddhism is *nirvana* – a state of perfect peace that awaits the immortal souls of those who have freed themselves from the cycle of birth, death and rebirth.

TRUE / FALSE

TEN THINGS A GENIUS KNOWS

1 The Vedic tradition
Siddhartha Gautama was born in what is now Nepal, some time around 560 BCE. At that time, understanding of the world and the wider cosmos was shaped by the mythology and cosmology of the Indian Vedic religions, the precursors of Hinduism. While Gautama came to reject many of the beliefs of these religions, there were certain fundamental elements that were universally taken for granted, and which he accepted as a basis for his own philosophy: the concepts of *samsara* (the cycle of birth and rebirth), *karma* (cause and effect) and *dharma* (virtue, and the natural order of the Universe). Even these, however, he subjected to rational scrutiny, dismissing those aspects he saw as merely blind faith.

2 Samsara, the cycle of birth and rebirth
Since the earliest Vedic cultures, a core belief of all the major Indic religions (such as Jainism, Hinduism and Buddhism) has been *samsara* – the cycle of birth, death and rebirth. The ultimate aim is to achieve *moksha*, escape from *samsara*. Connected with this is the idea of *karma*, that a person's fate in subsequent lives is affected by his or her behaviour in this one, determined by his or her adherence to *dharma*, cosmic order and virtue. Gautama, however, challenged the idea that this was a journey of an immortal, eternal soul (the *atman* of Hindu belief) on its way to salvation, but rather the progress of a consciousness towards freedom from existence.

3 Is Buddhism religion or philosophy?
Buddhism is widely regarded as a religion, one of the five major faiths of the world, but is arguably as much a philosophical system. Some elements of Buddhism are a matter of belief rather than reason, such as the concept of *samsara*, but this could be regarded as a cultural rather than religious belief. Gautama makes no reference to gods or supernatural beings, and his ideas are based on rational thought, not divine revelation, and although he is revered (and even in some places worshipped) as the Buddha, he is not considered to be a deity, messiah or even prophet.

4 Meditation
Gautama arrived at his interpretation of *samsara* and *moksha*, a realization he described as *bodhi* or enlightenment, after a long period of meditation. He had learnt the techniques of meditation in the years he spent as a religious ascetic, but instead of experiencing spiritual inspiration or divine revelation, he reached his enlightenment through rational thinking. Consequently, in Buddhism much emphasis is placed on the practice of meditation, rather than ritual or worship. The process of attaining enlightenment through meditation, a solitary occupation, chimes with the central ethos of Buddhism, which is concerned almost exclusively with individual ethics and personal development, and little to do with the individual's place in society or the nature of morality.

5 The middle way
Having been brought up in a position of comparative luxury, and with the freedom to indulge in worldly pleasures, Gautama came to realize they did not bring him true happiness. After his first experience of the harshness of the world outside his sheltered home, he decided to try to find spiritual satisfaction through extreme asceticism. At one stage, he nearly died of starvation and neglect, but had still not found the insight he was looking for. Reflecting on his experiences, he realized that neither seeking sensual pleasure nor denying your basic needs bring any satisfaction, and the route to happiness is a 'middle way' between self-indulgence and self-mortification.

6 The Four Noble Truths

Gautama's enlightenment came, it is said, while he was calmly meditating under a tree. Free from distraction, he turned his thoughts to what it is to be human, and concluded that our existence is characterized by *dukkha*, or suffering. *Dukkha*, he said, is the first of what he called the 'Four Noble Truths'. The second, *samudaya*, is that suffering is caused by our attachments – our egotistic desires, and craving for worldly goods and pleasures, and not accepting that we will grow old and die. The third truth, *nirodha*, is that we can end suffering by giving up these attachments. In the fourth truth, *magga*, he explains that this can be achieved by following his 'Eightfold Path'.

7 Not-self

The *dukkha* that Gautama identifies as the cause of our unhappiness is generally translated as 'suffering', but as well as the ideas of pain and deprivation that the word implies, it carries the additional connotation of dissatisfaction or unsatisfactoriness. This idea is explained more fully in the second noble truth as resulting from our wants, the things we desire for ourselves, but that are either unobtainable or ultimately incapable of satisfying. Attachment to these desires is a product of our self-centredness, or ego; in order to escape *dukkha*, we must overcome ego and find our place in the 'not-self', to become at one with the eternal and universal.

8 The Eightfold Path

The Eightfold Path Gautama advocates is essentially an ethical code of conduct, identifying the various ways in which to overcome self-centred attachments that cause suffering. The first of these, Right View, is the acceptance of the Four Noble Truths, which is followed by Right Intention, making a commitment to spiritual development. More practically, Right Speech, Right Action and Right Livelihood give guidelines for our day-to-day lives, while Right Effort, Right Mindfulness and Right Concentration provide the conditions for being in the correct frame of mind for meditation.

The spoked dharma wheel is often used as a focus for meditations on the eightfold path.

9 Nirvana

The goal of following the Eightfold Path is to achieve enlightenment, through which one can overcome the attachments of the ego and be free of the cycle of suffering continual birth and rebirth. According to Gautama, we do not have immortal souls, but instead our consciousness ceases to exist when we become at one with the not-self. This, he says, is the state of *nirvana*, 'extinguishing', and the final liberation from the suffering of existence.

10 Buddhism and Western philosophy

The teachings of Gautama, although enthusiastically followed by many in countries across Asia, were almost unknown in the West until the 19th century. And although it has gained some followers in Europe and America, especially in the 20th century, its influence on Western philosophy has been slight. A notable exception is Schopenhauer, who read some of the first translations of Hindu and Buddhist texts and discovered some striking similarities with his own ideas about human suffering and becoming one with the universal 'will'.

TALK LIKE A GENIUS

❛ Buddhism doesn't demand blind faith, but rather encourages its adherents to seek out the truth for themselves, using rational thought. That, and the absence of worship of, or even reference to, any supernatural being distinguishes it as a philosophy rather than a religion. ❜

❛ Gautama's idea of the "middle way" is strikingly similar to Aristotle's "golden mean"; they both advocate moderation, even in virtue. ❜

❛ The Four Noble Truths present us with a rather bleak and cynical view of the human condition – that suffering is an inherent part of our existence – but also offer us a way of ending that suffering. ❜

THE BLUFFER'S SUMMARY

Suffering is an inevitable part of our lives, until we can overcome our egotistic attachments and find our place in the 'not-self'.

Politics, society and the individual

'Man is by nature a political animal.'

ARISTOTLE

When Aristotle described man as 'a political animal', he used the word derived from the Greek πόλις (*polis*), a city-state, to suggest that we humans have a natural tendency to form organized societies. In prehistory, these social groups had a simple hierarchical structure, but as larger and more complex societies evolved, such as the Greek city-states, philosophers began to think about how best they should be structured and governed. Philosophers such as Socrates, Plato and Aristotle laid the foundations of Western political philosophy in the newly democratized city-state of Athens, examining forms of government and their ability to foster ideals such as justice and liberty.

How much of a political animal are you?

1 Political structures were devised to govern early civilizations, but it was not until the sixth century BCE that philosophers identified and examined the criteria for choosing a system of government.

TRUE / FALSE

2 The ancient Greeks were the first to apply philosophical reasoning to questions of political organization and government.

TRUE / FALSE

3 Plato's *Republic* presents arguments for an ideal state, in which the welfare of the citizens is protected by a government of representatives of the people, not a hereditary monarch.

TRUE / FALSE

4 The idea that natural law is the universal basis for morality and overrides man-made positive law was used to challenge the divine right of kings.

TRUE / FALSE

5 Greek *tyrannos*, meaning 'tyrant', described any authoritarian ruler. It only acquired its negative connotations of a despotic, lawless leader after the establishment of democracy in Athens.

TRUE / FALSE

TEN THINGS A GENIUS KNOWS

1 Political philosophy
Moral and political philosophy evolved side by side in classical Greece – and in contemporary China – as philosophers turned their attention away from metaphysics and towards more practical matters of human life. But where moral philosophy focused on the ethics of the individual, political philosophy was concerned with the morality of society, and its relationship with the morality and well-being of its individual members. As sophisticated states emerged from tribal societies, it was recognized that there is a need for some form of government, and philosophers examined what form that should take. Fundamental to that discussion was the question of what the purpose of government is, as well as such concepts as justice, liberty, rights, power and authority.

2 The purpose of government
Government, in its broad sense, is the means by which a society is organized. More specifically, it relates to the person or people responsible for overseeing that system. In any social group, there are rules to ensure people can live together peaceably, but also to protect their welfare and administer justice. It was this aspect, the morality of government, that especially concerned Greek philosophers; government for them was a means of ensuring that the people could live a 'good life', moral as well as secure and prosperous. Government's role is to make and enforce laws that ensure justice, a public morality fostering morality in the individual members of society.

3 Divine, natural and human law
Just as in moral philosophy, religious laws have had a huge influence on political philosophy. Believed by adherents to be literally the word of God, these commandments are considered as overruling any human-made laws. But this raises the question of the legitimacy of governments, and the role of rational thinking in organizing political systems. A solution to the potentially conflicting laws of God and the state was the concept of 'natural law', first hinted at by Aristotle's assertion that humans naturally form political communities. This would seem not to fit comfortably with the idea of a society ruled by God, but Thomas Aquinas found a way of reconciling the ideas. There are, he argued, eternal and divine laws determined by God, but also natural laws that are inherent in human nature, that we can discover with our God-given ability to reason; these are the basis of the human laws of earthly government.

4 Plato's philosopher-kings
Unsurprisingly, given that the Athenian democracy was responsible for executing his mentor Socrates, Plato had a jaundiced view of government by the people. Democracy is one of five forms of government that he identified and ranked in order of desirability. Worse even than democracy, he said, is tyranny – government by an oppressive authoritarian ruler. Above that, he placed oligarchy, where power is in the hands of the few, and timocracy (rule by property-owners). At the top, he placed aristocracy, government by a ruling elite – but rather than the hereditary nobility the term implies today, he advocated a class of philosophers: wise men with the necessary knowledge of the ideal Form of the Good.

5 Aristotle's *Politics*
In characteristically methodical fashion, Aristotle approached the problem of the most just form of government by analysing and classifying the options. To identify these, he asked two simple questions: who rules – and on whose behalf? The state may be ruled by a single person, a select few or the people, but the crucial question is whether it is a true form of government for the common good, or a corrupt government ruling in its own

interests. The three true forms of government, according to Aristotle, are monarchy (a single ruler); aristocracy (a ruling elite); and what he calls 'polity' or constitutional government. Their corresponding corrupt forms are tyranny, oligarchy and democracy.

6 Monarchy and aristocracy

Although the words 'monarchy' and 'aristocracy' imply some form of hereditary royalty, Aristotle used them simply to mean government by a single ruler, or a ruling elite. The idea of a single leader at the head of a hierarchical social structure dates back to prehistoric times, and is deeply ingrained in almost every culture. It is a traditional model advocated by many philosophers, including Plato, Kongzi and Hobbes, as a means of imposing and maintaining social order, but few of them believe that the leadership should be hereditary, and most have questioned the 'divine right of kings'. Conservative philosophers such as Edmund Burke have, however, argued that hereditary monarchs and aristocrats are best qualified to rule, as they have been brought up specifically to do so, and educated to protect the heritage of their realm.

7 Tyranny and oligarchy

What Aristotle calls the 'corrupt' forms of monarchy and aristocracy, tyranny and oligarchy demonstrate the pitfalls of putting power in the hands of the few. It is all too easy for a ruler or small clique to use that power for personal gain, and for their rule to become tyrannical. In order to maintain control in the face of opposition, the tyrant or oligarchy becomes authoritarian, assuming absolute power and wielding it without regard for the law or the welfare of the state or its people.

8 Democracy

Today, democracy in one form or another is the norm worldwide, so it may seem odd that Aristotle classified democracy as one of the 'corrupt' forms of government. This is because he contrasted it with what he called πολιτεία, 'polity', or constitutional government, which he describes as rule by the people in the interests of the state, society as a whole. In democracy, on the other hand, the power is in the hands of the people, but exercised selfishly, in their own interests rather than for the good of community or the state.

9 Anarchy and anarchism

The reason any form of government comes into existence is to provide an ordered structure for a society. Without government, whether that be a single leader, a group or its members, that society is literally an anarchy, without rule. Indeed, the arguments for government often contrast it with the popular image of a state of anarchy: chaotic lawlessness and disorder. There is a respectable tradition, however, of philosophers who advocate an absence of government - anarchism – which allows people to organize their communities for their own good without rule being imposed upon them.

10 International politics

The first political philosophers were primarily concerned with ways in which their states might best be governed, and the relationship between the state and its individual citizens. Some, though, also considered the relationships between those sovereign states, such as the recognition of other sovereign states and diplomatic relations, and the moral justifications for war. Especially as international trade increased, philosophers turned their attention also to the ethical and philosophical rationale for foreign policy in general, and even the arguments for and against supranational organizations and laws.

TALK LIKE A GENIUS

❛ After weighing up the pros and cons, it looks like the world has come to the same conclusion as Winston Churchill – that democracy is the worst form of government... except for all the others. ❜

❛ Although it might seem arrogant, Plato had a valid point when he suggested that we should be ruled by unwilling philosopher-kings. They are best qualified to know what's in the best interests of the state and its people, and because they don't actually seek power, are unlikely to abuse it. ❜

❛ The hierarchical social structures of ancient tribal societies with a single ruler have proved to be remarkably resilient. Even in the 21st century, there are several constitutional monarchies with hereditary royalty, and every country in the world has a head of state, whether that be a king, president or prime minister. ❜

❛ Anarchism gets a bad press, mainly because of its association with anarchic chaos. But anarchists would argue that we've tried almost every other form of government throughout history, and found them susceptible to corruption, so perhaps the answer is to adopt some kind of anarchism and trust to natural law. ❜

WERE YOU A GENIUS?

1 TRUE – Many early civilizations had quite sophisticated social structures and even explicit constitutions.

2 FALSE – Confucius presented arguments for a meritocratic form of government in the sixth century BCE, before the establishment of Athenian democracy.

3 FALSE – Plato rejects the ideas of both democracy and royalty, and instead advocates rule by those who have had an education in philosophy.

4 TRUE – The theory of natural law implies that there are certain rights inherent in nature that apply equally to everybody.

5 TRUE – During the 'Golden Age' of Athenian democracy, the previous autocratic rulers, known as tyrants, were denounced as despots.

THE BLUFFER'S SUMMARY

Political philosophy is concerned not with the practical business of governing, but the basic principles of government: its purpose, constitution and powers.

Justice

'He is called just who has a constant will to render to every man his own, but he unjust who strives, on the contrary, to make his own that which belongs to another.'

BARUCH SPINOZA

One of the principal concerns of a government is to ensure justice for its citizens, by creating laws and overseeing a legal system to administer and enforce them. But, as with other abstract concepts, such as liberty and power, there are many different interpretations of the meaning of justice and, consequently, how it can be achieved. Political philosophers have approached the subject of justice from several different angles, examining ideas including the rightful ownership of material goods and property, and claims to rights of welfare and security, but also such issues as crime and punishment, and how best to prevent injustice.

Can you judge which are the just and unjust claims?

1 While an everyday definition of justice might be the proper administration and enforcement of the law, philosophical consideration would say that the law is a reflection of our ideas of justice.

TRUE / FALSE

2 According to utilitarian philosophers, distributive justice is not a matter of equality, but what has a net benefit for society as a whole.

TRUE / FALSE

3 John Rawls's 'veil of ignorance' thought experiment demonstrates that egalitarian principles of justice will only be adopted by those who know they will benefit from them.

TRUE / FALSE

4 Robert Nozick describes taxation designed to redistribute wealth as a form of theft.

TRUE / FALSE

5 Sentences for criminal wrongdoing, such as imprisonment, fines or physical punishment, are merely retribution or revenge, and serve no other purpose in administering justice.

TRUE / FALSE

TEN THINGS A GENIUS KNOWS

1 **What justice is**

Ideas of justice invariably hinge on the idea of ensuring that people have what rightfully belongs to them – not only material goods, but also such things as welfare, security and respect. Where theories of justice differ, however, is in what precisely people can claim a right to, and so these are often linked to various interpretations of rights, and other prevalent ideas in political and moral philosophy, including the social contract, natural law and utilitarianism. The notion of justice is not restricted to individual claims of ownership; since the 19th century especially, the focus has been on social justice, the just relationship between the individual and society and the basis for a just distribution of wealth.

2 **Distributive justice**

Sharing a cake out to children (who have a keen sense of justice) at a birthday party often leads to cries of 'That's not fair!' if one child is perceived to get more than he or she deserves. It need not be in equal shares – older children may receive a bigger slice, as might the birthday girl – but there is an underlying sense that there is a just distribution. So it is with theories of distributive justice: how do we decide a just distribution of wealth, welfare and power? Some 'egalitarians' argue that equality should be the primary consideration to ensure fairness, or a distribution according to need; but others argue that equality is not necessarily just, and factors such as merit, social status or a rightful claim to ownership should be given weight.

3 **Egalitarianism**

For the egalitarian, equality in one form or another is the basis of distributive justice, based on the principle that all humans deserve to be treated as equals. However, this leaves scope for differences of opinion as to whether this should mean equality of outcome – a simple equal distribution of goods – or if circumstances such as need should also be taken into account. A different solution is to ensure equality of opportunity, rejecting claims of preference due to social privilege. Although this may result in inequality, it can nevertheless be regarded as a means of assuring a just distribution.

4 **Utilitarianism and justice**

John Stuart Mill typified the utilitarian view of distributive justice as being equivalent to the moral concept of rightness, which is judged by what results in the best consequences. Justice, then, is what produces the greatest good for the greatest number of people. However, this may result in inequality, but this is justifiable if there is a net gain overall. For example, it would not be unjust for the majority of people to suffer a small loss, if this was outweighed by a large gain for the minority; and, conversely, a huge loss to a minority could be justified if it caused a gain for the majority.

5 **Justice as fairness**

John Rawls instinctively felt that the utilitarian theory of justice was unfair and, in his 1971 book *A Theory of Justice*, he presented his argument of distributive justice as fairness. He, too, believed that justice is judged by consequences, but that it could be achieved by offering equality of opportunity and equal rights, but also considering the interests of those most in need. As an alternative to the utilitarian idea that inequality can be justified by a net gain, he proposed the 'difference principle': distribution that results in inequality can only be just if it results in the worst-off gaining an advantage they would not have had otherwise. The justice of a distribution is determined by whether it favours one party at the expense of another, and whether it increases or decreases inequality.

6 **The veil of ignorance**

In his argument for justice as fairness, Rawls uses a thought experiment to show how we can reach a rational decision about just distribution. Imagine, he says, that you can choose the principles of distribution of the society you are to live in. But you do not know what your status will be in that society; you have no knowledge of your ethnicity, gender, social standing or your natural abilities or disabilities. From behind this 'veil of ignorance', you will choose the policies that do not disadvantage any group that you might discover you belong to.

7 Justice as entitlement

In response to Rawls's egalitarian justice-as-fairness argument, Robert Nozick proposed an alternative, libertarian idea: justice determined by property rights. Unlike the egalitarian theories, Nozick's idea of 'justice as entitlement' addresses the justice of individual claims to property rather than the distribution as a whole. In this theory, justice is when a person comes to have something through legitimate transaction, freely and consensually entered into (that is not by coercion, theft, fraud or suchlike). Nozick lists three criteria for this: justice in acquisition, justice in transfer, and rectification of injustice. The role of the state in this process is only to protect entitlement; redistribution of wealth without consent, for example by taxation for welfare payments, is therefore unjust.

8 Government and the law

It is part of a government's role to ensure justice for its citizens. To do this, it puts into law the policies that reflect its interpretation of justice, in line with its political leanings. Whatever that might be, the purpose of the law is to uphold what the government sees as rightful claims to property and other rights, and to act as a neutral arbiter in disputes. To prevent injustice, the law needs to be enforced. Justice has to be seen to be done, not only to deter wrongdoing, but also to reinforce authority, and to satisfy those who have been wronged. One approach to this is restorative justice, with its focus on making reparation, either by the return of property or compensation for loss or damages. More often, however, the administration of justice also involves some form of punishment for wrongdoing – retributive justice.

9 Crime and punishment

Although most theories of justice include reference to punishment of some sort for wrongdoing, theories of retributive justice differ about the purpose of punishment. Consequentialists, and especially utilitarians, argue that we should consider the possible benefits for society of different forms of punishment. An obvious example is the element of deterrence, but the rehabilitation of offenders is also given as a reason, and protecting public security by removing criminals from society. For the hardline retributivist, however, wrongdoing simply deserves punishment, and justice is served when a criminal is given a punishment proportional to the crime committed.

10 Justice vs freedom

Whatever theory of justice is favoured by any society, it has to be asserted by an authority, such as a government. Finding a balance between authority and liberty has been a problem that has occupied many political philosophers throughout history, notably the liberal J.S. Mill. Albert Camus made the connection between justice and freedom, pointing out that for justice to be done, it must have the authority of law, and this is necessarily an infringement of liberty. We can have justice, but only at the expense of liberty, and vice versa.

TALK LIKE A GENIUS

❝ Ideas of justice, and especially the just distribution of resources, vary from culture to culture, and even according to one's political beliefs; left-leaning people tend to equate injustice with inequality, while those on the right favour a more meritocratic approach. Rawls's "veil of ignorance" helps to remove those prejudices. ❞

❝ The gap between rich and poor in today's world has reached unprecedented levels. The inequality is manifestly unjust, but we are faced with the problem of how this can justly be rectified. It may be that robbing the rich to pay the poor is justifiable after all. ❞

❝ Restorative justice succeeds in so far as it returns property to its rightful owners, but falls short of preventing injustices, so some form of punishment is also necessary – not just as an "eye for an eye", but as a deterrent. ❞

WERE YOU A GENIUS?

1 TRUE – Laws and their administration are based on a society's notions of justice; philosophy examines the concept of justice.

2 TRUE – The utilitarianism view of justice is that which results in the best consequences for the greatest number of people.

3 FALSE – From a position of ignorance of their status in society, people are made to consider impartially, and so choose principles of fairness.

4 TRUE – Such taxes imposed by the state are an unjust transfer of property, made without the free consent of the entitled owner.

5 FALSE – Punishment can also be considered as deterrence, rehabilitation, security and a means of reparation.

THE BLUFFER'S SUMMARY

Justice may be defined in terms of fairness, entitlement or equality regarding a person's rights to property, welfare and respect.

Liberty

'The word *freedom* has
no meaning.'

DENIS DIDEROT

Having overthrown a tyrant to establish their
democracy, the Athenians were rightly proud of their
liberty, and keen to ensure it was maintained. Along
with justice, liberty was one of the key concepts
that classical political philosophers sought to define,
contrasting it with notions of tyranny and slavery.
However, it was during the Enlightenment, when
many nations freed themselves from imperial and
monarchical rule, that liberty became the watchword,
and philosophers began to examine the political as well
as philosophical implications of creating a state that
offers liberty to its citizens.

**Feel free to find out if you know what liberty
is all about.**

1 The words 'liberty' and 'freedom'
are, in practice, interchangeable.

TRUE / FALSE

2 Jean-Jacques Rousseau bucked
the trend when he suggested that
civilization, far from granting liberty,
actually restricted it.

TRUE / FALSE

3 Liberalism is at the opposite
end of a political scale from
authoritarianism, rather than a position
on the Left–Right political spectrum.

TRUE / FALSE

4 Adam Smith argued that the
'invisible hand' of free markets
should be allowed to determine economic
distribution, free from state interference.

TRUE / FALSE

5 Isaiah Berlin identifies two distinct
types of liberty: negative liberty, the
condition of being free from coercion;
and positive liberty, the condition of
being free do whatever one chooses.

TRUE / FALSE

TEN THINGS A GENIUS KNOWS

1 What liberty is
In broad terms, we understand liberty to be the condition in which we have the ability to act in the way that we choose, following our own will, and without coercion. Today, it is generally considered to be a basic human right, and fundamental for a civilized society – even its main raison d'être. Many states have been founded on the principle of liberty, after a hard-fought battle against oppressive rule or slavery. However, opinions continue to differ as to the nature of freedom, and especially how it can practically be achieved and maintained.

2 Liberty and authority
If liberty is to be considered a basic right in a civilized society, the government of such a society has a duty to ensure it for its citizens. Like other fundamental rights, liberty is often enshrined in a constitution or bill of rights, and protected by law. But therein lies something of a paradox: laws, to have any effect, must have authority, which is inimical to the notion of liberty. The philosophical question, then, is one of degree – to what extent government or state regulation protects or restricts the liberty of its people. Since the Enlightenment, philosophers have tended to examine concepts of liberty in the context of this relationship with authority.

3 Freedom of speech
Liberty became a hot topic in the mid-18th century, especially in the United States and France. But while the Americans were intent on freedom from colonial rule, French philosophers sought freedom from an oppressive and outmoded system of government. Enlightenment ideas of democracy and secularism posed a threat to the ruling aristocracy, and writers such as Denis Diderot (compiler of the *Encyclopédie*) and

Voltaire constantly battled against censorship. For them, the fundamental liberties necessary for progress were those of freedom of thought, speech and the press, and tolerance of dissent, difference and individualism. These principles of individual freedom and tolerance were also to become the mainstays of British liberalism in the following century.

4 Jean-Jacques Rousseau
Contemporary with Voltaire and the free-thinking '*Encyclopédistes*' was Jean-Jacques Rousseau, who not only railed against the repressive French aristocracy, but also argued that government by any kind of authority restricts liberty. Civilization, in its most literal sense, far from providing us with liberty, has created laws that protect property and systems that make slaves of us all: 'Man is born free; and everywhere he is in chains.' Liberty can only be achieved in a real democracy, ruled by the collective 'general will' rather than imposed by a government.

5 J.S. Mill's *On Liberty*
In Britain, the Enlightenment produced fewer revolutionaries, but rather a liberal tradition with its roots in empiricism and utilitarianism. Probably the greatest liberal philosopher to emerge was John Stuart Mill, whose book *On Liberty* set out to define the nature and limits of the power of society over the liberty of the individual. He recognized the inherent conflict between authority and liberty that exists in any form of government, and that a balance has to be found between the two. Working from his 'harm principle', that individuals should be free to do whatever they choose so long as that does not harm others or restrict their liberty to do likewise, he concluded that government should not intervene except to protect liberty.

6 Social and economic liberalism

Mill's liberalism, based on principles derived from utilitarianism, concerned the liberty of individuals from state interference. With its emphasis on personal freedom and tolerance, it is perhaps best described as social liberalism. The same principles had been applied to economic thinking, too. In *The Wealth of Nations* (1776), Adam Smith explained how the 'invisible hand' of free markets guides the efficient operation of an economy which is, in general, hampered by government interference. As with social liberalism, laissez-faire economic liberalism argues that governments should only intervene to protect the freedom of the market to do its job.

7 Liberalism and libertarianism

Since the mid-20th century, the word 'liberal' has acquired rather different meanings on either side of the Atlantic. In Britain it is still used to describe the political philosophy proposed by J.S. Mill and the Liberal Party (now the Liberal Democrats), of personal freedom, tolerance and the protection of individual rights, often known as 'classical liberalism'. In the United States, however, it has taken a more specific meaning of 'social liberalism', with its association with progressive and left-wing politics, and even used pejoratively by the Right. A less ambiguous word is 'libertarian', which describes all the beliefs that consider liberty as a primary value, especially freedom from government interference in an individual's affairs, or state intervention in free enterprise.

8 Small government

While the primary concern of liberalism was originally the maximization and protection of liberty, libertarianism has increasingly emphasized the flip side of that coin: the minimization of government regulation. As long ago as the 14th century, the Islamic philosopher Ibn Khaldun cynically described government as a necessary evil, 'an institution that prevents injustice other than such as it commits itself', an idea that has persisted among libertarians. The idea of 'small government' – minimal state intervention – has been especially prevalent in the economic policies of right-wing thinkers since the 1980s, contrasted with the failure of socialist state-controlled economies.

9 Liberty and anarchism

The libertarian principle of minimal state intervention was taken to its extreme by Henry David Thoreau when he said: 'that government is best which governs not at all.' This idea, which harks back to Rousseau's views of government being a restraint of liberty, is the basis for the various forms of anarchism. For the anarchist, liberty cannot exist in a hierarchical society ruled by any form of government. By doing away with the idea of a state and its authority, people will be able, individually and mutually, to establish liberty for themselves.

10 Isaiah Berlin's *Two Concepts of Liberty*

In 1859, J.S. Mill published his comprehensive exposition of liberal philosophy, *On Liberty*. Almost 100 years later, Isaiah Berlin picked up on an idea that Mill had identified: that there is a difference between liberty as the absence of coercion, and liberty as the freedom to act. In *Two Concepts of Liberty*, Berlin expanded on this, arguing that as well as 'negative liberty' – freedom from tyranny and excessive authority – there is 'positive liberty' – control over one's actions and being master of one's own life. It is not sufficient that government does not interfere with an individual's freedom; it should also aim to shape society so that the individual can achieve self-realization.

TALK LIKE A GENIUS

❝ Freeing a society from tyrannical rule, or a class from slavery is one form of liberty, but it does not address the question of the individual's freedom within society, the freedom to live as one chooses. That's where political opinion is divided. ❞

❝ Isaiah Berlin described the distinction between negative and positive liberty as the difference between saying "I am no-one's slave" and "I am my own master". ❞

❝ Absolute liberty is a chimera. Do anti-slavery laws restrict the freedom of slave-owners? Of course they do. But necessarily so. To achieve a reasonable degree of liberty, there has to be some regulation. ❞

1 TRUE – While 'liberty' is more often used than 'freedom' in a political context, their meanings are practically the same.

2 TRUE – The prevailing wisdom of Rousseau's time was that civilized society brought both prosperity and liberty from a restrictive 'state of nature'.

3 TRUE – Liberalism's emphasis on individualism and free enterprise has appealed especially to the conservative Right, but its ideas of democracy and civil rights to the progressive Left.

4 FALSE – Smith recognized that even 'laissez-faire' economies require some regulation to prevent abuses and compensate for market failures.

5 FALSE – Positive liberty, according to Berlin, is the ability to act upon one's free will, free from any internal as well as external restriction.

THE BLUFFER'S SUMMARY

Liberty is the ability to do as one chooses, but only within the constraints of regulation to protect the right to that freedom.

The Rights of Man

> 'We hold these truths to be self-evident, that all men are created equal, that they are endowed by their Creator with certain unalienable Rights.'

UNITED STATES DECLARATION OF INDEPENDENCE

Until the Enlightenment, ideas of rights were concerned mainly with claims on property, or the right of monarchs to rule over their subjects in a feudal system. The rights granted to people other than the aristocracy were few, and by no means universally applicable or automatic. That was all to change, however, especially with the revolutions in England, America and France, in which subjects challenged the old order, encouraged by notions of rights to justice and liberty proposed by the first of the modern political philosophers.

The Founding Fathers of the United States knew their rights, but do you?

ARE YOU A GENIUS

1 Thomas Paine's *Rights of Man* influenced both the US and French declarations of rights.

TRUE / FALSE

2 The idea of natural rights is based on the assumption that these have been divinely granted to us, so is rejected by secular societies.

TRUE / FALSE

3 Jeremy Bentham advocated a major increase in the number and scope of legal rights – including equal rights for women – but dismissed the idea of natural rights as 'nonsense upon stilts'.

TRUE / FALSE

4 The Universal Declaration of Human Rights (UDHR) was based on the premise that all human rights are indivisible and related.

TRUE / FALSE

5 Olympe de Gouges famously presented arguments for equal rights for women, and also used the same arguments against racial discrimination.

TRUE / FALSE

1 **What we mean by 'rights'**

As with so many other concepts in philosophy, the precise definition of 'rights' is much debated. In essence, however, the word refers to entitlement of some kind – to be treated in a particular way, to be given the freedom to act in a certain way and so on – that a member of a society can expect. These range from basic rights to life and liberty, through rights to a vote and equal treatment by the law, to rights to bear arms or go on strike. Many rights are connected with ideas of liberty and equality, and as such are fundamental to a nation's constitution and laws. Some have now been universally recognized, but there are many others that are a matter of local convention.

2 **Natural rights**

The idea of rights became a hot topic in the 17th century, especially in England following the political turmoil of the Civil War and restoration of the monarchy. Parliament needed to assert its right to govern, and passed legislation culminating with the Bill of Rights in 1689. But this was not only about the right to rule; it also contained ideas suggested by John Locke, about fundamental entitlements that he called 'natural rights'. He considered these God-given rights, not man-made, but a necessary part of human nature, and consisting of the right of everyone to defend their 'Life, Health, Liberty or Possessions'. In a social contract, these are the basic rights that should be protected by the state.

3 **Declarations of rights**

Locke's formulation of fundamental natural rights was profoundly influential, shaping the political ideals of the Enlightenment, echoed in the rights to 'Life, Liberty and the pursuit of Happiness' in the American Declaration of Independence. At the beginning of the French Revolution, a similar document was published, the *Declaration of the Rights of Man and of the Citizen*. Like the American declaration, it stressed the universality of natural rights; where it differed, however, was in describing those rights as derived from secular natural law, and not divine authority. Thomas Paine, a 'Founding Father' of the United States and active in the French Revolution, presented the arguments for natural rights in his book *Rights of Man*, explaining that they are not granted by government, but it is government's job to recognize and protect them.

4 **The rights of women**

In 1791, only two years after the *Declaration of the Rights of Man and of the Citizen*, Olympe de Gouges published her pointedly titled *Declaration of the Rights of Woman and the Female Citizen*, highlighting the hollowness of the original's claims to universality and equality. Along with Mary Wollstonecraft's *A Vindication of the Rights of Woman*, published the following year, it marked the beginning of the slow process of bringing women's rights into mainstream political thinking. Through the 19th century, women continued to campaign for their rights, but it was not considered a subject for political philosophers, until J.S. Mill took up the cause, in support of his wife, the writer Harriet Taylor. In his book *The Subjection of Women*, he presented arguments that first appeared in her essay 'The Enfranchisement of Women'.

5 **Legal rights**

Of course, the natural rights to life, liberty, property and the pursuit of happiness were at first painted with a broad brush. The terms are far from precise, and represented the basic minimum rights any person should expect. With time, the rights were clarified, and others derived from them by extension, such as rights to housing, security and health care. Other rights, however, fall into a different category: unlike natural rights, these are man-made, granted by governments, such as the right of citizenship, enfranchisement, right to a fair trial and so on. Such legal rights, also known as statutory rights, are today considered basic human rights, but are by no means universally recognized.

6 Civil rights movement

The rights recognized by governments and given legal status include both the basic 'natural' rights, and the class of political and civil rights. As well as giving individuals freedoms of expression and belief, and protecting them from interference by others, these civil rights provide entitlement to participate in political processes of the society or state. By the time of the Universal Declaration of Human Rights in 1948, most of these had been generally recognized, but the emphasis now shifted to their universality: members of the civil rights movement, like women before them, argued that these are human rights, applicable to all humans equally, regardless of ethnicity, gender, age, disability or belief.

7 Civil disobedience

Rights of all kinds are the basis of a large part of the laws of most countries, and reflect the relationship between the individual and the state. One of the basic civil rights is to freedom of speech and thought, and that includes a right to criticize the government or law, and in many places to protest peacefully against them. Some philosophers, such as Henry Thoreau, have suggested that disobeying a law to which you have a conscientious objection is a legitimate form of protest, and that civil disobedience should also be a right. Thoreau himself withheld taxes to protest the US government's use of public money in slavery and warfare, and advocated conscientious objection to military service.

8 Rights and responsibilities

Since Locke's identification of basic natural rights, the idea that these are unconditional has been implicit. However, if those rights, along with other civil rights, are seen as part of the social contract, there has to be some reciprocity. In return for the protection of our rights, we have certain responsibilities to the state; most obviously, we agree to abide by the law (and may forfeit the natural right to liberty if we don't), but we also have civic duties, such as paying taxes, serving on a jury and, in some places, military service. The right to education is also sometimes seen as an obligation, and even the fundamental political right to vote is considered a duty, too – to the extent that voting is compulsory in some countries.

9 Animal rights

While humans were first establishing their basic rights, another debate was taking place: whether or not animals are sentient. For Jeremy Bentham, however, the question was not 'can they think?', but 'do they suffer?', and if so, do they not deserve to be treated without cruelty. After Darwin's theory of evolution, it became generally accepted that we humans are a part of the animal kingdom, and that at least some animals are sentient. Then, in the 1970s, Peter Singer argued that just as humans have natural human rights, animals, too, had natural rights. These, of course, do not extend to the political rights of exclusively human institutions, but should include the rights to life and liberty.

10 Environmental philosophy

Jean-Jacques Rousseau was almost a lone voice in challenging one of the natural rights described by Locke: the right to property. 'The fruits of the earth belong to us all, and the earth itself to nobody', he proclaimed. But this chimed with another element of Enlightenment thinking – the scientific idea that we can tame and exploit the natural world, and we have a right to do so. In the 20th century, that right has been severely tested by increased pollution and depletion of resources, and balanced against the fundamental rights to clean air and water, and a healthy environment. In the face of disastrous climate change, we may have to forego some of our rights to safeguard the environment for the future.

TALK LIKE A GENIUS

❝ There are positive rights, those that give us permission to do things, or entitle us to be treated in a particular way. But there are also negative rights that allow us not to have to do things, and to be left alone to get on with our lives. ❞

❝ The list of what are considered universal and inalienable human rights has expanded over the years, and today is vastly greater than the rights to life, liberty and the pursuit of happiness identified in the 18th century. The fact that many of them have only recently been recognized, and are not universally accepted, suggests that they are legal rather than natural, and the concept of rights is a human invention. ❞

❝ One of the most fundamental political rights is that of voting in free and fair elections. And while there are still some who are denied that right, in some countries voting is compulsory – implying that it is not only a human right, but at the same time a civic duty. ❞

1 FALSE – Paine's book was written in 1791, after both the American and French declarations of rights.

2 FALSE – Although some regard these rights as God-given, many (including the French revolutionaries) saw them as 'laws of nature' discernible by human reason.

3 TRUE – As an atheist, Bentham especially disliked the idea that natural rights are God-given.

4 TRUE – A distinction is made between civil and political rights, and economic, social and cultural rights, but the UDHR stresses the interdependence of these rights.

5 TRUE – As well as being a pioneering campaigner for women's rights, de Gouges was a fierce abolitionist.

THE BLUFFER'S SUMMARY

It may be self-evident that certain rights are inalienable, but there are many others that have only recently been recognized.

The social contract

'The social contract is an agreement of man with man; an agreement from which must result what we call society.'

PIERRE-JOSEPH PROUDHON

One of the oldest theories in political philosophy concerns the way in which individuals come together to form societies, and agree amongst themselves how they should be governed. The nature of this agreement became a focus of interest in the 17th century, when Thomas Hobbes described a 'contract' in which people consent to become subjects of a sovereign authority in return for protection from anarchy. This idea of a 'social contract' providing political legitimacy was taken up by John Locke and Jean-Jacques Rousseau, and was influential in the establishment of the American and French republics. It was also revived in the 20th century by John Rawls.

Are you an authority on the subject of the social contract?

ARE YOU A GENIUS

1 To give legitimacy to a government, the terms of a social contract need to be explicit and formalized in a document such as a constitution.

TRUE / FALSE

2 Having witnessed the horrors of the English Civil War, Hobbes argued that the only way to maintain political order is for people to give up their liberty and subject themselves to the absolute authority of a monarch.

TRUE / FALSE

3 Locke argued that the state of nature is not lawless, but is governed by the laws of God and nature; however, these are not fairly or adequately enforced.

TRUE / FALSE

4 Proudhon interpreted the notion of the social contract as a mutual agreement among individuals, rather than between the people and the state.

TRUE / FALSE

5 Rawls's imaginary 'original position' presents a completely apolitical state from which the principles of a social contract can be decided.

TRUE / FALSE

TEN THINGS A GENIUS KNOWS

1 **What a social contract is**
When political philosophers talk of the 'social contract', they aren't referring to an actual document or agreement, but a way of describing how individuals come together to form a civil society or state. According to this theory, individuals in a 'state of nature' are naturally inclined to cooperate and reach an agreement – the social contract – of how their society should be organized. Typically, this agreement involves surrendering some freedoms, and submitting to the authority of a ruler, or government, in return for protection of their rights. The nature of the social contract determines the relationship between the individual and society, and the legitimacy of the state's authority.

2 **The state and the individual**
By means of this social contract, individuals collectively form organized societies, such as nations, for their mutual benefit. Often simply referred to as the state, this collective enterprise has an identity of its own. Its individual members determine its structure by mutual agreement, more often than not giving power to some form of government – a single ruler, or a select group – to oversee its operation. The relationship between the state and its individual members is dependent on how freedom is surrendered by the people to the government: a balance between individual liberty and state authority, individual rights and state responsibilities.

3 **The responsibilities of government**
The social contract is, then, an agreement between the individual members of a society and their collective identity, the state. And, as with any contract, there are obligations on both parties. The individuals cede some of their autonomous freedoms, effectively transferring control of them to the state, by giving the government this power. In return, they expect state protection of their rights;

it is the responsibility of the government to ensure the welfare of the people, defend them from attack and ensure that justice is maintained.

4 **A mandate to govern**
If this social contract is to work in practice, the relationship between individual and state has to be consensual; the government must have the permission of the people to exercise power. Traditionally, the authority of monarchs was seen as legitimate because of what the ancient Chinese called the 'mandate of heaven', a divine right of kings. In a social contract with a government, the mandate is given by the governed. So to have legitimate authority, a government has to fulfil its obligations and to be accountable to the people. British statesman Tony Benn summed up this mandate by suggesting five questions to any person in power: 'what power do you have; where did you get it; in whose interests do you exercise it; to whom are you accountable; and how can we get rid of you?'

5 **The 'state of nature'**
In explaining the origins of civil society through a social contract, several philosophers describe an imagined 'state of nature' in which there is no political order, and humans act only according to their own individual desires and conscience. From this starting point, social contract theorists describe the reasons for individuals to give up their natural freedoms and establish a political order. Thomas Hobbes presented one of the first explanations of the social contract, an idea that was also pursued by John Locke and Jean-Jacques Rousseau. Unlike Hobbes, Locke and Rousseau each had a very different interpretation of the state of nature (a term coined by Hobbes) and the reasons for voluntarily abandoning it in favour of a civil society.

6 **Thomas Hobbes's *Leviathan***
Published in 1651, at the end of the English Civil War, Hobbes's *Leviathan* paints a gruesomely

pessimistic picture of man in a state of nature. Without social and political order, he says, individuals have unlimited freedom to act only in their own interest resulting in a constant 'war of all against all'. Life in this state is 'solitary, poor, nasty, brutish and short'. No wonder, then, that individuals should consent to giving up that natural freedom to gain some security. Such is the horror Hobbes had of this anarchic state that he argued that only by subjecting themselves to an absolute sovereign authority (a person or an assembly of people) can individuals be made to respect each other's rights.

7 John Locke

John Locke, writing some forty years later than Hobbes, had a more benign view of human nature. He believed that even without any social or political order, humans have a natural, innate moral sense that governs their behaviour. Nevertheless, without an authority to protect them, they live in fear of others harming them. Each individual has the right to self-defence, he argued, to protect his or her life, liberty and property. By agreeing to form a state, the individuals do not give up that natural right, but instead delegate to the government the right to act as an impartial judge and enforce the law, with the collective authority of the people: 'The legislative and executive power used by government ... is nothing except the natural power of each man resigned into the hands of the community.'

8 Jean-Jacques Rousseau

Yet another perspective of social contract theory came from Rousseau, writing in a time of political discontent before the revolution in France. In his book *The Social Contract*, he rejects Hobbes's pessimistic picture of man in a state of nature, and points out that the people in the civil society he saw around him were enslaved and exploited by those in power. Rousseau suggested there is a stage in human development between brute animals and decadent civil society, an ideal state of nature in which people

acted according to their uncorrupted morals. It is, he argues, civilization that has corrupted them, a failure of the social contract. The solution, in Rousseau's view, is for each individual to submit to the authority of the 'general will'; in place of individual self-interest, society collectively acts in the interests of all.

9 Pierre-Joseph Proudhon

Enlightenment political philosophers examined the transition from a state of nature to a social contract, in order to argue the case for a particular form of government. In contrast, Proudhon looked at the nature of the social contract itself. Where previously, thinkers had focused on the agreement between the people and the state, Proudhon went back a stage, and pointed out that the social contract is from the start an agreement 'of man with man', a consensus to form a society. Proudhon, a pioneer of anarchism, argued that 'As man seeks justice in equality, so society seeks order in anarchy' – individuals agree among themselves to give up any idea of governing one another. They retain their individual sovereignty and cooperate freely and equally.

10 John Rawls's 'original position'

Interest in social contract theory was revived in the late 20th century, notably inspired by the innovative approach of John Rawls in his 1971 book *A Theory of Justice*. He suggested an alternative to the 'state of nature' as a starting point for constructing a civil society, and called it the 'original position'. This is a similar, imagined condition with no political order, but is inhabited by participants in a thought experiment rather than a stage of human development. People in this original position select the principles for forming a society, but without any knowledge of their status, gender, ethnicity, talents or physical ability, within that society – which ensures they make impartial decisions.

TALK LIKE A GENIUS

❛ Interestingly, Hobbes uses the idea of a social contract to justify an absolute sovereign power, while Locke and Rousseau interpret it as an argument for forms of democracy, and Proudhon sees it as a basis for anarchism. ❜

❛ The key word in all social contract theories is "consent". Whether the contract is explicit, such as in a constitution, or tacit, a government only has legitimate authority if the contract is freely entered into with the consent of the governed. ❜

❛ Being intimately connected to the concepts of rights and freedoms, social contract theory emerged in the politically volatile atmosphere of the 18th century, and was revived in the late 20th century after the heyday of the Civil Rights movement. ❜

THE BLUFFER'S SUMMARY

Civil rights can be protected if the members of a society agree to surrender some natural freedoms and submit to the authority of a government.

Political realism

'The philosophers have only interpreted the world in various ways; the point is to change it.'

KARL MARX

Karl Marx's frustration with philosophers is understandable, if not wholly justified. Political philosophy had, until that time, been largely concerned with examining various models of an ideal society and political ideologies, based on rational arguments and ethical considerations. It was not, in the main, so concerned with finding ways of achieving this in practice; this was considered the realm of politicians and political theorists. Some philosophers, however, recognized the need to examine the political world as it is, not as it ought to be, and to consider the balance between ideal ethical ideology and the real-world problems of maintaining law and order and dealing with conflict.

Not all political philosophers were idealistic dreamers, but do you know which ones had a grasp of political reality?

ARE YOU A GENIUS

1 Political realism asserts that a government should use its power to do what is in the best interests of the state, and so should seek to maximize its power.

TRUE / FALSE

2 The principles of just war are not universally accepted; some realists believe that moral rules do not apply to war, while pacifists believe war can never be morally justified.

TRUE / FALSE

3 Working as a diplomat in the Florentine Republic, Machiavelli saw first-hand the effectiveness of the unscrupulous and brutal tactics used by the Borgias and Medicis.

TRUE / FALSE

4 In *Das Kapital*, Karl Marx presents capitalism as a strong economic model; it is only its tendency to inequality that will lead to its overthrow by socialism.

TRUE / FALSE

5 Ludwig von Rochau believed ideology and morality have no place in politics, which he argued should be conducted on purely practical lines.

TRUE / FALSE

TEN THINGS A GENIUS KNOWS

1 **What political realism is**
Realism, in political philosophy, is the acknowledgement that people and states act in ways that put their interests before ethics and ideology in political relations. Sometimes summed up as 'might is right', political realism actually recognizes that power and force do not necessarily have moral justification, but in practice will override any purely ethical or ideological considerations. Some philosophers accept this as a basic feature of human nature, and so suggest that the aim of politicians and states should be the maximization of power; others have sought to find moral justification for exercising power.

2 **Chinese legalism**
Before the establishment of civil societies, the idea that 'might is right' was the basis of social structures, both within social groups and in their relationships with one another. China was among the first to break with this notion, organizing society according to the ethical principles of Confucianism (see pages 124–7), but faced with the reality of factionalism and social unrest, Chinese political philosophers advocated a realist alternative: 'legalism'. This was not simply a return to the pre-political hierarchy, but a political system that starts from the premise that human nature is self-interested; in order to ensure order and justice, the government has to have a strict legal framework and the power to enforce it (a conclusion similar to the one reached by Hobbes; see pages 149–50).

3 *The Art of War*
As the pendulum swung from moralist Confucianism to realist legalism, it was clear that whatever the domestic politics of the Chinese empire, it had also to contend with other states and their ambitions for territory, resources and power. Even the Confucians accepted that armed combat was sometimes unavoidable, and that it is the duty of the ruler to protect the interests of the state. For that reason, a treatise on warfare, attributed to military strategist Sun Tzu, was respected as a classic alongside philosophical and literary texts. More than a mere military handbook, Sun Tzu's *The Art of War* presents a rationale for waging war as well as how it is best waged, without reference to morality or ideology.

4 **The Arthashastra**
Ancient Indian philosophers were also conscious of the necessary balance of morality and expediency in politics and relationships between states. In the classic epic the *Mahabharata*, a section known as the *Bhagavad Gita* is devoted to a dialogue between a prince and an incarnation of the god Krishna on the moral dilemmas of a ruler taking his people to war. The treatise known as the Arthashastra ('the science of politics'), although revered as a classic Hindu text, also acts as a practical guide to the world of politics, diplomacy and economics. Among many other things, it describes the duty of a ruler to use his power to ensure the welfare of his people, using whatever means are necessary.

5 **Just war**
For societies in the ancient world, armed combat was regarded as something of a necessary evil, but with the advent of Christianity, philosophers started to address the question of whether war could be morally justifiable. St Augustine was the first to suggest that, in certain circumstances, war can be compatible with the Christian ethos of peace and can be justified by God-given natural law. This idea was formalized into a 'just war' theory in the 13th century by Thomas Aquinas, who laid down three basic criteria for morally justifiable war: proper authority (waged by a legitimate government); just cause (in self-defence or to protect or restore territory or goods); and right intention (the restoration of peace).

6 The School of Salamanca

During the Renaissance, philosophers turned their attention away from the medieval concern with the compatibility of human rules of morality with God's law, and towards the more practical question of natural laws of morality in human affairs. In this spirit, philosophers of the School of Salamanca reassessed Aquinas's just war theory, giving it a more realist slant. Their premise was not that war is contrary to Christian doctrine, but that it is simply a great evil; therefore, it should only be used as a last resort, in order to combat a greater evil. War should, then, only be waged in self-defence, either in retaliation or to prevent attack, and with a likelihood of victory. They also specified that the force used should be proportionate to the threat, and that although government has the authority to declare war, a war is unjust if their people oppose it.

7 Niccolò Machiavelli

Another Renaissance philosopher, Machiavelli, took political realism to an unprecedented level, separating political philosophy from morality altogether. Political matters, he argued, are practical problems requiring practical solutions, and a ruler or government cannot let personal morality overrule the principle that its first responsibility must be to protect the welfare of the state. That means it is sometimes necessary to revert to force; violence, torture and deceit, while not ethical, are justifiable, as the ends justifies the means. It has been disputed whether he was actually advocating this amorality, or simply describing political reality. It is possible that he, a Republican, was simply exposing the true nature of the aristocratic ruling class.

8 Dialectical materialism

Karl Marx had no patience for abstract philosophizing, and sought to base his political theory on a quasi-scientific analysis of political and economic reality. He wrote a massive and comprehensive critique of capitalism, *Das Kapital*, pointing out its strengths and weaknesses, and predicting its collapse. The inherent economic instability of capitalism will lead to its downfall, he claimed, but this will be brought about by socialist revolution which, according to his analysis of the historical process, is inevitable. The methodical study of economics, history and political systems, rather than philosophical theory, provides not only a forecast of what is to come, but also a vision for future action to bring about change and progress.

9 Darwinism

Political realism got an unexpected boost when Charles Darwin published *On the Origin of Species*. As the theory of natural selection became mainstream, the maxim 'survival of the fittest' was applied not just to biological evolution, but to social sciences, too. A popular misconception was (and still is) that it means the survival of the strongest or most powerful, instead of best suited to the environment, an equivalent of the idea that 'might is right'. Inadvertently, Darwinism conferred a degree of scientific respectability to political realism, and a justification for some political opinions that would otherwise have been unacceptable.

10 *Realpolitik*

The political philosophy of the Enlightenment had, to a great extent, been based on moral principles of justice, equality and freedom, and inspired political change and social reforms. Among these reforms were the abolition of slavery and the promise of liberty. By by the mid-19th century, however, the rich industrial nations were jostling for power, and expanding their colonial empires. The German statesman Ludwig von Rochau noted that while the Enlightenment had shown the world that might is not necessarily right, it was still a force that should not be ignored. To maintain its power in the world, a state has to deal in what he called '*Realpolitik*', politics and diplomacy based on the reality of circumstances, not ideological or ethical premises.

TALK LIKE A GENIUS

‘ In an ideal world, governments would not need to resort to force to maintain political order, and states would resolve conflicts of interest by peaceful diplomacy. But it isn’t an ideal world, and sometimes justice demands the use of force. ’

‘ The original philosophical arguments of just war theory dealt with the question of *jus ad bello*, the right to go to war, and later tackled the concept of *jus in bello*, the morally acceptable conduct of war. It is only recently that the idea of *jus post bellum*, a just settlement after war, has been addressed. ’

‘ All the moral arguments in the world are useless in combating injustice and tyranny, unless they are backed up with a credible threat of resistance or retribution. ’

WERE YOU A GENIUS?

1 TRUE – A political realist would argue that governments need to build and assert power for the good of the state.

2 TRUE – Both realists and pacifists, from different perspectives, challenge the very notion of the morality of war.

3 TRUE – Machiavelli’s experience of the fall of the Florentine Republic helped to shape his pragmatic political philosophy.

4 FALSE – Marx praised the achievements of capitalism, but pointed out inherent weaknesses in the system itself that would lead to its collapse.

5 FALSE – Rochau acknowledged the role of morality and ideology in policy-making, but argued that practical problems need practical solutions.

THE BLUFFER'S SUMMARY

Political philosophy isn’t just about abstract ideas of ethics and ideology, but has also to take practical reality into account.

Political power

> 'The proletarians have nothing to lose but their chains. They have a world to win. Working men of all countries, unite!'

THE COMMUNIST MANIFESTO

From the respected tribal elders of early societies, through monarchs ruling by divine right, to the elected governments of democracies, rulers and governments throughout history have claimed or been granted the authority to govern societies. But it is only comparatively recently that philosophers have examined not only the scope of their power, but the nature of power itself. Political realists acknowledged the importance of power, as opposed to authority, and Machiavelli was perhaps the first Western philosopher to specifically address the concept of power. With Marxist ideas of transferring power to the people, power became a particular focus of philosophical interest, influencing a 20th-century examination of ways the establishment uses power to coerce and control.

Do you know who really wields the power in politics?

1 In *The Prince*, Machiavelli advises that, to govern effectively, a ruler must first gain, and then maintain power, with or without legitimate authority.
TRUE / FALSE

2 Marx interpreted political power in terms of class: in capitalist societies the bourgeoisie exercise their economic power over the proletariat by controlling the means of production.
TRUE / FALSE

3 In a bid to raise class consciousness in the proletariat, Gramsci fostered a working-class culture to counter the existing capitalist cultural hegemony.
TRUE / FALSE

4 Foucault is quoted as saying that 'Power is everywhere', suggesting that the structure of society allows those in power to control every aspect of our lives.
TRUE / FALSE

5 According to Chomsky, the media in capitalist societies is controlled by the establishment to produce propaganda in exactly the same way as the state-controlled media of totalitarian regimes.
TRUE / FALSE

TEN THINGS A GENIUS KNOWS

1 What power is

In politics, the word 'power' is used to describe the capability – generally of a ruler or government – to influence or control people's actions. It is, however, a loaded term, with negative connotations; when applied to a government, it often implies the excessive or illegitimate exercise of control. In that respect, it is contrasted with 'authority', the control and influence given legitimacy by the consent of the governed. Power, however, is a significant concept in political philosophy – how it is acquired, its scope and limits, and how it is exercised.

2 Machiavelli: maintaining power

Niccolò Machiavelli had no illusions about the importance of power in government. In *The Prince*, he said that it was an obligation of rulers to maximize their power to remain in control of the state. He posed the question 'Is it better to be feared or loved?' The ideal, he said, is to be both feared and loved, but that is seldom practicable. Being loved, ruling with the consent of the people, puts the ruler in a position of obligation where, if he has to make an unpopular decision, he risks overthrow. On the other hand, being feared means that a ruler can do unpopular things that may be in the best interests of the state, as the people fear the consequences of opposition. Being loved might give moral authority, but being feared gives actual power.

3 The will to power

Both Benito Mussolini and Adolf Hitler cited Friedrich Nietzsche's idea of 'the will to power' in justification of their brutal fascism – but this was a flagrant misreading of his philosophy. Rather than political power, and more particularly the power to control other people, Nietzsche was referring to personal strength, the power to achieve one's full potential. He believed that traditional morality, derived from Judaeo-Christian teachings, is the morality of oppressed people – a 'slave morality'. The idea that it is good to be meek and mild holds us back, and we should instead overcome this and regard strength, rather than weakness, as a desirable quality, in order to realize our innate 'will to power'.

4 Authoritarianism

The amount of power a state may have over its people depends on the political ideology of its government. This ranges from libertarianism, in which government has minimal influence in the lives of its people, to authoritarianism, in which control takes precedence over freedom, and individual behaviour is regulated by law. Tyrants and dictators who have taken power by force are obvious examples of authoritarian government, while others have some legitimate claim to their power. Totalitarian regimes – where authoritarianism is taken to extremes – include some theocracies, but more typically are ruled by governments that have progressively exceeded the limits of their authority in order to exercise authoritarian power, such as the fascist regimes of Mussolini and Hitler.

5 The class struggle

Karl Marx, in his characteristically methodical way, analysed the idea of power from a historical perspective. Using Georg Hegel's idea of the dialectic of historical progress, he argued that power had, at one time, been exercised by masters over slaves, then by aristocrats over serfs, and now economic power is exercised by the capitalist bourgeoisie over the working proletariat. His conclusion was that 'The history of all hitherto existing society is the history of class struggles', which could be ended once political and economic power is transferred from the ruling class to the people.

6 Cultural hegemony

Marx's forceful description of a ruling class's power to control and exploit people inspired a number of Marxist philosophers in the 20th century to investigate the ways in which that power is exercised and maintained. Antonio Gramsci, for example, did not believe that capitalism maintains its power solely by economic means, nor by force. Instead, he said, it is reinforced by cultural hegemony, control of the beliefs, perceptions and values of society, so that the capitalist ideology is accepted as the cultural norm. Change is thus rendered unthinkable, or at least unacceptable, and the status quo is maintained.

7 The power elite

The traditional concept of power as something imposed by force had been shattered by Marx and Gramsci, and replaced by ideas of economic and cultural control. It was still implicit, however, that this power was exercised by governments, consisting of members of the bourgeoisie acting in their own interests. But an American sociologist, Charles Wright Mills, suggested that power in society is not purely political. In his book *The Power Elite*, written during a period of anticommunist paranoia in the United States, he highlighted the interconnections between the interests of political, corporate and military sectors of society, and how this 'power elite' together control the lives of effectively powerless individuals.

8 Michel Foucault: the structure of power

Another Marxist-inspired philosopher, Michel Foucault, developed even further the idea that power is a manipulation of society to remove individual autonomy. The power relationship, he explained, is not a simple domination, a top-down exercise of control, but relies on a pervasive network of power relationships. The structure of this network is such that individuals become the unwitting agents of the apparatus, their apparent freedom in fact designed to increase their dependence on one another and the power structure itself. The power structure is controlled by government, and the power 'machine' is operated by shaping the lives of its individual components who, unaware of the manipulation and unable to locate any single source of power, offer little resistance.

9 Foucault: social control

Foucault, like Gramsci, regarded power as being exercised by hegemony, but not merely cultural hegemony. Society (rather than 'the state') wields its power by controlling knowledge of all kinds, and especially the knowledge that is used in shaping our social behaviour. Scientific knowledge, for example, is used as a form of social control: he cites the example of psychiatry's role in defining 'insanity', which is used as a label for many forms of behaviour seen as undesirable, or even simply individualist. This categorization of behaviour as 'normal' or 'abnormal' extends beyond the psychiatric, stigmatizing anything that falls outside the desired social norms, including illness, sexuality and even poverty.

10 Noam Chomsky: the media

One of the ways that a state can exert power is by control of its media. Under totalitarian regimes, the press and broadcasting media are owned and controlled by the state, operating as effective propaganda machines. In contemporary capitalist societies, however, much is made of the freedom of the press – but Noam Chomsky argues the media is nevertheless a means of reinforcing the power of the state. In the atmosphere of free-market capitalism, the mainstream mass media is owned by corporations, which have a vested interest in supporting the ideology of the state. Rather than using it for overt propaganda, however, debate and investigation are encouraged, though restricted to issues that do not undermine the fundamental ideology. This limits the spectrum of acceptable opinion, while giving the sense that the state's power does not extend to freedom of thought.

❛ Machiavelli makes a good case for authoritarian government. If you rely on popularity and the consent of the people, your authority isn't secure, but you can get things done if you make them respect your power. ❜

❛ Political power on its own is not enough to exercise control effectively. To exercise power effectively, a government must have the support of the military and the police, large corporations and, crucially, the mainstream media. ❜

❛ It's not just dictators who use their power to control what we can and can't do. There are subtler ways of exerting influence over our thoughts and actions than force, and they are as widespread as they are insidious. ❜

1 TRUE – In order to ensure order, a ruler needs to exercise power rather than seek the consent of his subjects.

2 TRUE – With the rise of capitalism, the bourgeoisie replaced the aristocracy as the ruling class, and maintained political power by economic means.

3 TRUE – Rather than simply inform the working class of Marxist principles, Gramsci believed they should be encouraged to establish a counter-hegemony.

4 FALSE – The full quote is: 'Power is everywhere: not that it engulfs everything, but that it comes from everywhere'.

5 FALSE – Chomsky says that while in totalitarian states dissent is forbidden, under capitalism there is the illusion of a free press.

THE
BLUFFER'S
SUMMARY

The difference between political authority and power is that authority is legitimized by consent, but power can be abused to influence and control.

Political ideologies

'The real division is not between conservatives and revolutionaries but between authoritarians and libertarians.'

GEORGE ORWELL

As well as suggesting ways in which society can, or should, be organized and governed, political philosophers have tried to identify and categorize different shades of political opinion. During the Enlightenment, as some form of democratic government increasingly became the norm in the West, various distinct political ideologies emerged: most obviously, some were resistant to the new order (conservative, or right wing) and others sought political change (progressive, or left wing). But there were also differing attitudes to social and economic issues, how much control the government should have in our businesses and everyday lives, and more sophisticated ways of classifying ideologies across the political spectrum evolved.

There are all sorts of different political ideologies – but can you tell Left from Right?

1 The terms 'Left' and 'Right' originate in the French Revolution's *états généraux* assembly: revolutionaries sat to the left side, and supporters of the *Ancien Régime* to the right.

TRUE / FALSE

2 A drawback of categorizing political ideologies on scales of Left/Right or libertarian/authoritarian, is that it does not accurately show differences between social and economic policy.

TRUE / FALSE

3 Joseph P. Overton suggested a 'window', near the centre of the libertarian-authoritarian axis, containing political ideas acceptable to the public; its size and position change over time, according to public opinion.

TRUE / FALSE

4 Left-wing ideals were precipitated by the emergence of capitalism from the Industrial Revolution.

TRUE / FALSE

5 Smith regarded public ownership of any producer of goods as inimical to the efficient working of free markets.

TRUE / FALSE

TEN THINGS A GENIUS KNOWS

1 The political spectrum

A rudimentary method of describing different political stances developed in the 19th century, representing the range of opinion as a simple scale on a line. At one end is the Right, the conservatives, and the other the Left, the progressives. But political beliefs are not so clear-cut, and political scientists suggested refining the model by adding another scale, and using the two lines as the axes of a two-dimensional graph covering a wide political spectrum. The question then arises: what should this second axis represent? A popular suggestion was that this should be a scale ranging from libertarianism to authoritarianism; other models suggest axes showing differences of attitude to social and economic issues.

2 The Right

The political attitudes identified as right wing, at the right end of the simple Left–Right scale, are generally regarded as being conservative, preferring traditional values and institutions, and resistant to change. Consequently, right-wing politics tend to advocate a hierarchical society with a paternalistic ruling elite, justified by tradition and natural law. Edmund Burke, the 18th-century British philosopher, suggested the aristocracy were not only entitled to rule, but best suited to the job; but with the rise of capitalism, the nobility has largely been replaced by a political ruling elite. Other right-wing values include an emphasis on law and order to protect private property rather than individual liberty, militarism and nationalism. These tendencies, when taken to their extremes of authoritarianism and xenophobia, are hallmarks of far-Right ideologies such as fascism and Nazism.

3 The Left

Left-wing politics are generally associated with progressive ideas, including egalitarianism and a collective government for the welfare of society as a whole, and a shift of power from a ruling class to the people. These principles of left-wing politics have their roots in Jean-Jacques Rousseau's vision of a civil society governed by the 'general will', in which everyone is free and equal, and resources are fairly distributed. Left-wing ideologies range from centrist social democracy, through socialism to communism, and those to the extreme Left advocate revolution to bring about the overthrow of the ruling class and the abolition of private property.

4 Individualism v communitarianism

As distinct political beliefs developed from the ideas of philosophers such as Jean-Jacques Rousseau and John Locke, it became clear that they did not fit neatly into the broad categories of Left or Right. The ideals that inspired revolutions also gave rise to quite different ideologies: ideas of collectivism and equality became the cornerstone of socialism, but classical liberalism was based on individual liberty and rights. A second axis on the graph of political opinion would take this into account. This is often shown as a scale ranging from libertarian to authoritarian, reflecting the amount of control given to government, but (quite apart from the negative connotations of the word 'authoritarian') an individualist–communitarian scale better reflects the aims of the ideologies, either for freedom of the individual or the welfare of the community.

5 Capitalism

Another complication arises when using the terms conservative and progressive when talking of left- and right-wing politics. Karl Marx pointed out that after the Industrial Revolution, a new ruling class emerged to fill the gap left by the waning power of the aristocracy: the bourgeoisie, owners of capital. This was not the traditional hierarchy favoured by conservatives, but capitalists became the natural successors to the nobility, and the political landscape changed, driven by economic considerations. As the polar opposite of socialism, capitalism, despite its capacity for innovation and change, became regarded as belonging on the right-hand side of the scale.

⑥ Marx and the dialectic

Marx recognized that this was more than a simple conflict between opposing Right and Left ideologies; there were also social and economic factors. Taking Hegel's model of historical progress as a dialectic, he applied this to the socio-economic and political process. According to the dialectic, each notion (or thesis) has within it a contradictory notion (the antithesis). Tension between these forces is what drives change and brings about progress to a resolution, the synthesis. Marx argued that the opposing forces of masters and slaves brought about the synthesis of the nobility in the feudal system, and in turn the tension between nobility and peasants produced the synthesis of a capitalist bourgeoisie. The next stage, socialism, will come about through the opposing forces of the bourgeoisie and the proletariat or working class.

⑦ Revolution vs evolution

Marx's analysis of the opposing sides of the conflict was based not on political theory, but the social consequences of material, economic reality. It is a class struggle between a ruling class who own the means of production, and the workers who provide their labour but have no economic or political power. Socialism, the synthesis of this conflict, will be achieved by the overthrow of the ruling class and ownership of the means of production passed to the workers. Marx unapologetically advocated revolution – not necessarily violent, but rapid and decisive. His followers, however, have been divided on this issue; some have taken him at his word, and cheered on the socialist revolutions in Russia, China and elsewhere, but others have argued that the path to Marxist socialism should be a process of gradual reform.

⑧ Socialism, communism and anarchism

Whether achieved by revolution or reform, what Marx forecast as the successor to capitalism is socialism. But this is not the end of the story; socialism is not quite the polar opposite of capitalism, and Marx saw it as only another stage in the process towards communism. Under socialism, he explained, the means of production will be taken over by the state, governed by the people. But this could be regarded as little more than state capitalism, a 'dictatorship of the proletariat'. Communism, on the other hand, requires the establishment of a classless society in which everybody benefits from production, and the eventual abolition of both private property and the state – a far-Left ambition also held by anarchists.

⑨ Economic liberalism

Differences between social and economic attitudes provide another complication to the Left–Right scale. As Adam Smith explains, the liberal principal of freedom has an economic significance. When producers of goods and services are allowed to trade in free markets, supply and demand regulate prices and ensure a fair distribution. Economic liberalism respects this principle, advocating free enterprise with minimal government interference. Economic liberalism's preference for private business – as opposed to collective industry – of course appeals to the right wing, but conservatives are less likely to take the same laissez-faire liberal approach to matters of social law and order.

⑩ Liberal democracy

In practice, the extremes of Left and Right, libertarianism and communitarianism, and so on are comparatively rare, and the majority of states today have governments whose political attitudes form a cluster in the centre of the spectrum. These are loosely known as liberal democracies: representative democracies with more or less universal suffrage and protection of individual rights and liberty, and a varying mixture of centre-right and centre-left social and economic policies.

TALK LIKE A GENIUS

❛ Conservatives will tell you that societies have evolved organically, that there is a natural order to things, and that rejecting traditional values and social structures can only cause problems. ❜

❛ The libertarian–authoritarian axis of the political spectrum is just as significant as the Left–Right axis, and in practice maybe more so. For the ordinary person living under a totalitarian regime, it makes little practical difference whether it's Stalinist or fascist. ❜

❛ Whatever you think about Marx's communist ideas, they have had an enormous impact. For a time in the last century, around a third of the world was ruled by governments inspired by Marxism – and much of his critique of capitalism has stood the test of time. ❜

❛ Interestingly, classical liberalism upsets both Left and Right: socialists don't like the idea of capitalist free enterprise, and conservatives don't like liberal attitudes to law and order. ❜

1 TRUE – The terms were then adopted during the 19th century to denote progressive and conservative ideologies.

2 TRUE – Shades of political opinion – especially among centrist ideologies – do not fit comfortably in a simple two-axis model.

3 TRUE –The 'Overton window' is now also loosely applied to acceptable ideas on the Left–Right axis.

4 FALSE – Ideas of egalitarianism and collectivism go at least as far back as the Athenian democracy.

5 FALSE – Smith recognized that certain essential goods and services would not be produced if left solely to private enterprise.

THE BLUFFER'S SUMMARY

Political ideologies are not simply either Left or Right, conservative or progressive: other parameters, both social and economic, allow for a broad spectrum of political opinion.

What is beauty?

> 'There is no excellent beauty that hath not some strangeness in the proportion.'
>
> FRANCIS BACON

Although aesthetics only emerged as a distinct branch of philosophy in the 18th century, its principal concerns – the nature of beauty, and the nature of art – have been a subject of philosophical enquiry since ancient times. In classical Greek philosophy especially, beauty was considered along with truth, justice and virtue as a fundamental value. In a similar way, it was also considered in much the same terms as morality. In the 18th century, philosophers including Hume and Kant revived interest in the concept of beauty from the perspective of their Enlightenment thinking, but by the 20th century, the emphasis in aesthetics had shifted from ideas of beauty to an examination of the nature of art.

How discerning are you when it comes to judging the truth about the nature of beauty?

1 Pythagoras challenged the ancient Greek idea that our ideas of beauty are derived from nature by arguing that beauty can be analysed in terms of mathematics.

TRUE / FALSE

2 Aesthetic relativists argue that there are no universal standards of beauty, but these vary from time to time and place to place, so are human constructs that are culturally conditioned.

TRUE / FALSE

3 British empiricist philosophers, such as Hume, shifted the focus of aesthetics from the object to the person perceiving that object, suggesting that there is no objective definition of beauty.

TRUE / FALSE

4 Evolutionary biology has proved that ideas of beauty are not subjective, but are simply a preference for the things necessary for survival and reproduction.

TRUE / FALSE

5 Kant noted that certain things are universally considered beautiful, and that the thing they have in common is their inherent quality of beauty.

TRUE / FALSE

TEN THINGS A GENIUS KNOWS

1 The nature of beauty
When Socrates quizzed citizens in the agora in Athens, he tried to elicit from them their understanding of abstract qualities that most took for granted, such as justice and goodness, but also posed the question 'What is beauty?' In his quest for a definition, he examined whether beauty is a quality, a property that is inherent in some things, or a subjective experience, setting the agenda for the debate that is at the core of this branch of philosophy. Linked to this fundamental issue is the question of how beauty can be judged – whether there are any objective standards of beauty, or if it is simply a matter of taste.

2 Is beauty an inherent property?
In everyday speech, we often speak of things having beauty, implying that it is a quality that exists in the object itself. But is beauty really an inherent property, in the same way as redness or hardness? The ancient Greeks, in the main, believed it is, and discussed it in the same way as they did the moral quality of goodness. The question then arises: if it is an inherent quality of some things, surely there would be no disagreement about what is or isn't beautiful? Plato's answer was that to appreciate beauty, one must understand what beauty is, which only comes from a knowledge of ideal beauty in the realm of Forms.

3 Objective standards of beauty
We appreciate the beauty of an object by recognizing certain characteristics, such as symmetry, harmony, simplicity and so on, that it exhibits. Those who believe that beauty is an inherent property, argue that these are the characteristics of that property, and the criteria we use to judge an object's beauty. And, being inherent in the object, they are objective standards of beauty. So are there degrees of beauty? Plato thought not: beauty, he said, is truth, and truth beauty, it is an absolute – but it is an ideal that exists only in the world of Forms, and things in this world exhibit the characteristics of that ideal standard of beauty only to a greater or lesser extent.

4 Formal beauty
For the ancient Greeks, the idea of objective criteria for assessing beauty was not merely theoretical; their aesthetic standards were defined and even measurable. Particularly important to them was beauty of form, such things as symmetry and harmony – an idea reinforced by the mathematical discoveries of Pythagoras. He showed that there are rules of mathematics that govern the underlying structure of the Universe, and can be found in the things we find beautiful, including musical consonance and the shapes of natural objects, such as snowflakes and seashells. What's more, these mathematical relationships provide an objective and ideal standard by which formal beauty can be judged.

5 Beauty and perception
Those who regard beauty as a property of an object tend to define it in terms of the characteristics it exhibits, but this does not address the question of what effect it has on the person who perceives it. An important characteristic of beauty is that it gives pleasure to those who experience it. But is an object beautiful if there is nobody to appreciate it – does it still have that inherent quality if it is not giving pleasure to a subject? Many philosophers have argued that beauty is dependent on perception, that an object is not in itself beautiful, but is perceived to be beautiful; beauty is in the eye of the beholder, determined subjectively.

6 Subjective judgement
When the subject of beauty was revived by Enlightenment philosophers, opinion tended towards the idea that beauty is subjective. Empiricists, such

as David Hume, rejected the notion that beauty is a quality of things, arguing instead that it 'exists merely in the mind which contemplates them; and each mind perceives a different beauty.' We each have an idea of what is beautiful, and aesthetically judge things by measuring them against our internal model of beauty. However, Hume concedes that this is not a purely emotional response of what he calls the 'passions', but also involves a critical faculty requiring rational thought – and to this extent, at least, there are some generally accepted standards of beauty.

7 Aesthetic relativism

Is judgement of beauty then a matter of personal taste? If the criteria are in the mind of the subject, rather than a quality of the object, judgements of beauty vary from person to person and have no absolute validity. Yet there are, as Hume pointed out, some commonly held views of what is beautiful. Relativists argue that these standards of beauty are culturally conditioned: there may be widely accepted norms of beauty, but these vary from culture to culture and time to time. Our personal criteria of beauty are shaped by these norms, and we find only those things that conform to them beautiful.

8 Natural beauty

In most cultures, the natural world is regarded a thing of beauty. The landscapes, flora and fauna, sunsets and the night sky are all held to be models of beauty, and philosophers from Pythagoras onwards have suggested that we derive our notions of beauty from nature. In the 19th century, the Romantics were inspired by even the savage and threatening aspects of nature. But not all philosophers agreed; Friedrich Nietzsche, for example, regarded this as anthropomorphism. We do not derive our ideas of beauty from nature – quite the reverse. Beauty, according to him, is a man-made concept, which we then impose upon nature, arriving at the mistaken belief that the world is filled with beauty.

9 Evolutionary aesthetics

Chalres Darwin's theory of evolution has had a profound impact on the biological sciences and psychology, and a knock-on effect on philosophy. In the 20th century, psychologists suggested that some of our aesthetic preferences have a biological function, for survival and reproduction. Far from imposing our ideas of beauty on nature, it is nature that determines them. For example, we find certain things repellant because they are harmful to eat, or dangerous; and our concepts of physical beauty are shaped by the choice of a suitable mate. Even our appreciation of landscapes is influenced by our instinctive preferences for a safe and fruitful environment.

10 Kant's aesthetics

Like Hume, Immanuel Kant thought that aesthetic judgements are not merely emotional, but that beauty has also to give sensory and intellectual pleasure. It is, nevertheless, subjective, but Kant argues it is also universal. When we make judgements about beauty, they are based on a subjective response, but the subject will argue that that judgement has universal validity, in much the same way that he or she would defend a moral opinion. It is different from a simple matter of taste, such as liking or disliking coffee; when we describe something as beautiful, we describe our appreciation of the object as if it has the quality of beauty, based on a 'commonsense' notion rather than any absolute ideal. Differences of opinion are, then, about the object and whether it has that property, not about the subject and his or her perception of it.

TALK LIKE A GENIUS

⚬ When I say that some food is delicious, nobody could dispute that it is delicious to me, even if they find it disgusting; so if I say something is beautiful, is that any different? The Romans had a phrase for it: *De gustibus non est disputandum*, "In matters of taste, there can be no disputes." ⁹

⚬ We get pleasure from appreciating the beauty of things, and we tend to find the things that give us pleasure beautiful. That pleasure may be sensual, emotional or intellectual, but might also be an instinctive reaction to what is most useful for our survival. ⁹

⚬ To the ancient Greeks, beauty was an ideal, an abstract quality of perfection. But at the same time, they found beauty in Nature, with all its imperfections. Perhaps Nietzsche had a point in suggesting that we impose our ideals of beauty onto Nature – and indeed anything we find beautiful. ⁹

⚬ There's a Chinese proverb that neatly sidesteps the debate over objective and subjective theories of beauty by saying that there is beauty in everything, it's just that not everybody sees it. ⁹

1 FALSE – Pythagoras saw mathematics as the fundamental framework of the natural world and, for that reason, of the notion of beauty.

2 TRUE – For the relativist, beauty is not an absolute value, but depends on the subject's perception.

3 TRUE – Hume argued that ideas of beauty are in the mind of the perceiver, but conceded that we have a common critical faculty for making judgements of taste.

4 FALSE – Theories of evolution suggest that biological necessity is one factor shaping our notions of beauty, but not the only one.

5 FALSE – Kant insisted that beauty is not a property of an object, and that our claims to its universality are not based on rational grounds.

THE BLUFFER'S SUMMARY

There's a difference between saying that something is beautiful, and saying that you find it beautiful.

What is art?

'The aim of art is to represent not the outward appearance of things, but their inward significance.'

ARISTOTLE

Central to all philosophical approaches to the subject of art is the problem of definition: what is it that characterizes something as a work of art? Traditionally, attempts at definition have considered criteria such as representation or expression, or the formal qualities of an artwork, and the implicit question of the purpose of art. Allied to that is another aspect of the philosophy of art: what criteria can exist for a critical assessment of an artwork, and whether that judgement can be truly objective. In the 20th century, when the bounds of what is considered art were pushed further than ever before, traditional definitions became inadequate, and philosophers sought new means of identifying and judging art.

Is it only art buffs who know what art is, or can you tell the difference between a fake and the genuine article?

1 In Plato's *Republic*, Socrates states that art that aims to represent or imitate things in the natural world has no place in a just city-state.
TRUE / FALSE

2 Aristotle found the characteristics of art exemplified in Greek drama, as it has beauty of form, is a representation of human experience and elicits an empathetic response.
TRUE / FALSE

3 Hume believed that appreciation of art is a subjective matter of taste, but argued that this was a critical faculty that could be cultivated; a greater knowledge of art leads to more rational judgement.
TRUE / FALSE

4 Judging a work of art by the skill of the artist within a formal framework is an example of Wimsatt and Beardsley's 'intentional fallacy'.
TRUE / FALSE

5 According to Dickie, anything that the artworld presents to the public as a work of art, is a work of art.
TRUE / FALSE

TEN THINGS A GENIUS KNOWS

1 Philosophy of art
As well as examining the notion of beauty, aesthetics is concerned with the philosophy of art: how we can assess the artistic value of a work of art, what its purpose is and, more fundamentally, defining exactly what we mean by 'art'. For the early philosophers, definitions were derived from ideas of what art sets out to achieve (and how well it succeeds), whether it is a representation of reality, a presentation of a compositional form or an expression of an idea or emotion. Later definitions have sought to identify in more detail the characteristics an artwork exhibits, but have also shifted the focus to the question of critical appraisal.

2 Art as representation
For the ancient Greek philosophers, art was regarded as what they called 'mimesis' – a representation of reality – inspired by their ideas of beauty in the natural world. This is most obvious in the visual arts, depicting the human form and the world around us. It is also seen in literature and drama, which simulate human experience of the world, and even in the decorative arts and music, which are inspired by the formal elements of beauty, such as symmetry and harmony.

3 Plato: imperfect imitation
Plato had a rather jaundiced view of art. In his philosophy, notions of art, beauty and morality are all interconnected, and the value they are judged by is truth. He regarded art not so much as representation, but imitation of things in the world, and even at its best not a faithful imitation. Since the physical world we inhabit is itself a mere imitation of the perfect reality of the realm of Forms, art is a distortion of the truth, the true nature of reality. A tree, for example, exists as an idea, a Platonic ideal tree; a tree we see in the natural world lacks the perfection of that ideal, and an artist's representation of that tree is less perfect still.

4 Aristotle: art as expression
Although Aristotle agreed that art is mimetic, he regarded it as much more than mere imitation. Rather than a simple representation of the outward appearance of something, he thought that art also tells us something of its inner significance, and is an expression of the artist's interpretation of it. Classical Greek drama, for example, is not a faithful representation of life, but emphasizes some elements and omits others to express an idea or emotion and evoke a response in the audience. Sculpture, too, is a stylized representation, in which mathematical ideals of beauty in composition are more important than simple depiction. The idea of art as expression also makes more sense when referring to the abstract arts, especially music, which do not set out to explicitly represent anything in the physical world.

5 Universal characteristics of art
The properties that characterize works of art identified by classical Greek philosophers provide only a partial definition of art. In the 20th century, philosophers suggested additions to the list of characteristics, and examined them to see which, if any, are universally applicable. Denis Dutton, for example, offered a set of what he considered universal characteristics of art: artistic skill and expertise; style, and satisfying rules of composition; imitation or representation; art for art's sake, simply to give pleasure; separation from ordinary life; and criticism, that it is a focus for appreciation and interpretation. Whether these characteristics are universal is, however, debatable. Instead, works of art may have what Ludwig Wittgenstein calls a 'family resemblance' – they have no one feature in common, but rather exhibit one or more of a set of several features.

6 High and low culture

A bad-tempered debate between Jeremy Bentham and John Stuart Mill brought up another aspect of assessing the value of a work of art. In Bentham's down-to-earth utilitarianism, it is simply a question of what gives the greatest happiness to the greatest number. There is no 'hierarchy among pleasures', so if, say, a popular song gives pleasure to a huge number of people, it is just prejudice to claim it has less value than an avant-garde string quartet appreciated by only a handful. Mill rejected the idea, arguing that the pleasures of high culture are qualitatively different from sensual, instinctual pleasures, as they are also intellectually satisfying, and 'It is better to be a human dissatisfied than a pig satisfied'.

7 The intentional fallacy

Twentieth-century aesthetic philosophers were also becoming increasingly interested in the ways in which art's aesthetic merit can be judged. Traditionally, this had been according to how well it measures up to apparently objective criteria of representation or compositional rules, and how well the artist succeeds in his or her intentions. However, two literary critics, William K. Wimsatt and Monroe Beardsley, argued in an essay titled 'The Intentional Fallacy' that a literary work should be judged solely by the words on the page – the intended meaning of the author is irrelevant to its artistic worth, and may even get in the way of an objective assessment.

8 Fakes and forgeries

Wimsatt and Beardsley's intentional fallacy was influential, and extended from the world of literature to all the arts, but was also controversial. If we accept that it is the work alone, regardless of the intention of the artist, that determines its artistic merit, provenance is irrelevant. It is of no consequence that the creator of a work might intend to hoodwink the audience

for fame and fortune, or pass it off as the work of someone else. A forgery, for example, if it's good enough, would have the same artistic value as if it were genuine. And a bad painting is bad, even if painted by Leonardo. The work should be judged on its own merits, no matter who created it or why.

9 The 'affective fallacy'

In a follow-up essay, 'The Affective Fallacy', Wimsatt and Beardsley threw another spanner into the works of literary criticism. Analysing and assessing a text should be as objective as possible, they argued, and so it is a mistake to use the reader's personal or emotional response as a criterion. This proved even more contentious than their intentional fallacy, as it contradicts the notion of art as expression, with the purpose of evoking a response. The argument was widely discredited by critics and philosophers. Some years later, Roland Barthes, one of the pioneers of structuralism in France, argued that artistic judgement is necessarily subjective: it is the reader (or viewer or audience) who decides what the significance of a work of art is, and even if it is art.

10 The institutional theory of art

Modern art has often baffled the public throughout history, but in the 20th and 21st centuries, works such as Marcel Duchamp's 'readymades' and John Cage's 4'33" of silence have challenged traditional notions of what actually constitutes art. An apparently simplistic answer was provided by Arthur Danto in 1964: if it's presented as art by the artworld, it's art. So a pile of bricks on a building site isn't art, but in a gallery it is. The idea was refined by George Dickie into what has become known as the institutional theory of art, in which he describes a work of art as an 'artefact' (a product of intentional human creativity) on which the artworld public (institutions with a knowledge and understanding of art) has conferred the status of candidate for appreciation.

TALK LIKE A GENIUS

⟡ Although understanding the cultural and historical context of a work of art can help in appreciating it, we have to be careful to judge the art rather than the artist. Knowing that Beethoven was an embezzler has little or no bearing on the artistic value of his symphonies. ⟡

⟡ A painting bought for £45 has recently been sold for $450 million, after it was authenticated as a work by Leonardo da Vinci. It's still the same picture, but has suddenly become revered as a masterpiece. It seems we don't judge an artwork simply on its own merit. ⟡

⟡ If the "artworld" decides what is and isn't art, it implies that the ordinary art-lover's uninformed opinion carries little weight. On the other hand, if the public were left to decide, soap operas would probably be credited with more cultural value than opera. ⟡

1 TRUE – As art is an imperfect imitation of nature, it is not truthful, and truth is a fundamental value in a just society.

2 FALSE – In his *Poetics*, Aristotle analyses drama and poetry and identifies their basic elements as the characteristics of art.

3 TRUE – Hume anticipated Dickie's argument that those in the know are better placed to judge the worth of a work of art.

4 FALSE – Wimsatt and Beardsley argue that the artist's intended meaning is irrelevant, but the compositional integrity of a work isn't.

5 FALSE – Only what Dickie calls 'artefacts', conforming to specific criteria, qualify for consideration as works of art by the experts of the artworld.

THE BLUFFER'S SUMMARY

Traditionally, art is defined in terms of its formal, representational or expressive function, but recent definitions are in terms of critical judgement.

Reason and logic

'Logic and mathematics seem to be the only domains where self-evidence manages to rise above triviality.'

WILLARD VAN ORMAN QUINE

Because philosophy is characterized by its use of reasoning to enquire about the world and our place in it, a major branch of philosophy – logic – is devoted to examining the structure of rational thought. This has developed from the simple dialectic method used by Socrates to point out the inconsistencies of an opinion, into a sophisticated logical framework for presenting a philosophical argument. The basic rules were established by Aristotle, and refined over the centuries, but at the beginning of the 20th century Bertrand Russell showed that the link between mathematics and logic demanded a profound change in the way that philosophy is practised.

Can you provide evidence to support your claim of knowing about philosophical reasoning?

ARE YOU A GENIUS?

1 The Socratic method of debate consisted essentially of a dialogue in which he contradicted each argument put forward by the other participant.

TRUE / FALSE

2 In the syllogism, 'All dogs like bones; Rover is a dog; so Rover likes bones', the argument is valid, so the conclusion must be true.

TRUE / FALSE

3 Until the end of the 19th century, the Aristotelian syllogism was accepted by most philosophers as the only system of logic.

TRUE / FALSE

4 A counterargument to a proposition can be a demonstration of faulty reasoning in the original argument, or that one or more of the premises is false.

TRUE / FALSE

5 Syllogistic logic was discredited when 19th-century philosophers pointed out the impossibility of expressing propositions precisely in ordinary language, and suggested new systems of logic.

TRUE / FALSE

TEN THINGS A GENIUS KNOWS

1 Reason and debate

The distinguishing feature of philosophy, as opposed to superstition, religion or mere convention, is the use of reasoning. The ideas that a philosopher proposes are the conclusions of a thought process, of rational thinking. Philosophical theories are not simply a matter of belief, as a philosopher has to support any idea or opinion with evidence, and a sound rational argument for reaching a particular conclusion. Rational argument is the nuts and bolts of philosophical debate, and logic provides the framework on which it is built.

2 The Socratic method

Although many philosophers come to their ideas through solitary contemplation, the roots of philosophical reasoning lie in a debate of ideas: presenting an argument for a particular point of view that can then be analysed. In its simple form, this is a dialogue, such as the method that Socrates used to elicit ideas and presumptions. His dialectical method involved inviting someone's opinion, and then subjecting them to a barrage of questions to elicit evidence for it, and to point out the flaws and inconsistencies of their position.

3 Aristotle: the syllogism

In practice, the simple back-and-forth of the dialectical method only produces a convincing argument in the hands of an interlocutor like Socrates. A more formal framework for argument is the syllogism, a presentation of statements from which a conclusion can be inferred. This is generally in a three-step form of two statements, or premises, and a conclusion. The ever-methodical Aristotle, although not the inventor of the syllogism, defined the form and codified the rules that determine whether the conclusion necessarily follows from the premises. The basic form of the syllogism remained the foundation for the study of logical argument from then until the 19th century.

4 Inference: deductive reasoning

In its classic form, a syllogism consists of two statements, or propositions, which are assumed or have been shown to be true. These are the premises of the argument; typically, there is a general statement, the major premise, in the form: 'All X are Y'. This is followed by a specific proposition, the minor premise, in the form 'Z is X'. The now clichéd example is 'All men are mortal. Socrates is a man.' From the premises, we can infer the conclusion 'Socrates is mortal' by a process of deduction from a general rule to a specific case. In essence, this gives the basis for a sound argument – if the propositions in the premises are true, and the argument is valid, then the conclusion must also be true.

5 True and false

But it is the idea of truth and falsity that exposes some of the weaknesses of the syllogism as a logical form of argument. For the argument to hold water, the premises have to be accepted as true. But that may not be a simple matter. We may have to provide empirical evidence to verify the proposition, or a further logical justification based on additional premises, which themselves need verifying, and so on, ad infinitum. Another problem is that, often, things in the world are not black and white, and the traditional binary true–false way of thinking cannot take into account degrees of likelihood that something is true.

6 Validity

While mathematicians will happily talk about proving a theorem, philosophers are rightfully wary of the word 'proof', and its meaning of incontrovertible truth. Instead, they examine the structure of the argument to see if it is valid.

Not all syllogisms are as straightforward as the example above: premises are sometimes in the form of 'All X...', but could equally be 'No X...' or 'Some X...', in various combinations, leading to various forms of conclusion. There is an infinite number of possible arguments in the form of a syllogism, for example, but only some satisfy all the rules of validity. The argument is said to be sound (that is, the conclusion is true) only when it is valid and the premises are true.

7 Language and logic

Philosophers face another hurdle when they want to present an argument or put someone else's argument to the test. Philosophical ideas are expressed using language, and language is often not precise enough for logical examination. Terms such as 'some', 'not all', or 'may be' can be interpreted in different ways. And some words have different meanings in different contexts, which can lead to ambiguity. For example, in one of Groucho Marx's cleverest quips, there are two propositions, each of which is unremarkable, but when juxtaposed highlight the problem: 'Time flies like an arrow. Fruit flies like a banana.'

8 Fallacy and paradox

Quite apart from the drawbacks of imprecise language and the rigidity of the notion of true and false, there are a number of ways that faulty reasoning may lead to a wrong conclusion. It may, for example, be based on false assumptions in the premises, or an incorrect inference from the premises. In either case, the argument is not sound, and any conclusion of an unsound argument is known as a fallacy. Sometimes, the conclusion of a fallacious argument is a paradox – it is demonstrably untrue – or involves some kind of logical contradiction, such as the proposition 'this sentence is false'. Although paradoxes are often obviously absurd, it can sometimes be very difficult to detect the flaw in the argument.

9 Symbolic logic

To overcome the problems of using language in logical propositions, several logicians suggested ways of 'translating' statements from words into symbols, similar to the ones used in mathematics. By doing this, they hoped to remove any ambiguity, imprecision or connotation, and make clearer the logical structure of the argument. Various conventions, a sort of shorthand, evolved to represent frequently used terms of logic, such as 'all', 'some', 'are/is' and 'if', and, as in algebra, letters of the alphabet are typically used to represent the subjects of propositions. To do this, however, presents another task: analysing the original proposition to ascertain its exact meaning, free of the imprecision of language.

10 Logic, science and mathematics

Aristotle's systematic approach to philosophy provided the basis for a logical way of constructing and testing rational arguments. In addition, he laid the foundations of a methodical way of establishing scientific knowledge, using a process of inductive reasoning – that is, inferring a general rule from specific instances – rather than the syllogistic process of deduction. Although this provided a methodology for the natural sciences that worked well in practice, it was built on shaky logical ground – the 'problem of induction' described by David Hume. Unlike the natural sciences, however, mathematics and logic have been found to be not only compatible, but intimately interconnected.

TALK LIKE A GENIUS

💧 Philosophers use a process of reasoning to arrive at and support their ideas and theories. But to support their arguments, they need to show that that reasoning is sound; logic is the means of doing that. 💧

💧 Although Aristotle didn't invent the syllogism, the form of logical argument where a conclusion follows from two premises, in his typically methodical fashion, he identified the multitude of combinations of different kinds of premise, and the various ways an argument can be shown to be valid or not. 💧

💧 Logic provides an objective means of analysing and assessing an argument, but it isn't always conclusive. It can show, for example, that the conclusion may be true, but doesn't necessarily follow from the premises. And unless the truth of the premises is established, they cannot be used as grounds for an argument. 💧

THE BLUFFER'S SUMMARY

Philosophy is a process of presenting ideas that are the result of reasoning, and logic provides the framework for those rational arguments.

Fallacies and paradoxes

'The point of philosophy is to start with something so simple as not to seem worth stating, and to end with something so paradoxical that no one will believe it.'

BERTRAND RUSSELL

Although the word 'fallacy' is commonly used to describe a widely held but false belief, to the logician it denotes faulty reasoning rather than an untrue assertion. Specifically, there are 'formal' fallacies, arguments that are invalid because they have a flaw in their logical structure; and 'informal' fallacies, in which the flaw lies in the content of the premises and the way it is used, rather than the logical form of the argument. Sometimes, a logical argument presents us with a paradox, or a conclusion that is patently untrue or involves a logical contradiction. With a paradox, there's either something wrong with the argument (that is, it's a formal or informal fallacy), or there's something wrong with the logical system it uses.

Philosophers have often puzzled over paradoxes; can you spot the fallacies?

1 A paradox uses faultless reasoning and a valid logical argument, yet leads to an obviously incorrect, absurd or contradictory conclusion.

TRUE / FALSE

2 Although the term 'fallacy' is used loosely to describe something that is commonly believed but not true, a logical fallacy is an error of reasoning, an invalid argument, but its conclusion is not necessarily false.

TRUE / FALSE

3 Paradoxes always produce results that are manifestly untrue.

TRUE / FALSE

4 A coin is tossed and comes up heads four times in a row. The chances of that happening are pretty slim, but the probability of it happening five times in a row is even smaller. So it is much more likely to be tails than heads next time.

TRUE / FALSE

5 The statement 'This statement is false' is self-referential and self-contradictory, and cannot be either true or false.

TRUE / FALSE

TEN THINGS A GENIUS KNOWS

1 *Petitio principii*

The fallacy of *petitio principii* (confusingly known in English as 'begging the question' – a phrase often mistakenly taken to mean 'raising a further question') is when acceptance of one or more of the premises of a logical argument is dependent on acceptance of the conclusion. The classic instance, cited by René Descartes, is: the Bible says that God exists; the Bible is true because it is the word of God; therefore God exists. Without accepting the conclusion, the premises are on shaky ground. A particular case of *petitio principii*, known as circular logic, occurs when the conclusion is actually included (albeit in a different wording) in the premises – for example: the word of God is true; the Bible says that it is the word of God; therefore the Bible is true.

2 The irrelevant conclusion

Also known as the *ignoratio elenchi* fallacy, this is not so much a case of faulty reasoning as simply missing the point. The argument presented may be (and often is) perfectly valid, but its conclusion does not address the point at issue. It often takes the form of refuting an opponent's argument by disproving an assertion that has not been made. If done deliberately, it creates a 'red herring' to divert attention away from the main issue.

3 *Ad hominem, ad verecundiam, et cetera...*

There are a number of fallacies that could be categorized as the 'appeal to...' fallacies. Best known is the *ad hominem* attack, on the person advancing an argument, rather than the evidence per se, either by pointing out a personal fault, an element of self-interest, or that the person does not herself follow the view she presents. Other examples of mistakenly believed evidence include *ad verecundiam*, the appeal to authority ('That must be true, because Professor X says so'); *ad*

populum, appeal to popular opinion ('fifty million voters can't be wrong'); and appeals to emotion ('Innocent children will suffer as a result of this policy').

4 Faulty analogy

Analogy can be a useful tool in arguments, but is only valid when comparing like with like – which it very often isn't. For example, likening a country's economy to a household budget, as most economists will point out, is a gross oversimplification. Related to the faulty analogy are the fallacies of composition and division, wrongly conflating the properties of a composite with those of its constituent parts. For example, a football team may consist of the finest players in the world, but that does not necessarily mean it is the best team.

5 *Post hoc ergo propter hoc*

'Same-sex marriage is legalized, and the next day there's an earthquake. Don't you think God's trying to tell you something?' Just because something happened after something else doesn't mean there is a causal relationship. It may be that the fall in inflation in the last quarter is a result of government policy, but simply saying *post hoc ergo propter hoc* (after this, therefore because of this) isn't sufficient evidence. This fallacious argument can also lead to a 'slippery slope' fallacy, that one small thing will inevitably lead to a much bigger thing: legalizing cannabis will encourage drug use generally, this is a gateway to addictive drugs, and will lead to an epidemic of heroin-related deaths.

6 Complex question fallacy

Sometimes an argument comes in the form of a question, inviting an answer that is the conclusion of a line of questioning. This can be a valid form of argument, but is susceptible to the 'complex question' or 'many questions' fallacy. The question may in fact involve an implicit assumption, which may not be established as true, such as in the classic leading question 'When did you stop beating your wife?'. This may also be in the form of a question demanding a simple yes or no answer to a complex question: for example, 'Are you still a member of a terrorist organization?'

7 Zeno's paradoxes of motion
Zeno of Elea (c. 490–c. 430 BCE) originated a number of paradoxes apparently showing the impossibility of motion. Probably the best known is the paradox of Achilles and the tortoise: given a head start, the tortoise will always be ahead of Achilles, because by the time Achilles has reached the tortoise's starting point, the tortoise will have moved on, and once again has a head start – Achilles can never catch up. Using similar logic, Zeno shows that a runner can never reach his goal, as first he must reach the halfway point, then halfway from there and so on, ad infinitum. Zeno even apparently demonstrates that motion is an illusion. An arrow, when at rest occupies a space just its own size; at any moment in flight, it occupies just that space, so is at rest; therefore it is at rest at every moment of its flight. Solutions to these and similar paradoxes eluded logicians until the development of calculus in the 17th century.

8 The horned man
The paradox of the man with horns (and several others including the *sorites* and liar paradoxes below) is attributed to Eubulides, a contemporary of Aristotle. The argument runs: What you have not lost, you have; but you have not lost horns; therefore, you have horns. This paradox is, however, reasonably simply resolved. It hinges on the ambiguous word 'lost', which the first premise gives the meaning 'used to have, but no longer have'. The 'lost' in the second premise is subtly different, though, with the implication of 'never had, so didn't lose'. This ambiguity creates a fallacy of the 'complex question' variety, to which there cannot be a simple answer.

9 The *sorites* paradox
Imagine a heap (Greek *sorites*) of sand. Let's say it consists of 10,000 grains of sand. If you remove one single grain, it is still a heap. Imagine a heap of 9,999 grains. You remove one grain, and it's still a heap... continue with this logic and you end up with one grain, yet still call it a heap, which it obviously isn't. The fallacy of this paradox lies in the use of the vague term 'heap', which has no distinct meaning (such as a specified minimum number of grains). But more problematic is the variation: I can lift a sack of 10,000 grains; if I add one grain, I can still lift it (of course, one grain won't make it noticeably heavier); so I can lift a sack containing any number of grains.

10 Antinomy
A paradox that involves contradiction, either between two apparently valid logical arguments or the conclusions reached by them, is known as an 'antinomy'. The classic example is the statement, 'Everything I say is a lie' – the so-called liar paradox – variations of which include assertions such as 'This sentence is false'. The contradiction highlights a shortcoming of the binary true/false values of traditional logic, because if the statement is true, it's false, and vice versa. Bertrand Russell pointed out a related antinomy in his critique of set theory: there is a set of all sets that are not members of themselves; is it a member of itself? If it is, it isn't and if it isn't, it is. He also offered a less technical (but just as perplexing) version of 'Russell's paradox': a male barber shaves all and only those men who do not shave themselves; does he shave himself?

TALK LIKE A GENIUS

❝ Paradoxes are more than simply philosophical puzzles or entertainment. Russell's paradox exposed the flaw in the argument of set theory that sought to define mathematics in logical terms. The contradiction inherent in the set of all sets that are not members of themselves apparently undermined the foundations of mathematics, showing that no mathematical proof could be known to be valid. ❞

❝ Zeno's assertions that motion is impossible, and that Achilles will never catch up with the tortoise, are obviously untrue, but it took more than 2,000 years for anybody to find a way of attacking his logic – and not everybody is convinced by those solutions even today. ❞

❝ It's comparatively easy to spot and refute a formal fallacy, an argument that is invalid because of a flaw in its logical structure; more difficult are the "informal" fallacies, which usually involve flawed content rather than structure. ❞

WERE YOU A GENIUS?

1 FALSE – Paradoxes use apparently sound logic, but are, in fact, fallacious – although it is often difficult to show why.

2 TRUE – Just because an argument is invalid doesn't mean that the conclusion is false.

3 FALSE – Many paradoxes do indeed lead to false conclusions, but there are some that, although apparently absurd, are actually true – what W.V. Quine calls 'veridical paradoxes'.

4 FALSE – This is the so-called 'gambler's fallacy'. No matter what has happened in the past, the odds of a tossed coin coming up heads are always the same, 1 in 2.

5 TRUE – If the statement 'This statement is false' is true, it's false; if it isn't true, it is.

THE BLUFFER'S SUMMARY

A fallacy presents a plausible conclusion supported by faulty logic, but a paradox uses apparently impeccable logic to support a manifestly untrue conclusion.

Scientific enquiry

'The game of science is, in principle, without end. He who decides one day that scientific statements do not call for any further test, and that they can be regarded as finally verified, retires from the game.'

KARL POPPER

For much of history, science was a part of philosophy – sometimes known as natural philosophy – and it only developed gradually into the separate disciplines of the natural sciences, such as physics and chemistry. The subject of enquiry, understanding the natural world, was one of the first concerns of philosophy. Philosophers and, later, scientists, observed phenomena in the world about them, and tried to discern patterns from which they could infer general rules that govern the way everything in the world is structured. And to do that with any degree of certainty, they had to devise a systematic methodology, which evolved into what is known now as 'scientific method'.

Based on your observations, can you formulate a hypothesis to test your knowledge of the scientific method?

1 The idea of conducting repeatable experiments to verify a hypothesis was first suggested by Francis Bacon in his *Novum Organum Scientiarum*.
TRUE / FALSE

2 A pioneer of experimental medicine and clinical research, the Persian physician Rhazes (Ibn al-Razi) explained the idea of testing treatments using a control group to compare results to.
TRUE / FALSE

3 The various different elements of scientific methodology have now been standardized into one single scientific method.
TRUE / FALSE

4 From observation, scientists can propose theories, which can then be proved by scientific methods.
TRUE / FALSE

5 The majority of religious beliefs can be dismissed as pseudoscience.
TRUE / FALSE

TEN THINGS A GENIUS KNOWS

1 Scientific methods

The 'scientific method' is often held up as the definitive acid test for new ideas in science, but there is actually no single scientific method; rather, there is a general methodology following certain principles that characterizes scientific method. In its modern form, it consists of a sequence of procedures including observation, measurement and experiment, that are used to formulate and test a hypothesis. Typically, a scientist will observe a phenomenon, and then suggest an explanation for it – a hypothesis. The hypothesis is then tested by experiment and further observation, and the results are recorded and analysed. From this information a conclusion about the validity of the hypothesis can be inferred.

2 Aristotle: observation and analysis

In its very simplest form, this was the way that the very earliest rational explanations of the natural world came about. Prehistoric people observed the changing of the seasons, the waxing and waning of the Moon and so on, and inferred from what they saw that such things follow a general rule – a 'law of nature'. But the first step towards systematic scientific enquiry came from Aristotle. Taking a break from Athens for a few years, he travelled around the eastern Mediterranean studying the flora and fauna, and making meticulous notes about the characteristics of the various animals and plants. He then classified them all according to these characteristics, and inferred some general rules applying to different classes of living things.

3 Science in the Islamic world

Aristotle was particularly influential in Islamic philosophy. While in Europe philosophy and learning were eclipsed in the Dark Ages, intellectual activity thrived in the Islamic empire. Scholars in the 'houses of wisdom' tended to be polymaths, and as well as studying philosophy and theology, developed Aristotelian principles into a recognizable scientific method – which they applied practically to make discoveries in all the sciences. In the 10th and 11th centuries, Islamic philosophers were also pioneers in the fields of physics, astronomy, chemistry and medicine, and Alhazen (Ibn al-Haytham) and Avicenna, in particular, devised ways of confirming their hypotheses by experiments and observation.

4 Francis Bacon

When Islamic philosophical and scientific ideas filtered in to Europe, they inspired a sea change in intellectual activity. Although as yet no distinction was made between science and philosophy, during the Renaissance the first great European scientists emerged. Among them was Galileo Galilei, who did much to establish a rigorous methodology for the study of the physical sciences. In Britain, Francis Bacon specifically addressed the question of applying reason to scientific enquiry in his *Novum Organum Scientiarum*. He argued that the deductive reasoning of the syllogism is not suited to scientific research and, instead, recommended a process of induction to formulate general laws. This has to be methodical, and most importantly sceptical, not simply observing examples that confirm a hypothesis, but also seeking negative instances that test the idea.

5 Descartes's *Discourse on the Method*

Bacon's notion of scepticism became an essential component of the evolving scientific methodology. And it was a central idea of René Descartes's *Discourse on the Method of Rightly Conducting One's Reason and of Seeking Truth in the Sciences*, a landmark in the history of scientific method. In the discourse he stresses the need to find incontrovertible truths: 'The first precept was never to accept a thing as true until I knew it as such without a single doubt.' He then advocates a step-by-step process of deduction of one truth from another, so that 'Each problem that I solved became a rule, which served afterwards to solve other problems'.

⑥ Comte's positivism

By the time of the Enlightenment, the method of sceptical deductive reasoning was well established as a means of ascertaining scientific hypotheses. Science became recognizably different from 'natural philosophy', and among the first to acknowledge the difference was Auguste Comte, a leading figure in positivism, or positive philosophy. Science, he asserted, distinguished by the systematic methods of observation and theory, provides us with verifiable information about the world, in a way that metaphysics cannot, and so our search for knowledge should be scientific rather than philosophical.

⑦ Philosophy of science

With the separation of science from philosophy, philosophers began to turn their attention from scientific matters to science itself. Beginning in the early 19th century, the philosophy of science is concerned with such things as the ways that scientific enquiry is conducted, and the nature of scientific progress.

⑧ Paradigm shifts

When Aristotle's model for methodical natural philosophy was adopted by Islamic philosophers, it was refined and made more powerful, and allowed groundbreaking advances in all the sciences. Similarly, Islamic scientific method gave a foundation for the discoveries of the European Renaissance, which in turn led to the beginning of a 'scientific revolution' that continued into the Enlightenment period. Throughout its history, science has not progressed smoothly, but in sudden revolutionary leaps: the theories of Copernicus, Newton, Darwin and Einstein are prime examples. These were described by Thomas Kuhn as 'paradigm shifts' – when an idea or discovery upsets conventional wisdom and causes a fundamental change in scientific thinking. During periods of what he calls 'normal' science, research is done within an accepted paradigm or framework, and anomalies in results are often discounted as experimental error. But if the anomalies are significant, contradicting the paradigm, there is a 'crisis' that calls for alternative theories and a shift to a new paradigm.

⑨ Feyerabend's *Against Method*

A friend of Kuhn's, Paul Feyerabend, used his idea of paradigm shifts as the starting point for what he called an 'Anarchist Theory of Knowledge'. In his book *Against Method*, he argued that as there are paradigm shifts, there is no single permanent method for scientific enquiry; the framework changes with each crisis. Moreover, advances in scientific knowledge occur when the accepted rules of 'normal' science are broken, when somebody thinks 'outside the box'. So, he concluded, the search for a definitive set of rules of scientific methodology is more than pointless, it actually hinders progress.

⑩ Pseudoscience

The snag with Feyerabend's otherwise attractive suggestion is that, without some rigorous method of testing, it's difficult to separate a genuinely groundbreaking theory from all the pseudoscientific nonsense. With the benefit of scientific method, such pseudosciences as astrology, young earth creationism and homeopathy have been discredited as unscientific – although they still have their adherents. Many of these theories claim to be scientific, but fail to satisfy the criteria of modern scientific methodology. When challenged though, some believers in the various pseudosciences question the authority of science, which they see as just an alternative belief system offering theories and not proofs – and not entirely without justification, given the 'problem of induction' (see pages 184–7).

TALK LIKE A GENIUS

❛ The methods used in the natural sciences are the legacy of Aristotle's argument that knowledge of the world is gathered empirically, by experience and observation, but in order to make sense of this raw data, it must be analysed by rational thinking in a sytematic logical way. ❜

❛ Aristotle may have started the scientific ball rolling, but medieval Islamic polymaths picked it up and ran with it. Using rigorous methods, they made advances in all the sciences, and their legacy is reflected in the international vocabulary of science, including words such as algorithm, alkali, chemistry and algebra. ❜

❛ The physicist Niels Bohr is quoted as saying, "No, no, you're not thinking, you're just being logical", apparently supporting Feyerabend's idea that the game-changers in science are the ones who don't follow the rules. ❜

WERE YOU A GENIUS?

1 FALSE – Medieval Islamic philosophers and scientists first developed the method of seeing whether results of experiments could be reproduced.

2 TRUE – Rhazes divided patients into two groups, treating one group and not the other, to test the efficacy of blood-letting for meningitis.

3 FALSE – Variations of the methods of observation, experimentation and analysis, have evolved as appropriate to different branches of science.

4 FALSE – Scientists propose hypotheses, and if empirical evidence supports them they are regarded as theories – but these can be shown to be wrong by negative instances.

5 FALSE – Pseudosciences make false claims of scientific credibility, whereas religions, in the main, base their beliefs on faith, not science.

THE BLUFFER'S SUMMARY

The principles of scientific methodology, deriving a theory from a hypothesis by observation and experimentation, are based on inductive reasoning.

The problem of induction

'Custom, then, is the great guide of human life.'

DAVID HUME

From our experience of the world, we build up a picture of the way things behave. We see the Sun rise every morning, and infer that the Sun always rises in the morning, and we can predict that it will rise again tomorrow morning. The methods that evolved to establish scientific theories work on the same principle: a theory is inferred from empirical observation by a process of induction. But, as David Hume pointed out, inductive reasoning is an unsatisfactory way of reaching a conclusion, and gives no rational justification for believing scientific theories to be true.

Inductive reasoning was a real problem for David Hume, but do you know what it is all about?

1 Inductive reasoning provides us with information about the world, but not a means of establishing its truth.

TRUE / FALSE

2 Hume argued that 'causality' is a human invention; even when one event always follows another, there cannot be a causal connection between them.

TRUE / FALSE

3 According to Hume, it is simply human nature to assume a general rule from our experience of recurrent events, and our 'common sense' misleads us into believing our conclusions.

TRUE / FALSE

4 Popper's idea of falsifiability creates a paradox, because for a theory to be considered a matter of scientific enquiry, it has to be shown to be false, and if is not shown to be false, it is unscientific.

TRUE / FALSE

5 Bacon's 'New Method' of scientific enquiry was based on inductive reasoning, but stressed the importance of seeking negative instances as well as positive to test a hypothesis.

TRUE / FALSE

1 Deductive vs inductive reasoning

For an argument to be valid according to the rules of Aristotelian logic, it has to follow a definite pattern of deductive reasoning. There is a major premise, a general statement such as 'All bears like honey', followed by a minor premise, a particular instance such as 'Pooh is a bear', from which can be inferred the conclusion 'Pooh likes honey'. But while deduction infers the particular from a general rule, inductive reasoning aims to formulate a general rule from particular instances – and Aristotelian logic tells us that a conclusion does not necessarily follow from such premises. For example, from the premises 'My dog likes bones' and 'Every dog I know likes bones', it does not follow that 'All dogs like bones', even though it may happen to be true.

2 Aristotle's classification of nature

As well as setting the standard for deductive reasoning, Aristotle laid the groundwork for methodical scientific enquiry using a process of induction. In his systematic study of living things, he classified them according to their characteristics. So, for example, he classified birds as two-legged creatures with feathers, and that lay eggs. Every bird he had come across had these characteristics, and so he concluded that all birds are two-legged, feathered, oviparous creatures, deriving a general rule from a number of particular instances.

3 David Hume

The principle of inductive reasoning established by Aristotle became the foundation of the evolving scientific method – Francis Bacon even explicitly argued that induction is better than deduction for scientific enquiry. By Aristotle's own logic, however, induction does not provide any necessarily true conclusions. David Hume famously pointed out the elephant in the room in *A Treatise of Human Nature*. Although induction doesn't give us rational grounds for thinking something is the case, we have a natural predisposition to interpret regular repetition as uniformity. And so, he suggests, we should use our common sense to assess the likelihood of whether it is true, and let 'custom', our experience of what has normally been the case, be our guide.

4 Post hoc ergo propter hoc

Hume noted another quirk of human nature that has no foundation in reason: our tendency to assume a causal connection when there is a 'constant conjunction' of things. If, in your experience, event B has always followed event A, you infer that A has caused B: the post hoc fallacy (*post hoc ergo propter hoc* – 'after this, therefore because of this'). But there is no rational reason for coming to that conclusion. If two alarm clocks are set a minute apart, one will always ring a minute before the other, but there is no causal link between the two. Again, Hume advises 'custom' and experience rather than logic. Common sense tells us that the two clocks are not causally connected, but we know from experience that drinking hemlock does cause death.

5 Matters of fact

Despite Hume's highlighting of the problem of induction, he recognized that it is our only basis for scientific enquiry. This is because the natural sciences are based on empirical evidence – what he called 'matters of fact' – rather than 'relations of ideas'; contingent rather than necessary truths. And, as he explained (see also page 93), contingent truths can only be verified by empirical observation, not reason; and reason alone can tell us nothing about the world. Science, unlike logic and mathematics, is concerned with matters of fact, not truths of reasoning, and cannot be logically proven in the same way.

6 Proof vs theory

Because the natural sciences derive their information from empirical observation and experience, the propositions of science are matters of fact and not relations of ideas. And because science uses a process of inductive reasoning to reach its conclusions – deriving a general rule from a number of specific instances – these, too, are not necessary truths, but contingent propositions; not proofs, but theories. In this regard, mathematics is distinct from the natural sciences, as mathematical theorems are tested by reason alone, not empirical observation, and so some can be proved true or false – although some remain unproved and possibly unprovable.

7 Pragmatism

The 20th-century American pragmatists (see page 94) had no problem with the idea that science deals in theories rather than truths. For them, truth is not an absolute, but something that is valid so long as it is useful, good enough for practical purposes. So a scientific theory, such as Newton's theory of gravity, didn't need to be true in order to be good enough to give us a better picture of the workings of the Solar System than before; it was subsequently shown to be inadequate by Einstein's theories, which gave a more accurate picture of things, and have enabled technological progress.

8 Popper and falsifiability

The problem of inductive reasoning in science was largely ignored after Hume until the 20th century. In his book *The Logic of Scientific Discovery,* Karl Popper argued for a new approach to the justification of scientific theories, as it was clear that they cannot be justified by inductive reasoning. Instead, he suggested that scientific methodology should be based on falsifiability: the truth of a theory cannot be proved by any number of experiments or observations, but can be contradicted by a single instance showing it to be false. In order to be considered as scientific, a theory

does not have to prove its truth, but must be falsifiable, capable of being shown to be false.

9 The black swan

The classic example to demonstrate the notion of falsifiability is the proposition 'all swans are white'. What we are proposing with this is: after extensive observation, all the examples of swans we have found in the world are white, so we propose the theory that all swans are white; it can be falsified by finding just one example of a swan of a different colour, but as yet we have no evidence of one. It meets Popper's requirements for being scientific, because it is capable of being falsified – and in fact the theory has been shown to be false, by the discovery of black swans in Australia.

10 Pseudoscience and falsifiability

Imposing the qualification of falsifiability on a scientific theory helps to weed out those ideas that are mere pseudoscience. An example of how this works was provided by the astronomer Carl Sagan, who claimed to have an invisible, incorporeal dragon in his garage. The problem with this claim is that it very difficult to refute, but that in itself shows the strength of Popper's falsifiability criterion. As Sagan puts it: 'Your inability to invalidate my hypothesis is not at all the same thing as proving it true'. As it is impossible to devise an experiment or series of observations to contradict the claim, it is not falsifiable, and so should not be considered a matter of scientific enquiry, even if it is true.

TALK LIKE A GENIUS

❦ Aristotle's legacy included a system of logic based on deductive reasoning, and a tradition of scientific enquiry based on inductive reasoning. Until the 20th century, at least, the two were never satisfactorily reconciled. ❧

❦ The analysis of the problem of induction in Hume's *A Treatise of Human Nature* is slightly uncomfortable reading, as he's telling us our scientific knowledge is not based on solid, provable facts, but on experience tempered with a dose of common sense. ❧

❦ It is often said that Karl Popper "solved" the problem of induction, but it would be more accurate to say that he showed that philosophers of science had been barking up the wrong tree. Scientific enquiry is by its nature an inductive process, but can be made more rigorous by applying criteria such as falsifiability. ❧

THE BLUFFER'S SUMMARY

It is not possible to construct a logically valid argument using inductive reasoning, yet induction is the basis for scientific enquiry.

Logic and mathematics

'Every good mathematician is at least half a philosopher, and every good philosopher is at least half a mathematician.'

GOTTLOB FREGE

For over 2,000 years, the system of logic established by Aristotle – inferring a conclusion from two or more premises by deduction – was assumed to be the only model for logic. But at the end of the 19th century, the German mathematician Gottlob Frege demonstrated the intimate connection between logic and mathematics, and showed that there is vastly more to logic than had previously been thought. The mathematician-turned-philosopher Bertrand Russell was the first to recognize the implications of Frege's work for philosophy, marking the beginning of a new approach to philosophy in the 20th century.

Frege and Russell inspired a whole new way of doing philosophy. Do you know what they did to bring about the change?

1 Frege's interest in logic was purely as a mathematician. He had little knowledge of philosophy, and no idea of the implications of his work to the study of philosophy.

TRUE / FALSE

2 It was Frege's *The Foundations of Arithmetic* that inspired Russell to write his own *Principles of Mathematics*.

TRUE / FALSE

3 As an illustration of 'Russell's paradox', which pointed to a contradiction in naive set theory, Russell told of the village barber who shaves all those, and only those, who do not shave themselves – but who shaves the barber?

TRUE / FALSE

4 Russell's co-author of *Principia Mathematica*, A.N. Whitehead, later turned to metaphysics rather than mathematics and logic as his main philosophical concern.

TRUE / FALSE

5 Frege's *Begriffsschrift* was the first system of symbolic notation in logic.

TRUE / FALSE

TEN THINGS A GENIUS KNOWS

1 Objective truths

Until comparatively recently, it was assumed that the system of logic described by Aristotle is derived from the way we think, its rules the laws governing our thought processes. As such, it was regarded in the same way as language, a human construct. It was not until the late 19th century that that assumption was challenged, when Gottlob Frege suggested what seems today to be obvious: something either does or does not follow from something else, and that would be the case even if we did not exist, it does not depend on the way we think. Logic is independent of human thought, its rules are universal and its propositions are objective truths.

2 Gottlob Frege

As a mathematician, Frege was keen to see how his insight into the objectivity of logic could be used in mathematics. The procedures of mathematics – like logic – consist of conclusions following from premises. The problem, however, was that those procedures and premises had not been proven: it isn't possible to demonstrate the validity of mathematical premises and laws using mathematics, an argument assuming what it is trying to prove. But now that Frege had shown the rules of logic to be objective, he could go on to show that the premises of maths can be derived from logic. He demonstrated that the laws of arithmetic are objective truths, but also went on to show that arithmetic (and probably all of mathematics) is a part of logic.

3 Mathematics as universal truth

Frege's aim was to set mathematics on a solid foundation, putting an end to the long-running debate as to whether it is a human invention, like language, or exists independently. Using logic, he established that the rules of mathematics are universal and objective, independent of human thought. Having discovered that mathematics is a branch of logic, and vice versa, Frege was able to use the techniques of modern mathematics to free logic from the bounds of Aristotelian syllogisms, and show its potential as a more powerful and effective system.

4 Begriffsschrift

There was, however, one significant difference between logic and mathematics: while a system of signs and symbols had been devised for mathematics, logical propositions were still expressed in ordinary language. Frege was well aware of this, and its drawbacks, and in 1879 suggested a system of symbolic notation for logic in his book *Begriffsschrift* ('Concept Script'). The symbols were intended to remove the imprecision and ambiguity of language, and also to expand the vocabulary of logic beyond the Aristotelian syllogism. As well as symbols for variables, Frege suggested a calculus using quantifiers that clarified terms such as 'some', 'not all' and so on. Although Begriffschrift was influential, a slightly different set of symbols evolved during the 20th century, some of which are shown in the table below.

Symbol	Meaning	Example
¬	Negation (NOT)	¬P means 'It's not the case that P'
∧	Conjunction (AND)	P∧Q means 'P and Q'
∨	Disjunction (OR)	P∨Q means 'P or Q'
→	Conditional (if/then)	P→Q means 'If P, then Q'
↔	Biconditional (if and only if, or iff)	P↔Q means 'P if, and only if, Q'
∀	Universal quantifier, 'for all'	$\forall x P x$ means 'Px is true for every x'
∃	Existential quantifier, 'there exists'	$\exists x P x$ means 'Px is true for at least one x'

5 Russell: *The Principles of Mathematics*
Frege set out his explanation of the logical foundation of mathematics in his 1884 *The Foundations of Arithmetic*. Apart from a small readership of mathematicians in his native Germany, its publication went largely unnoticed. However, a young British mathematician, Bertrand Russell, was working on the same idea independently of Frege and, in 1903, published his own *The Principles of Mathematics*. In this, he argued that arithmetic, and probably the whole of mathematics, could be derived from logic, and that the laws governing mathematics are universal, objective truths.

6 *Principia Mathematica*
As it happened, Russell was a German-speaker, and in the course of his work came across *The Foundations of Arithmetic*. Having discovered Frege's work, he was inspired to undertake (with Alfred North Whitehead, his former tutor at Cambridge) a thorough study of the logical foundations of mathematics, which culminated in the three-volume *Principia Mathematica*, definitively showing the objectivity of mathematical propositions, and the mutual relationship between logic and mathematics. Russell was also, like Frege, a philosopher as well as mathematician. But while Frege's ideas were ignored by philosophers in mainland Europe, which was dominated at the time by German idealism, Russell recognized how they fitted with the British empiricist tradition.

7 Logic as an analytical tool
What Frege and Russell had demonstrated was of obvious importance to mathematics. Less obviously, it was to have a profound significance for philosophy. The overlap between mathematics and logic showed that there is far more to logic than the Aristotelian syllogism; using the principles of mathematics offered new possibilities for increasing the power and sophistication of logic, and for analysing and clarifying philosophical propositions. Perhaps more importantly for philosophy, the two had also shown that logic (and mathematics) are not a human construct, but based on universal and objective truths, and so can be used to talk about truths in the world – the things previously thought of as contingent 'matters of fact'.

8 Logic vs epistemology
As a result, logic was thrust into the limelight, eclipsing centuries of philosophical enquiry based on metaphysics and especially epistemology. Logic, which focuses on what is the case and what does or doesn't follow from that, exists independent of human thought. Epistemology, the study of how we acquire knowledge, should not, therefore, take a central role in philosophical enquiry, seeking explanations for things in the world. Our attempts to understand the world should not centre on the way our minds apprehend that knowledge, or what we can know, but on a logic-based search for objective truths in the world that are independent of the ways our minds work.

9 A logical foundation for knowledge
Where, previously, philosophers had considered knowledge a matter of epistemology, Russell approached it as a matter of logic. He set out to provide a solid logical foundation for scientific knowledge, a means of analysing and examining propositions to establish their truth. In place of metaphysical and epistemological speculation, Russell proposed, we can use logic to provide knowledge of the external world with objective certainty.

10 Analytic philosophy
Russell's championing of a new approach to philosophical enquiry was a turning point in philosophy, setting the agenda for philosophers in the English-speaking world in the 20th century. What became known as analytic philosophy earned him a reputation as the most influential philosopher of his generation, which was enhanced by his ability to write accessible and readable books that brought philosophy to a wider public. In contrast, Frege remained something of an unsung hero, as philosophers in Europe took a different, language-based path, widening the rift between the British and Continental traditions of philosophy.

TALK LIKE A GENIUS

❛ Once it had been established that logic is objective and universal, and not simply a reflection of the way our minds work, philosophers such as Russell realized that it could be used as a tool for identifying objective truths, replacing metaphysical and epistemological speculation. ❜

❛ By demonstrating that mathematics is a part of logic, Frege and Russell showed that there is far more to logic than had previously been thought. The syllogism, until then regarded as the whole of logic, turned out to be only a tiny part of it. ❜

❛ If it hadn't been for Russell's nanny, he may never have come across Frege and developed analytic philosophy. She was German, and young Bertrand was brought up with German as his first language; and Frege's work was considered too obscure to merit translation. ❜

WERE YOU A GENIUS?

1 FALSE – Frege studied philosophy and theology as well as mathematics and sciences, and wrote several philosophical papers.

2 FALSE – Russell was unaware of Frege's work until after the publication of his work.

3 TRUE – The contradiction inherent in the set of all sets that do not contain themselves was at the heart of his *Principia Mathematica*.

4 TRUE – Surprisingly, Whitehead became a leading figure in the field of process philosophy.

5 FALSE – Logicians through the ages have suggested various ways of expressing logical statements, using letters, numbers and symbols.

THE BLUFFER'S SUMMARY

Logic and mathematics are two sides of the same coin, and both can provide propositions that are universal, objective truths.

Analytic philosophy

'Every philosophical problem, when it is subjected to the necessary analysis and justification, is found either to be not really philosophical at all, or else to be ... logical'

BERTRAND RUSSELL

Having established that the laws of logic are objective, not the product of human thinking, Bertrand Russell concluded that logic can be used to assess, with certainty, if a philosophical proposition tells us something about the nature of the world. Philosophical debate, however, had traditionally been conducted in the form of language, with all its grammatical and semantic complexities; before any judgement can be made, it has to be analysed and 'translated' into a logical form to express the meaning precisely and unambiguously. The process of clarifying philosophical propositions and presenting them in a logical form was a primary concern of analytic philosophy.

Russell showed ways of finding what meaning a statement has before assessing whether it is true or not. Can you do the same?

1 In order to express ordinary language statements in the form of logical propositions, Russell suggested creating an 'ideal language'.

TRUE / FALSE

2 The two statements 'My dog is a boxer' and 'My brother is a boxer' have the same grammatical form, and so have the same logical implications.

TRUE / FALSE

3 Logical positivism is also known as neopositivism, to distinguish it from the 19th-century school of thought led by Auguste Comte.

TRUE / FALSE

4 Logic, according to the logical positivists, can be used to verify empirical knowledge, such as scientific discoveries.

TRUE / FALSE

5 G.E. Moore's commonsense analysis of statements in ordinary language went almost unnoticed for more than 40 years.

TRUE / FALSE

TEN THINGS A GENIUS KNOWS

1 Analysis, not construction

The impact of Russell's work on logic and mathematics was huge. By showing that logic give us an objective assessment of propositions, he provided an alternative to 19th-century German idealism, and challenged the relevance of metaphysics and epistemology. He said that 'The true function of logic ... as applied to matters of experience ... is analytic rather than constructive'; the purpose of philosophy is to help us understand the nature of the world, and logic is the means to examine statements about the world. Logic does not provide those statements; they come from our empirical experience of the world, and constitute our scientific knowledge. By applying techniques of logical analysis to statements about our knowledge we can make an objective evaluation.

2 Linguistic vs logical form

A perennial problem with philosophical propositions has been the language in which they are presented, which is seldom as simple and straightforward as the classic 'All A are B' statement. Before the truth of a statement can be judged, it is necessary to ask the question 'What do we really mean when we say such-and-such?'. Often the way a proposition is presented – the linguistic form – obscures its meaning, which can be seen when it is presented in a logical form, and can even be shown to have no real meaning at all.

3 Meaning and truth

In order to judge a philosophical statement then, it has to be 'translated' into the formal language and grammar of logic, similar to the way in which propositions in mathematics are presented. Even the simplest statements may use language that is imprecise, ambiguous or misleading, requiring careful analysis to render it in a logical form. This can then be verified by checking with known facts, and judged as being part of a valid argument. The process of analysing a statement in this way is not so much to show its truth or falsity, however, as to reveal its meaning, and whether or not it is actually meaningful.

4 The king of France is bald

One such problem of presenting a statement in a logical form involves what Russell called 'definite descriptions' that do not directly refer to a specific thing. For example, 'the president of the United States', as opposed to the specific person, George Washington. Take a statement such as 'The king of France is bald'. Is it true, or false? If it's false, then 'The king of France is not bald' is true. But France is a republic, and has no king, so both the statement and its negation appear to be false – a logical impossibility. The original statement makes linguistic, but not logical sense. Presenting the statement in a logical form resolves the inconsistency. If instead of 'The king of France is bald', we say 'There is a king of France; no more than one thing is the king of France; and if anything is a king of France, then it is bald', we can contradict this by denying the first part of the proposition by saying 'There is not a king of France', rather than 'The king of France is not bald'.

5 The Vienna Circle

Russell's analytic philosophy was most enthusiastically taken up in his native Britain, but also found a following among European philosophers unhappy with the widening gulf between science and philosophy. A particularly influential group of philosophers and scientists gathered at the University of Vienna to discuss the philosophical foundations of science. This 'Vienna Circle' argued that while science provides information about the world, it is the purpose of philosophy to provide a logical framework for scientific enquiry, a view known as 'logical positivism'.

6 Verifiability
The central question posed by logical positivism is the way the truth or falsehood of a statement can be established, how it can be verified. Logic can show if the statement follows from particular premises, but unless it refers to the way things actually are in the world, it has no meaning. Only statements that are empirically verifiable, that can be observed to be true, have any empirical meaning. If logical or empirical verification is not possible, for example in statements such as 'God exists', the statement is neither true nor false, but meaningless, and so not a consideration of science or philosophy.

7 Logical positivism vs continental philosophy
The emphasis on logical and empirical verification broke from the German tradition of idealism, and set logical positivism apart from the subjective nature of the emergent 'continental philosophy' of phenomenology and existentialism. By focusing on only those things that can meaningfully tell us something about the world, logical positivism separated knowledge from opinion and belief, and freed philosophy from metaphysical and epistemological theorizing. Just as importantly, it provided a way of cutting through religious dogma, and the political propaganda of Nazism, fascism and Soviet communism that was prevalent at the time.

8 The spread of logical positivism
In the first decades of the 20th century, the Vienna Circle attracted philosophers and scientists from across Europe, and even some from Britain and the United States. Among them was the English philosopher A.J. Ayer, who had studied at Oxford University before moving to Vienna. After his return to Oxford in 1933, he published *Language, Truth and Logic*, which brought the ideas of logical positivism to the English-speaking world. At the same time, members of the Vienna Circle were fleeing from Nazi-occupied Austria and many of them took up posts in the United States.

9 G.E. Moore
Russell's groundbreaking idea of analytic philosophy dominated British philosophy at the beginning of the 20th century, overshadowing other philosophers working along similar lines. One such philosopher was G.E. Moore, who also took an analytical approach, especially to the subject of morality, in his *Principia Ethica*, published the same year as Russell's *Principles of Mathematics* (1903). Rather than mathematically styled logic, however, Moore used what he called 'common sense' to analyse ethical propositions, continuing a tradition of down-to-earth argument that dates back to Locke and Hume.

10 Reaction to analytic philosophy
Although many philosophers, especially those from the empiricist tradition, found inspiration in Russell's analytic philosophy and logical positivism, it was by no means universally accepted. European 'continental philosophy' was taking an entirely different direction, eschewing the focus on logic and science; but even some in the British philosophical tradition were uncomfortable with the application of scientific standards to philosophical problems. Influenced by Moore's commonsense approach, they considered logical analysis imposed restrictions on the way that statements are made, and philosophers should instead focus on understanding the ways in which we use ordinary language.

TALK LIKE A GENIUS

❝ Russell provoked a sea change in philosophical thinking with his analytic philosophy. The role of philosophy is no longer to provide us with knowledge of the world – that is the job of science – but to analyse and evaluate statements of the knowledge that we have. ❞

❝ The problem of evaluating statements is that, because of the language we use, we don't always say what we mean, or mean what we say. Before we can apply logic to a statement, it has to be analysed and its meaning unpicked, then converted into the form of a logical proposition. ❞

❝ Analytic philosophy's rejection of metaphysics and epistemology as a source of knowledge of the world in favour of scientific enquiry and strict logical analysis derived ultimately from the very British tradition of empiricism. That's one reason it didn't catch on in France – but it did appeal to the German mentality, inspiring "circles" of logical positivist thinkers in Vienna and Berlin. ❞

1 TRUE – Most analytic philosophers adopted some form of symbolic notation in their search for an ideal logical language.

2 FALSE – Although they are linguistically similar, the ambiguities of 'my' (belonging to me, and related to me) and 'boxer' (the breed, and a person who boxes) mean that they have different logical forms.

3 TRUE – Logical positivism saw philosophy as providing a logical framework for the natural sciences; Comte's positivism advocated establishing a scientific basis for philosophy and the social sciences.

4 FALSE – Empirical knowledge can only be verified empirically, and logic can only be used to analyse propositions and arguments.

5 TRUE – Moore's idea of ordinary language analysis was revived by J.L. Austin in the late 1940s.

THE BLUFFER'S SUMMARY

Analytic philosophy examines statements to determine their sense, and whether they meaningfully tell us something about the world.

Tractatus Logico-Philosophicus

'What can be said at all can be said clearly, and what we cannot talk about we must pass over in silence.'

LUDWIG WITTGENSTEIN

While Bertrand Russell set the agenda for philosophy in Britain in the 20th century, it was a Viennese-born philosopher, Ludwig Wittgenstein, who led the debate. In the principles of analytic philosophy, he saw a way to explain the way language is used to describe reality, and ultimately how this defines the limits of philosophical enquiry. This was the task he set himself in his first book, the *Tractatus Logico-Philosophicus*, on which he worked while serving in the Austro–Hungarian Army during the First World War. Its publication in 1921 marked the end of the period referred to as the 'early Wittgenstein.'

Wittgenstein claimed the *Tractatus* resolved all the problems of philosophy – can you match his boast?

ARE YOU A GENIUS

1 Wittgenstein asserts that reality is the 'totality of facts, not of things': that things themselves do not exist, but facts do.

TRUE / FALSE

2 Wittgenstein's colleague G.E. Moore came up with the title *Tractatus Logico-Philosophicus*, a glib homage to Spinoza's *Tractatus Theologico-Politicus*.

TRUE / FALSE

3 Russell regarded the *Tractatus* as a continuation of the analytic philosophy he had initiated, rendering ordinary language into meaningful logical propositions; but Wittgenstein felt that Russell had missed the point.

TRUE / FALSE

4 It was Wittgenstein's membership of the Vienna Circle that led to the development of logical positivism – the view that only empirically verifiable statements can be meaningful.

TRUE / FALSE

5 Wittgenstein makes it clear in the *Tractatus* that statements of religious faith are meaningless, so it is senseless to believe in any supernatural being.

TRUE / FALSE

TEN THINGS A GENIUS KNOWS

1 Ludwig Wittgenstein
Born into a large and wealthy family in Vienna in 1889, Ludwig Wittgenstein was brought up in an atmosphere rich in *fin-de-siècle* Viennese culture, but also of domestic tensions. His father demanded much from his children, who were privately educated, and expected them to become industrialists like himself. Three of his four brothers committed suicide, but Ludwig went on to study mechanical engineering in Berlin, then moved to England to study aeronautics at Manchester. There, he came across Russell's *Principles of Mathematics* and, on Gottlob Frege's advice, applied to Cambridge University to study mathematical philosophy under Russell.

2 The *Tractatus*
Russell quickly recognized the young man's genius, and as his mentor, hoped that Wittgenstein would continue the work of analytic philosophy he had started. For his part, Wittgenstein was inspired by Russell, and especially the idea that logic could give a firm foundation for knowledge of the world. In 1913, he began work on his magnum opus, the *Tractatus Logico-Philosophicus*, in which he aimed to define what can and can't meaningfully be expressed in language, and hence the limits of philosophical and scientific enquiry. Fundamental to this endeavour was an examination of the relationship between language and reality.

3 Logic vs epistemology
Wittgenstein had been introduced to the philosophy of Arthur Schopenhauer by his sister Gretl, and agreed with his idea that total reality is divided into two realms: one that we can have no conception of, and the phenomenal world that we can talk about and try to understand. Where he disagreed with Schopenhauer was in believing that philosophy is confined to the things that can be meaningfully expressed in language – the phenomenal world – and that this can be explained not by epistemology, but by logic.

4 The picture theory of meaning
Central to Wittgenstein's thesis in the *Tractatus* is his theory of how we use language to describe reality. The metaphor he uses is of a painter making a representation of what he sees: a landscape painting, for example, is a very different thing from its subject; it is composed of pigments on a sheet of canvas, not clouds, sky, grass and trees. But the elements of the painting, the colours and shapes, are arranged with the same relationships to one another as the elements of the reality it represents. So it is with language. The elements of language, the words and phrases, represent the elements of the reality that a statement is describing.

5 Logical form
To adequately 'picture' reality, the internal relationship of the elements of a painting should correspond to the relationship of the elements of whatever it represents. In Wittgenstein's words, they have the same 'logical form'. In the same way, only when the logical form of a statement is the same as the logical form of what it describes does it represent reality accurately, and only then can we use language to talk meaningfully about what is the case in the world.

6 Meaningful propositions
As one might expect of a book on logic and language, the *Tractatus* is written as a series of propositions, rather than continuous prose, setting out a logical progression or thought process. Wittgenstein starts out by defining his terms: the world, he states, is 'everything that is the case', and is 'the totality of facts, not of

things'; then he turns to language, asserting 'the totality of propositions is language'. But he adds that a proposition is only meaningful if it pictures a fact, not a thing, and can tell us something about what is the case.

7 The limits of language

Because propositions that do not picture facts are meaningless, our meaningful language is restricted to statements of fact about the world. This puts a limit to our thinking, or at least to the thoughts that we can express in language. The limit is drawn by what we can meaningfully express; our thoughts are restricted to the limits of our language, and whatever lies beyond those limits is meaningless to us, it is outside the bounds of logic – we cannot think what cannot be thought. As Wittgenstein puts it, 'The limits of my language are the limits of my world.'

8 The 'mystical'

According to Wittgenstein's theory, the propositions of morality, metaphysics, religion and so on, are not meaningful, as they do not picture facts. These subjects lie outside the limits of what can be expressed meaningfully, and so cannot be considered matters for philosophical debate. The final proposition of the *Tractatus* sums this up: 'Whereof one cannot speak, thereof one must be silent.' Although there are things that cannot be put into words, he asserts that they 'make themselves manifest. They are what is mystical'.

9 Influence on the Vienna Circle

The natural home of analytic philosophy was Cambridge University, where Wittgenstein had studied with Russell, but it also had an outpost in his native Vienna. A group of scientists and philosophers led by Moritz Schlick and Rudolf Carnap at Vienna University were building on Frege and Russell's ideas in what became known as logical positivism. When the group formally became the Vienna Circle following the First World War, they took as their 'bibles' Russell and Whitehead's *Principia Mathematica* and Wittgenstein's *Tractatus*. Although Wittgenstein had returned to Austria by then, he did not join the circle, and was only persuaded to take part in debates some years later; despite being an inspiration to the group, he did not share their objectives and felt that they had misunderstood the *Tractatus*.

10 The resolution of all philosophical problems?

There was another reason for Wittgenstein's reluctance to participate in the activities of the Vienna Circle: he felt that, with the *Tractatus*, he had resolved the outstanding problems of philosophy, and there was no more to be said. The 'cardinal problem of philosophy' according to him is, what can be expressed by propositions and consequently what can be thought, and what cannot be expressed by propositions but only shown. This, he believed, he had shown in the *Tractatus*. But while he genuinely believed in the truth of his theory, he admitted that he was not a good enough philosopher to express it adequately, and that anybody who understands the *Tractatus* will realize that the propositions in it are meaningless – they do not meet his own criteria of meaningful propositions.

TALK LIKE A GENIUS

❛ Like Locke and Kant before him, Wittgenstein set out in the *Tractatus* to define the limits of what we can know, but more specifically what we can express in language, and therefore think about. ❜

❛ In the end, he concluded that if we strip out all the questions and statements that can be verified empirically, and all the metaphysical and moral propositions that are meaningless because they don't refer to facts, there is nothing left for philosophy to examine. ❜

❛ Wittgenstein ends the *Tractatus* by saying that most philosophical propositions "are not false, but senseless", and that we cannot answer questions of this kind, but only point out their senselessness. So it is with his own propositions, but the reader who understands that and can recognize them as senseless surmounts the propositions, and then "sees the world rightly". ❜

WERE YOU A GENIUS?

1 FALSE – The distinction between facts and things is that a proposition is only meaningful if it pictures a fact, not a thing.

2 TRUE – Wittgenstein originally submitted it for publication as *Der Satz* (*The Proposition*).

3 TRUE – Wittgenstein had set out to show what can and cannot be expressed meaningfully, and therefore the limits of philosophy.

4 FALSE – The *Tractatus* was an influence on logical positivism, but Wittgenstein never joined the Vienna Circle and disagreed with their overly scientific approach to philosophy.

5 FALSE – He says that questions of religious belief are not meaningful, and so cannot be answered.

THE BLUFFER'S SUMMARY

In the *Tractatus*, Wittgenstein defined the limits of meaningful language, the limits of conceptual thought and the limits of philosophical enquiry.

Linguistic philosophy

'Philosophy is a battle against the bewitchment of our intelligence by means of our language.'

LUDWIG WITTGENSTEIN

In his *Tractatus*, Wittgenstein took up the cause of analytic philosophy, and showed what is and isn't logically meaningful, and therefore capable of philosophical enquiry. But there was a reaction to this hardline logical approach, defending the use of ordinary language in philosophy, that persuaded him to think again. In the interwar years, Wittgenstein came up with a completely different theory of language, which inspired the next generation of Anglophone philosophers. Instead of trying to change language to fit it into logical forms, linguistic philosophy set out to analyse language as it is used in its everyday contexts – that is, to determine what we understand by statements in ordinary language.

Wittgenstein prompted a 'linguistic turn' in philosophy. Do you know what that means?

1 When Wittgenstein returned to philosophy in the late 1920s, he was unable to teach at Cambridge University, as he did not have a degree in philosophy.
TRUE / FALSE

2 Wittgenstein's later philosophy was not published during his lifetime, and the only book he wrote after the *Tractatus*, the *Philosophical Investigations*, was unfinished when he died.
TRUE / FALSE

3 In the 'beetle in a box' thought experiment, Wittgenstein shows our inability to communicate a private meaning in public language.
TRUE / FALSE

4 Oxford philosopher J.L. Austin argued that not all language is expressed verbally, but can also be expressed by actions, in what he called 'speech acts'.
TRUE / FALSE

5 Looking back on the early 20th century, Bertrand Russell expressed dismay that his analytic philosophy had become preoccupied with *how* things are said, losing sight of *what* is said.
TRUE / FALSE

TEN THINGS A GENIUS KNOWS

1 **The origins of linguistic philosophy**
In the interwar years, British philosophers became increasingly critical of analytic philosophy, and especially Wittgenstein's *Tractatus*. Many felt that its focus on logical propositions was too narrow, and began to explore different ways of analysing statements. Where analytic philosophy sought to 'translate' statements into an ideal, unambiguous language of logical propositions, they argued that the task was in fact to examine and analyse ordinary language, to better understand its meaning. This ordinary language philosophy, or 'linguistic philosophy' as it became known, aimed to replace what was seen as the abstract theorizing of analytic philosophy with a more practical examination of language as it is actually used.

2 **Ordinary language philosophy**
The premise of linguistic philosophy was a simple one: philosophers (at least in the British tradition) were increasingly developing a separate 'philosophical' language that ignored or misunderstood the meanings of words in everyday use. Far from helping to clarify philosophical problems, it was creating them. In trying either to reduce ordinary language into logical propositions, or to dismiss it as having no philosophical meaning, analytic philosophers ran the risk of becoming out of touch with the business of philosophy, getting knowledge of the world. Wittgenstein was among the first to realize this and, with a group of like-minded philosophers at Cambridge University, initiated the change to linguistic philosophy.

3 **Language and context**
What quickly became apparent to ordinary language philosophers, from their linguistic analysis, was that there are many ways of using language other than simple statements. And although statements can comparatively easily be seen in logical terms, as propositions whose truth can be evaluated, other ways of expressing things have different sorts of logic, and may mean different things in different contexts. This, they argued was at the root of many philosophical problems: philosophers have misunderstood these modes of discourse, and have tried to analyse them in the context of philosophy, using inappropriate philosophical language. Linguistic analysis, however, set out to analyse not only the meaning of words, but how they are used, and in what context.

4 **Wittgenstein's later period**
With the *Tractatus*, Wittgenstein claimed to have resolved all the philosophical problems that could be resolved, and retired from philosophy. But he was persuaded out of retirement by the nascent ordinary language movement, and realized that he had to rethink his position completely. Where the 'early Wittgenstein' had focused on logic and what can meaningfully be said, the 'later Wittgenstein' turned his attention to ordinary language and its meaning, to bring 'words back from their metaphysical to their everyday use'. The problem, as he saw it, was that philosophers had tended to regard words and language in abstract terms, attempting to restrict them to a specific meaning, and had ignored the richness that comes from their many different uses in ordinary discourse.

5 **Language as a tool**
The philosophy of the later Wittgenstein was a complete departure from that of the *Tractatus* – not a rejection of it, but an admission that it was not as complete as he had believed. For example, he realized that language is used for more than simply picturing reality, it can be used for a multiplicity of tasks. So in place of his picture theory of meaning, he used the metaphor of language as a tool, and one that can be used in a variety of contexts. He also revisited his view of words as 'atomic' elements of propositions, as he realized that a word's meaning is not fixed, but is dependent on the way that it is used.

6 The meaning of words

The connection between a word, or concept, and the way it is used is central to Wittgenstein's idea of its meaning. A word can have many uses, and different meanings in those different contexts. The meaning of the word is the sum total of its different uses, and it emerges from the contexts in which it is used, the task it has to perform in different circumstances, cultures, professions and so on. As an example, he asks us to define the word 'game"; we can come up with many different uses of the word, but no single definition that captures all of its meaning. But we do not need a definition to understand the word 'game', as we can use it in its various contexts.

7 Family resemblance

In trying to find a definition for 'game', we will probably think of a number of activities (chess, football, hopscotch, solitaire, charades and the like) that are in some way related, but appear to have no one thing in common. This is what Wittgenstein refers to as a family resemblance: we recognize members of a family by certain physical features, mannerisms, and so on, and can tell that they are all related even though they may not have one common distinguishing feature. The same is true of words and concepts such as 'game'. We have enough experience of the different ways the word is used to recognize what is or isn't a game.

8 Public and private language

Wittgenstein took this idea of the use of language and its meaning a step further, and argued that we learn language from other people and the way that they use it. We derive its meaning from the way that it is used as tool, and so understand the intention of the user: language, therefore, is public, and if it were private we would not be able to communicate with one another. In a famous thought experiment, he describes each person as having a box that contains something its owner refers to with the word 'beetle'. No one can see inside any box except their own, but each will claim to know what a 'beetle' is. In this case, 'beetle' does not mean any specific thing, because each person's box could contain something different; yet they can talk about their 'beetles', with the meaning of 'what's in my box', and communicate publicly without needing to know what exactly is in other people's minds.

9 J.L. Austin: the speech act

After the Second World War, Wittgenstein's ideas were taken up and expanded upon by a group of philosophers at Oxford University, led by Gilbert Ryle and J.L. Austin. They were also inspired by G.E. Moore's 'common sense' approach of 40 years earlier. Like Wittgenstein, they argued that ordinary language consists of much more than statements with a truth value. As well as using language to state facts or describe things, we ask questions, give orders, apologize, thank and any number of other tasks. Language, according to Austin, is associated with action, and many words and phrases are part of that action; for example, saying 'I'm sorry' or 'I promise' is an inherent part of the action of apologizing or promising – a 'speech act'. To understand the meaning of a word or phrase, we must ask in what circumstances it might be used.

10 The application of linguistic philosophy

Russell intended his analytic philosophy to provide a sound logical basis for scientific enquiry, and linguistic philosophy had a similar aim. Its scope, however, was much wider: analysis of language in many different contexts, from everyday conversation to specialized jargon. But linguistic philosophers regarded that as the only purpose of philosophy; empirical problems are the domain of science, politics, social sciences and even everyday conversation, and the job of linguistic analysis is to clarify meaning and prevent misunderstanding.

TALK LIKE A GENIUS

❛ Between the two world wars, philosophy in Britain took a "linguistic turn" – the emphasis shifted from a logical to a linguistic analysis of discourse. Rather than forcing language into an ideal logical form, linguistic analysis examined ordinary language as it is, and attempted to clarify its many shades of meaning. ❜

❛ Wittgenstein is possibly the only major philosopher to have come up with two completely different philosophies, both of them highly influential. ❜

❛ Linguistic philosophy became so pervasive in British philosophy that other branches of philosophy all but disappeared from the scene. Metaphysics, epistemology and ethics were dismissed as meaningless, and describing and explaining the world was left to other disciplines. Philosophy had come to mean just one thing: language. ❜

THE BLUFFER'S SUMMARY

Linguistic philosophy shifted the focus from attempts to formalize the language of philosophy, towards an examination of the meaning of ordinary language.

Continental philosophy

'A work has two levels of meaning: literal and concealed.'

ROLAND BARTHES

A distinctively British tradition of empiricist philosophy evolved in the early modern period, in contrast with the rationalist and idealist traditions that emerged in mainland Europe. The term 'continental philosophy' was used somewhat pejoratively to refer to all non-Anglo-Saxon philosophies in the 19th century, but today it more often refers specifically to a mainly French approach to philosophy with an emphasis on the human condition and experience rather than a scientific worldview. In the latter part of the 20th century, this continental philosophy developed methods of philosophical analysis derived from theories of linguistics and literary criticism, shaped by aesthetic movements such as structuralism and postmodernism.

Anglo-Saxon or Continental – do you know the difference? And which side of the divide do you stand on?

1 Three French philosophers, Bergson, Sartre and Camus, have been awarded a Nobel Prize in Literature, yet no British philosopher has had that honour.

TRUE / FALSE

2 The critical theory advocated by the Frankfurt School arose as a reaction to the increasing dominance of science, and argued that the social sciences, because they are shaped by human activity, are different from the natural sciences.

TRUE / FALSE

3 Although Barthes rejected Sartre's existentialism, he shared his Marxist politics, and used structuralism to expose the way that capitalism moulds society.

TRUE / FALSE

4 Rather than applying the methods of literary criticism, Foucault took the viewpoint of a critical historian to examine various forms of discourse in society.

TRUE / FALSE

5 With his oft-quoted dictum '*il n'y a pas de hors-texte*' (there is nothing outside the text), Derrida suggests that philosophy is about nothing other than language.

TRUE / FALSE

TEN THINGS A GENIUS KNOWS

❶ The continental tradition

From the beginning of modern philosophy during the Renaissance, there was a discernible difference between British and Continental philosophy. With its roots in the rationalism of Descartes and Leibniz, the Continental tradition evolved during the 19th century as various forms of idealism, which in turn evolved into the more subjective phenomenology of Husserl, and through Heidegger to existentialism. But an especially French tradition also emerged in the 20th century, originating in the essentially literary nature of French philosophy. In contrast to the Anglo-Saxon philosophy of the time, late-20th-century Continental philosophy was not concerned with logic or the natural sciences, but was more human-centric, focusing on the social sciences, politics and the arts.

❷ The Frankfurt School

The emphasis on social sciences was particularly prevalent among the group of thinkers known as the Frankfurt School, founded during the interwar years by Max Horkheimer, a sociologist and philosopher. They developed a 'critical theory' based on Kant's idea of critical philosophy, specifically in reaction to the predominant logical positivism of the Vienna Circle, but also the political ideologies of capitalism, fascism and Soviet communism. Their goal was the Marxian ideal of social change, through a synthesis of ideas from sociology, psychology and political science as well as philosophy. Before it was forced to disband by the Nazis' rise to power, the school included such thinkers as the philosophers Herbert Marcuse and Theodor Adorno, and the psychoanalyst Erich Fromm, many of whom fled to the United States.

❸ Philosophy as literature

In the 19th century, European philosophy had been dominated by German idealism; but at the same time a new tradition of French philosophy began to emerge. In the vanguard was Henri Bergson, whose writings were admired as much for their literary merit as their philosophical content. Other French philosophers followed his lead, writing literary works with philosophical themes, rather than expositions of philosophical arguments, so that philosophy in France became regarded as much a part of the literary tradition as a discipline of rational enquiry.

❹ Linguistics

The literary nature of French philosophy was not its only distinguishing feature. With its emphasis on text and language, it gained credibility by reference to the new discipline of linguistics, a scientific approach to the study of language pioneered by Ferdinand de Saussure. Of particular importance was Saussure's theory of structural linguistics, which examines the linguistic structures of language and their relation to their usage in a particular context, or 'speech community'. Through analysis of the texts and conversations, the discourse – the underlying patterns of language and thought – can be discerned.

❺ Structuralism

Continental philosophy's interest in structural linguistics began in the interwar years, influenced to some extent by the 'linguistic turn' of British philosophy. Saussure's structural linguistics was part of the general movement known as structuralism, which sought to identify the structures of thought that influence every aspect of our behaviour. All discourse, including philosophical discourse, was considered by structuralist philosophers as a structure in language, and its meaning and significance are discovered by linguistic rather than logical analysis. Philosophers could thus apply the principles and methods of structural analysis to other, related disciplines, including literary criticism, political philosophy, psychoanalysis and anthropology.

6 Roland Barthes

One of the pioneers of this structuralist approach to philosophy was Roland Barthes, who took over from Sartre as the foremost Marxist philosopher in France, and marked the change from existentialism to structuralism as the predominant movement. He applied the principles of structuralism to literary criticism, advocating a structural analysis of texts, but also analysed the discourse of culture, in general, in the same way. By examining the way in which language is used in all kinds of discourse, he explained how cultural values can become established as norms in a society and, in particular, how bourgeois values have been imposed upon contemporary society.

7 Althusser, Lévi-Strauss and Lacan

Barthes's groundbreaking work in adopting structuralism as a tool for philosophical analysis of culture and society was very influential, and inspired Louis Althusser, a political philosopher, to apply the same principles to Marxism. Althusser's structuralist re-reading of Marx's texts provided a new interpretation of Marxist theory, in which the individual is a product of society, and made in its own image. Others who followed Barthes's structuralist path included the anthropologist Claude Lévi-Strauss, who discerned common structures in all human cultures and concluded that, regardless of the degree of civilization, all human minds work in the same way; and Jacques Lacan, a psychoanalyst whose analysis of Freud led to a radical rethink of the concepts of self and the Other.

8 Michel Foucault

Of the next generation, it was Michel Foucault who came to dominate French philosophy in the 1970s. A student of Althusser's, he shared his teacher's Marxist leanings, but concentrated less on political philosophy than social theory. Rather than the traditional perspective of political theory – the examination of the relationship of government and the governed – he focused on power itself, and how it is exercised at all levels in society. Specifically, he identified a ubiquitous network of relationships within society, and how power is exercised in all of these relationships. Although power is everywhere, its operation can only be detected by an analysis of the discourse of power relationships.

9 Jacques Derrida

A contemporary of Foucault, Jacques Derrida became the figurehead for the next movement in Continental philosophy, poststructuralism, which was closely associated with the wider postmodern cultural movement. He is perhaps best known for abandoning structural analysis in favour of deconstruction as a means of examining a text for meaning and significance. And it is the text, nothing else, that should be the object of this examination: in his words, 'Il n'y a pas de hors-texte' ('there is no outside text'). The meaning of words is what analysis of the text reveals, not the intentions of the author, or the context in which they appear.

10 Anglo-American criticism

Because of its emphasis on literary and linguistic analysis rather than logic, modern Continental philosophy was increasingly dismissed by British philosophers as lacking rigour. With the advent of poststructuralism, it was even regarded by some as meaningless, with Derrida ridiculed as pretentious or even a charlatan. In its defence, however, Continental philosophy has addressed human concerns such as politics, culture, social relationships and the human condition. Such issues can only be thoroughly studied by examining the discourse of human activities – and that may be outside the scope of purely rational analysis.

TALK LIKE A GENIUS

❝ In contrast to the British analytic method of trying to impose logical structure and meaning on to language, the French structuralist philosophers tried to identify the underlying structures of language to determine its meaning and significance in philosophical discourse. ❞

❝ Barthes showed how many of the ideas we take for granted, cultural norms and conventional wisdom, are established and maintained by the discourse, the language, signs and symbols, that are used within a society. ❞

❝ Several philosophers in the analytic tradition have ridiculed postmodern continental philosophy – and Derrida in particular – as illogical nonsense, not philosophy, but they may be missing the point: there's more to philosophical enquiry than logic alone. ❞

WERE YOU A GENIUS?

1 FALSE – Bertrand Russell was awarded the 1950 Nobel Prize in Literature.

2 TRUE – The Frankfurt School saw philosophy as a means to social and political rather than scientific ends.

3 TRUE – Barthes was particularly critical of Sartre's literary opinions, but shared his left-wing politics.

4 TRUE – Foucault developed his own idiosyncratic analysis of modern political history from a starting point of structuralism.

5 FALSE – The phrase is, perhaps deliberately, mistranslated to give this impression, but the implication is that there is no philosophy without language.

THE BLUFFER'S SUMMARY

While Anglo-Saxon philosophers tackled logic and language, Continental philosophy focused on human and social issues through an analysis of discourse.

Glossary

AESTHETICS
The branch of philosophy concerned with the nature of art and beauty, the arts, artistic values and criticism.

ANALYTIC PHILOSOPHY
An approach to philosophy based on logical analysis of statements and arguments to clarify their meaning and establish whether they provide objective knowledge of the world.

ANALYTIC STATEMENT
In philosophy, a statement that can be shown to be true or false by analysing it without reference to other facts. (c.f. *Synthetic statement*)

ANGLO-SAXON PHILOSOPHY
A broad school of 20th-century philosophy inspired by the work of Bertrand Russell and Ludwig Wittgenstein, which analysed philosophical problems through the tools of mathematics and logic.

A PRIORI / A POSTERIORI
An *a priori* proposition is one that is known to be true without evidence from experience. Propositions that can only be proved true from experience are *a posteriori*.

AXIOM
A statement that can be accepted without question within a particular framework and used as a basis for developing logical proofs.

COGITO (THE)
A widely used philosophical shorthand for the famous statement *Cogito, ergo sum* (I think, therefore I exist) – Descartes's attempt to identify an indubitable truth as the foundation for his system of philosophy.

COMPATIBILISM
A philosophical approach that attempts to reconcile the concept of free will with the apparently deterministic nature of the Universe.

CONSERVATISM
A political and philosophical ideology that seeks to retain traditional institutions and values.

CONTINENTAL PHILOSOPHY
A term today used specifically to refer to a primarily French approach to philosophy in the 20th century, in which philosophical analysis adopted theories of linguistics and literary criticism.

CONTINGENT
A contingent truth is one that happens to be true, but in other circumstances might not have been. (c.f. *Necessary*)

COSMOS
(see *World*)

DEDUCTION
A process of inference drawing a particular conclusion from a general premise. For example, 'All men are mortal. Socrates is a man. Therefore Socrates is mortal.' If the premises of a deductive argument are true, the conclusion must also be true. (c.f *Induction*)

DEMOCRACY
A form of government either formed from, or elected by, the entire eligible populace.

DEONTOLOGY
An ethical position that judges an action's morality based on its conformity to a set of established rules or duties.

DETERMINISM
The view that every event is determined by, and the necessary outcome of, a prior cause, and that nothing can happen other than what happens. Some philosophers see determinism as removing the possibility of free will.

DIALECTIC
The philosophical idea, particularly associated with Hegel and Marx, that any statement, action or state contains within it a contradiction that creates opposition, requiring the development of a synthesis that reconciles the two.

DUALISM
The philosophical view that the world is composed of two distinct elements, often perceived as the physical and mental realms. In the philosophy of mind, dualism refers to the view that mind and body are distinct.

EMPIRICISM
The philosophical view that knowledge must be acquired through experience; hence there is no such thing as *a priori* knowledge.

ENLIGHTENMENT
An intellectual period spanning the 18th century, marked by great advances in philosophy and setting the stage for modern politics and economics.

EPISTEMOLOGY
The branch of philosophy concerned with knowledge: what knowledge is; how we acquire knowledge; and what, if anything, we can know.

ETHICS
The branch of philosophy concerned with morality and how we should live our lives, including questions of right and wrong, good and bad, and duty.

EXISTENTIALISM
An approach to philosophy based on the subjective human experience of existence, and in particular the search for meaning in life.

FALLACY
An error of reasoning or false conclusion.

FALSIFIABILITY
In the philosophy of Popper, the concept that a theory (usually scientific) is capable of being proved false by empirical evidence.

FREE WILL
The ability for an individual to make choices and pursue courses of action entirely according to their own decisions. The question of whether free will can truly exist in a Universe ordered by a deity or running according to deterministic rules has been a long-standing problem for philosophy.

HUMANISM
An approach that considers humankind as more important than any supernatural world as a basis for philosophical enquiry.

IDEALISM
A philosophical view that reality is ultimately immaterial (consisting of minds, ideas or spirits) with physicality a mere projection or illusion created by the mental realm. (c.f. *Materialism*)

INDUCTION
A process of inference drawing a general conclusion from a particular premise. For example, the statement: 'Socrates, Plato and Aristotle were philosophers. They were all Greek. Therefore all philosophers are Greek.' The conclusion from an inductive argument may or may not be true, and is open to falsifiability. (c.f. *Deduction*)

INFERENCE
A process of reasoning in which a conclusion follows from premises, such as deduction and induction.

LIBERALISM
A philosophical and political outlook based on the freedoms and rights of the individual citizen.

LIBERTARIANISM
A political philosophy advocating liberty and the exercise of free will, with little or no government interference or taxation.

LINGUISTIC TURN
A renewed interest in looking at language within 20th-century Anglo-Saxon philosophy, inspired by Ludwig Wittgenstein's idea that philosophical problems arise through misinterpretation and misuse of language.

LOGIC
The branch of philosophy concerned with the methods, rules and validity of rational argument. Logic identifies techniques for the construction of rational proofs based on simple axiomatic statements and various mathematical or philosophical methods.

LOGICAL POSITIVISM
A 20th-century school of philosophy founded on the epistemological view that the only meaningful philosophical statements are those which can be verified by means of empirical observation or experiment.

MARXISM
A political and economic philosophy, derived from Karl Marx, that analyses society based on contrasts in power, money and social class.

MATERIALISM
The view that reality is ultimately material or physical, and that apparent mental or spiritual aspects arise ultimately from physical activity in the matter of our brains. (c.f. *Idealism*)

METAPHYSICS
The branch of philosophy concerned with the nature of reality, of what exists, including concepts of being and substance.

MIND-BODY PROBLEM
The long-standing philosophical problem of how the mental realm of our minds interacts with the physical matter of our bodies, and vice versa.

MONISM
The view that all things (for example the mental and physical aspects of the world) are ultimately made up of a single element manifested in different ways.

MORAL PHILOSOPHY
(see *Ethics*)

NATURAL PHILOSOPHY
The ancient branch of philosophy concerned with the ordering and origins of the natural world, which gave rise to and has ultimately been largely supplanted by modern science.

NECESSARY
A fact that is true in any circumstances, and could not be otherwise. (c.f. *Contingent*)

NOUMENON
The reality, also known as the 'thing-in-itself', that exists independent of our experience of it. In the philosophy of Kant, the noumenal world is the world of ultimate reality, as opposed to the world of the phenomenon, the world as it is experienced by human consciousness.

OBJECTIVITY
Describing ideas, concepts and experiences that should be considered as true irrespective of the point of view of the subject or subjects apprehending them. (c.f *Subjectivity*)

ONTOLOGY
The branch of philosophy concerned with the nature of existence and being.

PARADIGM

A widely shared framework of knowledge, assumptions and approaches used for addressing problems within a particular field (most commonly in science). In one model of scientific progress, major advances involve a 'paradigm shift' that disproves old approaches and requires the construction of new ones.

PARADOX

A statement based on apparently true premises and logical reasoning that nevertheless gives rise to an incorrect conclusion. Paradoxes are an indication that either the initial assumptions of the premises are incorrect, or some form of fallacious reasoning is present in the argument.

PHENOMENOLOGY

An approach to philosophy developed by Edmund Husserl in the early 20th century, which advocates concentrating only on the phenomena we can experience in the world, rather than the noumena that are beyond our apprehension.

PHENOMENON

In philosophy, a 'thing as experienced', channelled through the filters of human consciousness, as opposed to the noumenon or 'thing in itself' that objectively exists.

POLITICAL PHILOSOPHY

The branch of philosophy that attempts to discern rules for the organization of society and the governance of people.

POSTMODERNISM

A cultural view widespread from the late 20th century in which scepticism, irony and relativism are dominant, while attempts at 'grand narratives' are cast into doubt.

PRAGMATISM

The view that truth is valid explanation – in other words, that a statement can be considered true if it describes a situation accurately enough to be useful.

RATIONALISM

A philosophical approach that sees knowledge of the world as something best acquired through reasoning rather than experience, observation and experimentation.

RELATIVISM

The idea that ethical and other judgements are dependent on their cultural and historical context, and even the language framework in which they are described, and therefore cannot be judged as right or wrong in any absolute sense.

RENAISSANCE

A cultural movement spanning the 14th to 16th centuries and marked by a revival of classical learning and a newfound spirit of humanist inquiry.

REPUBLIC

Any state governed by an elected parliament and head of state, in which the people are citizens rather than subjects of a monarch.

RIGHTS

The fundamental rules arising in a society from a shared understanding of what individuals are owed as members of that society, and what they are permitted to do. Rights are often enforced by moral, legal and political structures.

ROMANTICISM

A cultural movement of the late 18th and early 19th century characterized by a rejection of rationalism and a reaction to the Industrial Revolution.

SCEPTICISM

The view that it is not possible to have certain knowledge of anything.

SCIENCE

A system of inquiry that builds knowledge through empirical observation of phenomena in the physical world, and the construction and testing of hypotheses to explain them. Science began as a branch of philosophy and has subsequently become our most successful way of understanding the rules that govern the physical Universe.

SOCIAL CONTRACT

The implicit mutual cooperation between the mass of individuals and the government that rules them, often framed in terms of a negotiation of rights.

SOCIALISM

A political ideology based on shared ownership of means of production and the fair distribution of their profits.

STRUCTURALISM

A critical approach to texts and social practices that aims to understand them in terms of rule systems and language frameworks.

SUBJECTIVITY

Describing ideas, concepts and experiences that can only be considered true from the point of view of a certain subject or subjects, rather than being universally true. (c.f *Objectivity*)

SYNTHETIC STATEMENT

In philosophy, a statement whose truth can only be determined by checking the facts it refers to. (c.f. *Analytic statement*)

TELEOLOGY

A philosophical approach that analyses entities in terms of their function or purpose. Once popular in natural philosophy until it was supplanted by scientific approaches, teleology is now principally an ethical position that the moral value of actions should be judged by their outcomes. raised to a given power (i.e. multiplied by itself a certain number of times).

UNIVERSE

(see *World*)

UTILITARIANISM

In ethics and political philosophy, the view that the morality of an action should be judged by its consequences, which should bring about the greatest good for the greatest number.

VALIDITY

In logic, an argument is said to be valid if its conclusion follows from its premises. In a valid argument, the conclusion will be true if the premises are true, but if any of the premises are false, the conclusion may not be true.

WORLD

In philosophy, 'the world' (and sometimes 'the cosmos' or 'the Universe') is used to mean everything that exists that we can have experience of, everything in empirical reality.

Index

a priori/a posteriori 94
absurd, the 122
acquired knowledge 78, 81
ad populum 177
ad verecundiam 177
aesthetic relativism 166
affective fallacy 170
afterlife 37, 102
agnosticism 72–5
alchemy 14
Althusser, Louis 206
analogy 177
analytic philosophy 190, 191, 192–5, 200, 201
anarchism 134, 135, 142, 162
anarchy 134
animal rights 118, 146
Anselm of Canterbury 62, 66
antinomy 178
Aquinas, Thomas 18, 61, 62, 66, 122, 133, 153
Aristotle 16, 17, 19, 21, 22, 37, 66, 67, 78, 80–3, 98, 101, 132, 133–4, 169, 173, 174, 181, 183, 185
art 168–71
Arthashastra, the 153

artificial intelligence (AI) 38, 56–9
atheism 72–5
atomists 14, 21
Augustine of Hippo, St 65, 153
Austin, J.L. 202
authenticity 121
authoritarianism 157, 159, 161
Avicenna 41
Ayer, A.J. 194

Bacon, Francis 89, 181, 185
Barthes, Roland 170, 206, 207
beauty 164–7
behaviourism 54, 90
being 8–11
belief 73, 77, 85, 93
Bentham, Jeremy 116, 117–18, 119, 146, 170
Bergson, Henri 33, 205
Berkeley, Bishop George 18, 19, 21, 62
Berlin, Isaiah 106, 113, 142, 143
Big Bang theory 61
black swan 186
Boethius 65, 69
boo/hurrah theory 110

brain in a vat 41, 50
Buddha/Buddhism 102, 128–31
Burke, Edmund 161

Camus, Albert 122, 123, 138
capitalism 154, 158, 161–2
categorical imperative 112–15
cave allegory 81
Chinese legalism 153
Chinese philosophy 124–7
Chinese room thought experiment 58, 59
Chomsky, Noam 90, 91, 158
Christianity 64–7, 69
civil disobedience 146
civil rights movement 146
class struggle 157, 162
cogito ergo sum 40–3, 85
commandments, religious 106
communism 162
communitarianism 161
compatibilism 69
complex question fallacy 177–8
Comte, Auguste 182
Confucius/Confucianism 102, 125, 126, 127, 153

consciousness 30, 37, 46, 49–50, 52–5, 58
consequentialism 113, 114, 117, 118, 119, 138
continental philosophy 34, 194, 204–7
cultural hegemony 157–8
cultural relativism 105, 106
culture, high and low 170
cynics 101, 102

Daoism 125, 127
Darwin, Charles 90, 154, 166
deceiving demon 41, 43
Declaration of Rights 145
deductive reasoning 173, 185
democracy 133, 134
Dennett, Daniel 54, 58
deontology 113
Derrida, Jacques 206, 207
Descartes, René 22, 37–8, 40–2, 57, 59, 73, 85, 87, 89, 181–2
determinism 68, 69, 71
dialectical materialism 154
Diogenes of Sinope 101
dogmatism 86
dualism 22, 26, 37–8, 41, 42, 43, 53, 59

economic liberalism 162
egalitarianism 137
Eightfold Path 130
elements 13, 14

emotivism 110
Empedocles 14
empiricism/empiricists 24, 25, 26, 78, 82, 86, 88–91, 165–6
Enlightenment 29, 117, 141, 145, 146, 154, 182
environmental philosophy 146
Epicurus/Epicureans 73, 101
epistemology 77–8, 80–3, 190, 197
Erasmus, Desiderius 66, 67
eternal Universe 17
ethics 97–115
eudaemonia 101
evil 73, 96–9
evolutionary aesthetics 166
existence 8–11, 13, 17
existentialism 34, 49, 70, 120–3
experience 25
experience machine 102

faith 61, 66
fallacies 174, 176–9
falsifiability 186
family resemblance 202
felicific calculus 117
Feuerbach, Ludwig 74
Feyerabend, Paul 182, 183
Fichte, Johann Gottlieb 29
Foucault, Michel 158, 206
Four Noble Truths 130, 131
Frankfurt School 205
free will 68–71, 113–14
freedom 70, 138
freedom of speech 141

Frege, Gottlob 188, 189, 190, 191
functionalism 54, 58

Gautama, Siddhartha 129–30, 131
Gettier, Edmund 77–8, 79
'ghost in the machine' 42, 53, 58
God, existence of 60–3, 66, 72–3, 75, 121
golden mean 98
good 96–9, 106
good life 97, 100–3, 117
government 133–4, 138, 142, 149
Gramsci, Antonio 158

happiness 97, 101, 117
harm principle 117
heaven, mandate of 125
Hegel, Georg 30, 31, 74
Heidegger, Martin 11, 33, 34, 49, 121
Heraclitus 13
Hobbes, Thomas 50, 57, 149–50, 151
horned man 178
Hume, David 22, 25, 49, 53, 63, 73, 75, 85–6, 95, 108, 166, 174, 185, 187
Hume's fork 93, 94
Hume's guillotine 109
Husserl, Edmund 33, 35, 121

I

idealism 20–3, 38, 42, 62, 193
  absolute 29, 30
  German 26, 28–31, 193, 205
  Kant's transcendental 24–7,
    29, 30, 31, 74, 86, 114
identity 48–51
immaterialism 18, 62
incompatibilism 69
individualism 161
induction 182, 184–7
innate knowledge 78, 81, 82
institutional theory of art 170
intentional fallacy 170
irrelevant conclusion 177
is and ought 108–10
Islam 64–7, 181

J

James, William 49, 53, 94,
  95
junzi 125–6
just war 153, 154, 155
justice 136–9

K

Kant, Immanuel 24–7, 28, 29,
  30, 33, 70, 73–4, 75, 86, 90, 94,
  110, 112–15, 166
Kierkegaard, Søren 121
knowledge 76–9, 80–3, 86,
  190
Kong Fuzi 125–6
Kuhn, Thomas 182

L

Lacan, Jacques 206
language 90, 174, 197, 198,
  200–3, 205
Laozi 125
law 138, 141
Left, the 161
legal rights 145–6
legalism 126, 127, 153
Leibniz, Gottfried 10, 25, 90,
  93, 95
Lévi-Strauss, Claude 206
liberal democracy 162
liberalism 142, 161, 162, 163
libertarianism 69, 142
liberty 140–3
linguistic vs logical form 193
linguistics 200–3, 205
Locke, John 18, 45, 46, 49, 53,
  55, 70, 86, 90, 145, 149, 150
logic 93, 172–5, 185, 187, 188–91,
  193, 194, 197
logical form 197
logical positivism 193, 194, 198

M

Machiavelli, Niccolò 113, 119,
  154, 157, 159
machine intelligence 57–8
Marx, Karl 30, 31, 74, 152, 154,
  157–8, 161–2, 163, 206
materialism 10, 20–3, 30, 38, 73,
  74, 154
mathematics 186, 188–91
matters of fact 185

meaning 193
mechanistic view 57
media 158
meditation 129
memory 50, 51
Merleau-Ponty, Maurice 34, 49,
  121–2
metaphysics 9–10, 11, 22,
  30, 34
middle way 130, 131
Mill, J.S. 45, 113, 117, 118, 137,
  141–2, 145, 170
Mills, Charles Wright 158
mind, philosophy of 37–8, 45
mind-body 36–9, 40, 42, 53
Mohism 126
monarchy 134, 135
monism 13, 21, 22, 42
Moore, G.E. 109, 194, 202
moral authority 113
moral luck 98
Mozi 126
mystical (Wittgenstein) 198

N

Nagel, Thomas 54, 58
natural law 133
natural rights 145, 146
naturalistic fallacy 109
nature vs nurture 90
neo-Platonism 65, 67
neuroscience 46
Nietzsche, Friedrich 30, 70, 74,
  102, 121, 123, 157, 166, 167
nirvana 130
nominalism 18

noumena 26, 27, 29, 30, 33, 70, 73–4, 86, 114
Nozick, Robert 102, 138

objective reality 33
objective truths 189
objectivism 105–6
oligarchy 134
ontology 9–10, 17
'original position' 150
other minds 38, 44–7

Paine, Thomas 145
paradigm shifts 182
paradoxes 174, 176–9
Parmenides 10, 13, 14
Pascal, Blaise 62, 63
Peirce, Charles Sanders 33, 86, 94
petitio principii 177
phenomena 26, 27, 29, 30, 33, 70
phenomenology 33, 121
philosopher-kings 133, 135
physicalism/physicalists 21, 42, 53–4
picture theory of meaning 197, 201
Plato 16, 17, 18, 19, 20, 21, 22, 37, 66, 78, 80–3, 105, 113, 133, 135, 165, 169
Plato's Forms 17, 21, 22, 37, 65, 81, 82, 83, 97, 98, 165, 169

Plotinus 65
political ideologies 160–3
political power 156–9
political realism 152–5
politics 132–5
Popper, Karl 186, 187
positivism 182, 193, 194
post hoc ergo propter hoc 177, 185
poststructuralism 206
power 156–9, 206
power elite 158
pragmatism 86, 94, 186
pre-Socratic philosophers 13, 15, 16, 21
prescriptivism 110
primary/secondary qualities 18
private language 45
proof vs theory 186
Protagoras 105
Proudhon, Pierre-Joseph 150
pseudoscience 182, 186
psyche 37, 48
psychology 42
punishment 138
Putnam, Hilary 41, 58
Pythagoras 17, 165

rationalism/rationalists 24, 25, 26, 78, 82, 88–91
Rawls, John 137–8, 150
reality 10, 11, 13, 16–19, 21, 29, 30, 32–5
Realpolitik 154

reason 26, 61, 73, 172–5
relativism 104–7, 166
Right, the 161
rights 144–7
Romanticism/Romantics 29, 166
Rousseau, Jean-Jacques 141, 146, 149, 161
Russell, Bertrand 10, 32, 61, 62, 74, 86, 87, 178, 179, 189–90, 191, 192, 193, 195, 197
Ryle, Gilbert 42, 43, 53, 58, 202

Sagan, Carl 186
samsara 129
Sartre, Jean-Paul 34, 121, 122, 123
Saussure, Ferdinand de 205
scepticism 73, 84–7, 181
Schelling, Friedrich 29–30
scholasticism 66, 67
School of Salamanca 154
Schopenhauer, Arthur 29, 30, 31, 70, 130, 197
science 89
scientific enquiry 180–3, 185, 187
scientific method 181
Searle, John 54, 55, 58
self 38, 48–51, 53
self-awareness 49, 121–2
self-realization 101
sensory information 45

Singer, Peter 118, 146
Sisyphus, myth of 122
Smith, Adam 142, 162
social contract 146, 148–51
social control 158
socialism 162
Socrates 16, 77, 81, 96, 97, 101, 165, 173
sophists 85, 105
sorites paradox 178
soul 37, 38
speech-act 202
Spinoza, Benedict 22, 29, 42, 89–90
state 149
'state of nature' 149
statements
    analytic and synthetic 93–4
    of fact and value 109
stoics/stoicism 102
structuralism 205–6, 207
subjective experience 45, 54, 121
subjective reality 32–5
subjectivism 109–10, 111
Sun Tzu: *The Art of War* 153
syllogism 173–4, 175, 181, 190
symbolic logic 174

teleporter thought experiment 50
Theseus's ship 50
thing-in-itself 26, 30, 31
Thoreau, Henry 142, 146
totalitarianism 157

transcendental idealism 24–7, 29, 30, 31, 74, 86, 114
trolley problem 118
truth(s) 92–5, 173, 185, 186, 193
truth relativism 105
Turing, Alan 56, 57–8
tyranny 134

universal grammar 90, 91
universal will 30
universals 18, 19
utilitarianism 29, 116–19, 137, 142, 170

validity 173–4
Vedic religions 129
veil of ignorance 137–8
verifiability 194
Vienna Circle 193, 194, 198
virtue 97, 98, 101, 125
Voltaire 74, 141

will 30
Wittgenstein, Ludwig 45, 47, 74, 75, 103, 169, 197, 201
    Tractatus Logico-Philosophicus 196–9, 200, 201
women, rights of 145
words, meaning of 202

Xenophanes 13, 14

Zeno's paradoxes 178, 179
Zhuangzi 125, 127
zombies 46, 47, 50

ABOUT THE AUTHOR

Marcus Weeks is the author of the popular *Philosophy in Minutes*, and several other titles in the same series, and has written and contributed to many books on philosophy, psychology and the arts. As well as his career as a writer, he has worked as a teacher, piano technician and restorer, and musician. He lives In Hastings on the south coast of England, with his partner, his dog Daisy and four hives of bees.

ACKNOWLEDGEMENTS

Marcus Weeks would like to thank Anna Southgate, Giles Sparrow and Tim Brown for their hard work in getting this book from manuscript to print.

In memory of Pete Burden,
a philosopher and gentleman

First published in Great Britain in 2018 by

Quercus Editions Ltd
Carmelite House
50 Victoria Embankment
London EC4Y 0DZ

An Hachette UK company

A CIP catalogue record for this book is available
from the British Library

HB ISBN 9781786485878
EBOOK ISBN 9781786485885

10 9 8 7 6 5 4 3 2 1

Printed and bound in China